BARBARA ANDERSON was born in 1926, and published her first book, the collection of short stories *I think we should go into the jungle*, in 1989. An immediate bestseller, and a finalist for both the Goodman Fielder Wattie Award and the New Zealand Book Award for Fiction, it launched a highly successful writing career which has seen the publication of eight novels and a further collection of short stories, all published to acclaim in New Zealand and by the prestigious British publisher Jonathan Cape. Barbara Anderson's best-known novel, *Portrait of the Artist's Wife*, won the Goodman Fielder Wattie Award in 1992. Her *Collected Stories* appeared in 2005. In 2009 she was awarded an honorary doctorate by the University of Otago.

PRAISE FOR BARBARA ANDERSON

'She is a novelist of great talent, well qualified to write black comedy. But she has, too, the comprehension of human incomprehension, the pity for human pity, that makes it possible to write tragedy.'

Penelope Fitzgerald, *Times Literary Supplement*

'Never portentous, never trivial, marvellously comic but with grey skeins of pathos, this is surely among the most powerful collections of stories produced in New Zealand. Its unerring economy of effects suggests at times the quality of a Flaubert, a Patrick White, a Grace Paley. To have achieved such brilliance in a first book is remarkable.'

Ian Reid, *Listener*

'I found *Portrait of the Artist's Wife* to be acutely observed, furiously gleeful, compulsively readable—and the work of a natural writer.'

Janet Frame

'[*Portrait of the Artist's Wife*] is a novel about context, specifically about two contexts, domestic and national, in which art is produced; it is not a dry book, and nor, amazingly enough, is it an insular one. The promise that was evident in *Girls High* has been splendidly fulfilled, and it now seems only a matter of time before Wellington replaces New York as the literary capital of the world.'

Nick Hornby, *Sunday Times*

BOOKS BY BARBARA ANDERSON

I think we should go into the jungle (1989)

Girls High (1990)

Portrait of the Artist's Wife (1992)

All the Nice Girls (1993)

The House Guest (1995)

Proud Garments (1996)

The Peacocks and other stories (1997)

Glorious Things and other stories (1999)

Long Hot Summer (1999)

The Swing Around (2001)

Change of Heart (2003)

Collected Stories (2005)

GETTING THERE

AN AUTOBIOGRAPHY

BARBARA ANDERSON

VICTORIA UNIVERSITY PRESS

TE WHARE WĀNANGA O TE ŪPOKO O TE IKA A MĀUI
VICTORIA
UNIVERSITY OF WELLINGTON

VICTORIA UNIVERSITY PRESS
Victoria University of Wellington
PO Box 600 Wellington
http://www.victoria.ac.nz/vup

First published 2008
Paperback edition 2009

National Library of New Zealand Cataloguing-in-Publication Data

Anderson, Barbara, 1926-
Getting there : an autobiography / Barbara Anderson. Pbk. ed.
Previous ed: 2008.
ISBN 978-0-86473-602-4
1. Anderson, Barbara, 1926- 2. Women authors, New Zealand —20th century—Biography. 3. Women authors, New Zealand —21st century—Biography. 4. Authors, New Zealand—20th century—Biography. 5. Authors, New Zealand—21st century —Biography. I. Title.
NZ823.2—dc 22 [B]

Printed by South Wind Production (Singapore) Pte Ltd

For Neil, with love

Parting is all we know of heaven,
And all we need of hell.

Emily Dickinson

PART I

CHAPTER 1

I was born with a full set of near relatives: mother, father, four grandparents, one brother, six aunts, two uncles. All were aware of the imminent arrival of Barbara Lillias Romaine Wright sometime in April '26. I assume some were pleased at the prospect. They had been when my brother David was born two years before, a child of exceptional beauty, the right sex, and the first grandchild on both sides.

Henry Cecil Wright, his English-born grandfather, was glad the male line of his strain of Wrights would continue and came down from New Plymouth to the nearby village of Manaia to say so. My Scottish grandfather, Frederick Arthur Jackson of Mangatahi, Rural Delivery, Hastings, Hawke's Bay, didn't rush into anything, but when the next trip into town was due he cranked up his Tin Lizzie and drove his wife Lillias into town where he stopped at Mr Baird's Drapery window and pointed out a pair of first-size shantung rompers. 'Go away in, Lil,' he said, 'and get that wee bit for Charlie.' A gesture which was taken as evidence of his extreme excitement at his grandson's birth.

I don't know my grandmothers' reactions to my arrival but my mother would have been happy, I'm sure, not only from maternal affection and the fact that I was now extant, but also because of her highly developed sense of order. A healthy girl born two years after a beautiful son had a tidiness about it, a neatness which would have pleased her. She must have been glad, and my father was always glad when she was.

My parents, Jessie Amelia Jackson and Cecil Govett Romaine Wright, met when he was a medical registrar at the Napier public hospital and she a highly regarded theatre sister. After they were married my father set up his practice in Manaia, Taranaki.

My mother had loved her job in the theatre, the height of achievement of a nursing career in the 1920s. Unless you aspired to the very peak and became Matron, which, Mum told us, was a different thing again. She remained proud of both her profession and expertise. Jessie Amelia Wright was a real nurse, we learned that young.

Early in childhood I became aware that the Jacksons and the Wrights belonged to different tribes. On one side of the forest were the Scottish Jacksons, on the other the English Wrights. Not only that but that they danced to the beat of different tom-toms. Our Jacksons danced with skill, our Wrights hardly at all. Also the Scots arrived here first which gave them a touch of pioneer pride, albeit their arrival was not until 1864 when my great-grandfather, Michael Jackson, emigrated from Inverness with his elder brother, Adam, who with his wife and family settled in Canterbury, while Michael headed for the West Coast of the South Island, an area known to all true Coasters as the Coast. The Jacksons were proud of their Scottish origins and memories, including Michael's son, Frederick Arthur, who loved all Scots but not the English. He was also suspicious of 'town men'. A true country Scot, there was the man for Fred Jackson.

In 1893 he married Lillias Russell, a beautiful young woman from Marsden, a little gold-digging town tucked away in the bush south of Greymouth. On their children's birth certificates Fred's occupation is entered variously: 'Butcher', 'Miner', and later 'Contractor'. At which stage he was a carrier, with his own cart and horse that, according to legend, wore a straw hat with holes for his ears, a story which appealed to David and me from earliest youth. Like some wiser or saddened miners, Fred turned from digging himself to providing services for the diggers who flocked to the 1860s gold rush. (Goldminers always 'flock'.)

Fred and Lily had five children: my mother Jessie, followed by Freddy, Lillias, Jeannie and Harry, all of whom were born between 1896 and 1902.

Frederick Senior and his family moved north to Hawke's Bay in 1906 when Olrig station, owned by the Smith brothers, was being broken into smaller holdings. Fred Jackson drew a ballot of an 800-acre block about twelve miles from the nearest town, Hastings. He rented a house in Hastings for Lily and the children and camped on the land while he made it liveable. When he arrived the only buildings in existence were an old iron shed, which was originally the cookhouse of Olrig, and an implement shed. He cleared, ploughed and fenced the property and built a house which still stands. The timber, which was sawn at the Kereru mill, was also used in the construction of a small woolshed which was in use until 1940.

He called the farm Craigieburn, or Rocky Stream, a name brought from Scotland via the Coast, a name and a place he was proud of, and which he left too soon.

An extract from a West Coast newspaper of 1927 reads:

The death is announced of Mr Fred Jackson, a former resident of the Coast. The late Mr Jackson, who had latterly resided at Maraekakaho, passed away at Hastings on Saturday morning, his sudden demise being the result of injuries sustained through slipping on some steps. Deceased was 58 years of age. When the Otira railway liner was first under construction the late Mr Jackson did a considerable amount of contracting. He left the West Coast about 23 years ago and went to the North Island to take up farming . . .

At which he succeeded. When Fred died in 1927, Craigieburn was a Scots shepherd's dream: 'A fine skelp of land with good steddings.'

Fred Jackson shared with many others of his tribe an illustrious forebear. My great, great, great, great grandfather, a previous Adam Jackson known as Yeddie, was born at Howpathy in Scotland in 1763, the son of a Border shepherd, William, and his wife Esther, from near Newcastleton, and died 94 years later.

He and his life are described by an unknown writer.

Adam Jackson (Yeddie) 1763–1857

To mention the name of Yeddie Jackson is to awaken the memory of many a Borderer whose hearts were young forty or fifty years ago. He had a threefold capacity; shepherd, host and king. As a shepherd, he was known and respected at all sheep and land fairs from Stagshawbank to Lockerbie. Then, as host or gudeman of the shepherd's sheiling, at the Dead Water Well where many an invalid found a home and wholesome faring, his memory endures with gratitude in the domestic annals of a thousand homes. His was the only house where lodgings could be had at the time when the Dead Water Well was a resort of invalids, of tourists and of anglers. It is, however, as The Hunter King that Yeddie's fame is widest spread. Poets have embalmed him in song and artists have preserved his likeness as The Hunter King. In that capacity, he acted as if he was monarch of all he surveyed. He and his fellow sportsmen followed the fox wherever it was to be found. The sublime and silent vale of Keilder, the gathering ground of North Tyne, the moorland and marshland of Dead Water, the links and fells of Liddlehead, were each and all the hunting ground of Yeddie. His sporting excursions sometimes extended on the West to the edge of Solway and as far South as the Humber. He kept foxhounds and terriers ready for the field, and the shepherds and farmers that he summoned to the meet also brought their dogs along with them, so that when they all were gathered, horsemen and footmen, hounds and terriers, a motley field they made. An eyewitness of a lay-on on Thorliehope Fell says that when the terriers were purring in the fox den and hounds in full music for the outcome of Reynard, Auld Yeddie clapped his hands and shouted 'Glorious, glorious'.

His enthusiasm was most exuberant and tended to inspire all around. A whole volume might be written about him and yet he would be no truer hit off than the description given of him by James Telfer, the poetic schoolmaster of Saughtree.

***The Hunter King** (abridged)*
(Tune – Bonnie Dundee)

Brave King of the huntsmen, we'll sing of thy glory
Old Cock of the Border, our praise is thy due
Thy years may be many, thy locks may be hoary,
But young is the heart that is honest and true.

O'where is the huntsman, in Tyne or in Teviot,
In England or in Scotland, that's equal to thee?
Thy fame loudly rings from Solway to the Cheviot,
Through all the wide Border by Muirland and lea.

Long life of thee, Yeddie, and fame be attendant,
The joys of the chase do thou never forget,
Thou prince of goodfellows, thou soul independent,
Thou hearty old hero, success to thee yet.

Come fill up a bumper, we'll pledge thee in glory
Tho links of green Liddel in echo shall ring,
Thy years may be many, thy locks may be hoary,
Oh young is thy heart yet, our brave Hunter King.

The unknown author continues:

The old couple, of whom many a story is told, now lie side by side in Castleton Kirkyard. They have left a numerous race behind them to cherish their memory and to perpetuate their honoured name. His gude wife rather objected to Yeddie's portrait being painted in case people would laugh at him. In the picture of him at Keilder Rigg he is lively looking with low crowned hat and blue coat and is seated on a crag with foxhound and terrier both in leash, eager for the fray. The likeness is a most correct one and is visited by tourists from far and near.

I wish our mother had known about Yeddie. Like him, she was friendly and welcoming, and she was deeply in love with a Scotland she never saw. Her sentiments were with those of the writer of the 'Canadian Boat Song' and millions of his fellows.

From the lone shieling of the misty island
Mountains divide us, and the waste of seas –
Yet still the blood is strong, the heart is Highland,
And we in dreams behold the Hebrides!

Everything about her old country was precious to her, the beauty of the place and the hard times and the heroes and Bruce and his spider and the history of it all. And Robert Burns and Sir Walter Scott and the bagpipes which her father had played like a dream. (And don't take any notice of your Father, he hasn't an ounce of music in his body.) An unknown man in a kilt playing on Waimarama Beach at dusk could reduce her to pulp. 'The Flowers of the Forest' was far far too much; to our astonishment, tears, real dripping tears, rolled down.

They were all musical, the Mangatahi Jacksons at Craigieburn. Ah, those evenings around the piano and the squabbling among the girls as to who should play and which songs they would have. And the fun of it all, and young Fred with his banjo which he took to Gallipoli and, what was more, they both came back. He then took it with him to his farm near Porangahau when he won a Returned Servicemen's ballot on return from the war. It was the second time his banjo kept him sane, he said, with him sitting up there like Jackie and the loneliness so tough, until he met his future wife Elsie.

All had learned the meaning of hard work at Craigieburn and learned well, according to Mum. However, they had fun, in fact it seemed to us fun came because of the hard work, in some mysterious way. Her story of the best fun of all happened during dipping when their sister Lillias (known as Bubba Lil), their mother's favourite and blessed with the most beautiful auburn hair in the whole wide world, fell bang, crash into the dipping trench alongside startled sheep and was drenched as well.

Glorious, glorious.

Henry Cecil Wright and his family sailed across the world in comfort in the early 1900s when the worst hardships of early pioneering were over. A timing which our father considered eminently sensible; none of the males of his family had a taste for hard physical work and, except for a few country parson relatives, knew little of the countryside of Britain, let alone of New Zealand. They were proud of being town men. Added to which, and this was a major irritant to my mother, my father boasted they had not a drop of Scottish blood in their veins. English, French Huguenot, yes, but Scottish? Not on your life.

The Wrights also took their pleasures differently. Music was not an interest for them. Cecil was tone deaf and his children could sing in tune but little else. I never heard Mum singing about the house though she was said to 'have a voice'.

Where the Jacksons had music the Wrights had books. 'Other men's flowers' in a different form. Dad quoted Montaigne in an airy way: 'I have gathered a posie of other men's flowers and nothing but the thread that binds them is my own.' A solid-looking bookcase, filled with equally solid-looking leather-bound books, stood four square among the sofa and chairs in the two houses in which we grew up. They had been handed down from Grandfather Wright, now in Wellington, because he was now half blind and Cecil 'was the reader'. David and I were not allowed to touch the books, let alone take them from their shelves. We were not tempted. Later when I could read I found even the titles hard going. *The Ingoldsby Legends*, Wood's *Natural History*, Burton's *Anatomy of Melancholy*, the *Life of Luther*, and Addison and Steele's *Spectator* essays remained unread. *Jorrocks' Jaunts and Jollities* sounded more cheerful and were so: 'Where I dines I wines and where I wines I breakfasts.'

Poetry was on the higher shelves above our hands which we

never attempted to reach. Dad and Grandfather knew by rote slices of Wordsworth and Chaucer and Kipling (always Kipling), and chanted them together with delight. But not Mum, who usually retreated to the kitchen when the chanting began.

Henry Cecil and his son's range was wide, from *The Canterbury Tales* to thundering Macaulay and solo versions of psalms from Grandfather Wright which dated from the days before he gave up his theological studies at Oxford and read law. His reason for doing so, according to our father, who told us at an early age and to our complete incomprehension, was that he could no longer accept one of the *Thirty-Nine Articles*.

These articles, I found years later in the *Oxford Dictionary of the Christian Church*, are statements to define the Anglican position against Roman Catholics or Calvinistics. Article 17, for example, contains 'masterly ambiguity about the difficult topic of predestination'; 'Article 28 is concerned with that old stumbling block, transubstantiation'.

However, by the time Grandfather Wright would have been ordained the Articles, having been altered in 1865, had lost their teeth. The church required only that their ordained Anglican priests affirm that the articles were 'agreeable to the Word of God' and undertake not to 'teach in contradiction of them'.

None of us knew which article had felled Grandfather Wright's faith. Something important, we felt, was missing. Having made this decision, Henry Cecil changed his college and began reading law, a subject he found boring after the cut and thrust of late nineteenth-century theology.

Having finished his law degree at Oxford, Henry Cecil married his bride Miss Blanche Baker and they began their peripatetic lives. First he attempted to grow pineapples in Queensland where our father was born. 'Never live in Queensland, child. A ghaster of a place, believe me. As for pineapples!' I think of Henry Cecil whenever I meet them.

They sailed to Britain where their elder daughter Angela was born. Then off to New Zealand where he bought a small farm near Auckland. The enemy there was clay. 'The soil was sour, the work was back-breaking, the cows foul-tempered and the bulls worse,' said our father who had disheartening memories of the Bombay Hills.

After this disappointment they arrived in New Plymouth where one of his cousins, Henry Govett, was vicar of St Mary's church and grandfather of Monica Govett, who much later donated money for a public art gallery which became the Govett-Brewster Art Gallery in 1962.

My grandfather put up his brass plate (or had someone do it for him) on a corner plot: Henry Cecil Wright, BA, LLB. And there they stayed until he and Blanche retired to Wellington.

My father and grandfather shared not only an interest in words, and the sound of them; they enjoyed Latin tags and swapped inexplicable jokes that none of the rest of us could understand. Here is one finally understood after much help from Dad: Three ibis are flying along. An Egyptian huntsman fires a Right and Left. Down fall both outside birds; the middle one flies on. The huntsman's friend says *In media tissimis ibis*. 'It is safest in the middle.' End of joke. Mispronunciations of words either worried or delighted father and son; poets and their poems pleased them immensely.

Another way in which male members of the Wright tribe differed from their Jackson counterparts was the attention the former took with their appearance, the care they took of their clothes. Grandfather Wright had a well-trimmed Vandyck beard of which he seemed proud, likewise Dad and his well-tended moustache. *A kiss without a mustache is like an egg without salt.* French joke.

Every pair of Dad's shoes had its own wooden shoe trees. His shoes shone from constant polishing, the buttons on his fawn gaiters which he wore in winter required a special little hook on a handle to do them up. He took care of his clothes and nothing was ever lost. Extraordinary. He had a hat for every occasion, including a black beret for holidays which came all the way from Paris and reduced his children to blushing shame every time he wore it.

Our Jackson men, though by no means their women, had little interest in sartorial matters. Frederick Arthur, a fine upstanding man according to his daughter, let his moustache take its chance, his working clothes were built for the job, and his town suit shone.

In the 1860s when Great Grandfather Michael Jackson arrived from Scotland to the Coast, my English great grandfather, Philip Wright, was ensconced in a village called Copford, a few miles from Colchester and not far from the church of St Michael and All Angels, the one in which his son Henry Cecil married Miss Blanche Baker. The church, or parts of it, have been in existence since the twelfth century and, as the church booklet says, it is noted for its antiquity and Saxon wall paintings.

It is also host to a gruesome find. In 1780 some pieces of parchment were found under the hinges of the door – not strange in itself, as cattle hide was often inserted between wood and iron to protect the wood. For many years it was thought to be the skin of a marauding Dane who had been caught plundering the church and paid for this sacrilegious act by being flayed. Forensic examinations this century confirmed that the 'parchment' was that of a 'fair-skinned male'. According to the hunting law of Henry I, flaying is known to have been a punishment meted out to bondsmen found hunting in the royal hunting grounds; freemen, apparently, only lost a hand.

Philip earned his living as the diocesan secretary to the Bishop of London, during which time he lived with his wife Sarah Louise (née Govett) and their six children near St Michael and All Angels. For many years the house was held by the Bishops of London but they were dispossessed when Bishop Bonner refused to take the oath of allegiance and supremacy to Queen Elizabeth. History does not relate how Philip and his family came to live there. It now belongs to an organisation called the Care of the Elderly.

Henry Cecil and Blanche had four children: Cecil, Angela, Philip (who was drowned fishing in Norfolk Island when young), and Margaret, who with a friend established the Blue Cross Kennels in Karori, Wellington, where they worked as hard as anyone at Craigieburn ever did and with as much dedication to their cause.

Frederick Jackson Senior died long before Henry Wright and my memories of their friendship came from my mother. The grandfathers were different in so many ways – even their facial hair was different both in form and barbering – but they saw each other often and enjoyed each other's company. Talked their heads off, said Mum.

On 28 December 1928 Colin Frederick Romaine Wright appeared in King Street, Hastings. I have little memory of him until he surfaced as an adjunct to the Earthquake. From then on I loved him dearly.

CHAPTER 2

I was fond of dentists as a child. They gave drama to a structured and overprotected life. The first one I met, Mr Tonks, started it with what I thought were a haze of exciting words. 'Open wide while I look for caries.'

I thought he meant fairies. Clutching the arms of the chair in an effort to keep calm I counted the power lines beyond the square sky of the window above his head. Sixteen there were, counting the more frail telephone lines drooping lower and ending in mysterious white china cups, but never a fairy in sight.

Later I was moved to Mr Bob Whyte in King Street. Why I have no idea and probably didn't ask. I was a vague and dreamy child with hay fever, unlike my brother David who was spirited and demanded answers.

Mr Whyte was kind and jokey and told me I was brave which was a surprise. Squeaky clean in his high-necked jacket he was loved by all, including his receptionist Miss Protheroe (Not Her Real Name) who sat behind a desk in a starched white cap like an upturned boat, gave you appointments and pined away while Mr Whyte flourished and made his patients laugh. You couldn't help it.

Another thing of interest near Mr Whyte's surgery was the ivy-covered house across the road. Half hidden behind its privet hedge, the house where I was born gave little away. For years I kept hoping for some reaction, some interesting memory dredged up from the time when David and I lived there and Colin was a baby. Nothing happened. Only three memories remain from King Street: Miss Morris's mother, the garage across the road and my fairies.

The last one puzzled my practical mother. I was head down, bottom up, searching among the pansies one day when she appeared to be greeted by my wail, 'You've frightened her away.' This interest in fairies came from my four small books, illustrated and written by an English woman called Cicely Mary Barker. I carried *Flower Fairies of the Spring, Summer, Autumn*, or *Winter* long before I could read. None of them were New Zealand fairies but then nothing ever was in the books of my childhood. I studied fairies endlessly, knew each one off by heart and had my favourites, such as the reckless Thistle Fairy swinging about on top of his purple cushion, or the red baby-faced Spindle Berry Fairy shaking his berried branch with force. All the boy fairies had pointed ears, so technically, I suppose, they were elves, but who cared. The only one I never warmed to was the Wild Rose of England. Dressed in a long pink robe with a crown of roses, she was, I felt, beyond me as she sat staring straight ahead on her high branch, holding a gold staff in her hand.

Each fairy painting had its own verse which meant nothing to me before I could read, and was a sad disappointment when I could. The Burdock Fairy remains, washed up on some useless tide of memory.

Wee little hooks on each brown little bur,
(Mind where you're going, O Madam and Sir!)

What on earth was a Burdock? Again, it didn't matter as I searched for Snowdrop or Primrose or Bluebell fairies among my father's Jerusalem artichokes.

I learned quite soon that not every child believed in fairies, let alone saw them. It was a shock at the time but I learned to keep quiet on the subject. Fairies, apparently, were sissy, or worse, babyish.

Miss Morris and Mother (my second memory) lived next door. Mother had white hair and was old. I had worked out that the two went together and found it vaguely interesting, but not much.

One day Miss Morris came to ask my mother if she would like to come next door and see Mother before they took her away because she looked so beautiful.

My mother, who always looked beautiful, said that was very kind but thank you no, she had a friend coming to tea and she didn't think Barbara would want to . . .

Miss Morris had a jar of humbugs for boys and girls on her desk.

'Yes, I do.'

Mum looked doubtful. 'Are you sure, Bub?'

'Yes.'

I took Miss Morris's hand and trotted beside her up the shingle path to Mother's house, through the shadowy hall, past the tall clock which bonged the hours away and into Mother's bedroom which was dark, with pulled curtains. The only light was a dim bedside lamp beneath a pink lampshade with silky tassels. On the bed lay Mother. I stared at the face, the closed eyes, the stillness. Something was badly wrong.

'Why's she there?' I whispered.

'Mother has passed away. They'll be coming to take her away soon.'

Worse and worse. What? Where? Why?

'I knew you'd like to see her, dear.'

'No, no, no,' I yelled and ran screeching down the path.

My mother apologised. Miss Morris forgave me. The humbugs continued.

My last memory of the Frederick Street house involved Mr Hursthouse's Garage across the road from our house. I suppose there were cars for sale behind the vast windows, but the thing I loved was a brightly coloured placard standing upright on the floor near the front. Watched by two cows and a pig, a 1920s roadster sped along a country road, its carefree young driver laughing at the wheel, his scarf flying in the wind. Beneath were words.

'What does it say?' I asked my brother David, who could read but was already car mad, and didn't like me much anyway.

'Ask Dad, dopey.'

I did so.

'It is better to be five minutes late in this world than fifty years too soon in the next,' intoned my father.

'But what does it say?'

'You'll understand when you're older.'

More puzzlement.

One of Katherine Mansfield's stories I read twenty years later tells of a child's excitement when her family moved into a new house, a dramatic day which involved trailing up the long hill from Wellington city to the developing suburb of Karori.

Nothing like that for the Wrights. Our new house in Roberts Street was only a few blocks away from our one in King Street. Hastings, a small country town in 1930, was, according to Grandmother Jackson, 'flat as your hat. Hadn't a hill to bless itself.'

The first people who saw the new house were our grandmothers. They shared the honorary title of Nana, with a long 'a', as in Nana in Peter Pan, or worse, Émile Zola's Nana. Both our Nanas were strong women and I don't know why they settled for the same name as a large hairy dog in a frilly cap pretending to be a Nanny, or Émile Zola's mid nineteenth-century prostitute.

The Nanas' reactions to 609 Roberts Street differed. Nana Jackson said there was plenty of room out the back for a henhouse and Mum must keep White Leghorns which were the best layers. Nana Wright said there would be more room for us all to frolic.

Fat chance.

For as long as I can remember I was aware that we were not a family who frolicked.

The house at number 609 Roberts Street remains for me as a series of spaces. The best one was the so-called Dolls' Cupboard, a small child-sized place behind an odd-shaped door in my bedroom where my People lived when fairies had departed. All of them – Jane, Bunty, Josie, Molly and Bella with the long yellow legs – were never babies. They were not fed or cuddled or put to bed or woken up. They waited in dark nothingness, flat on their backs, with arms at their sides and feet facing outwards, ready to swing into instant Adventures when I opened the door.

I had little interest in the sitting room downstairs except in winter, when the fire gave one of the few sources of heat in the house, and we were allowed to warm our behinds in front of it before sprinting upstairs to bed. No one was ever allowed to poke the fire except Mum. For years I thought there must be some skill in keeping a fire going, a skill known to Mum's Jackson tribe but not the Wrights. I discovered years later any fool can do it. Another myth gone poof.

Grandfather Wright's bookcase and its books now stood against one wall, the King Street sofa and chairs were still covered in flowery linen, padded window seats stood either side of the fireplace, and always, inevitably, a vase shaped like a miniature cattle trough sat on the left hand of the mantelpiece, filled with dahlias, or gladioli, or a Mixed Bowl. Troughs, with chicken wire crumpled inside to support the flowers, were the chosen vases for mixed bowls in 609 and Mum's were much admired. She was good at mixed bowls as well as fires. The thing I liked best in the room was a Tiffany vase, which also came from Grandfather, its curved rainbow colours sleeping inside, definitely not for touching, nor for flowers.

Blinds were always drawn unless people were in the sitting room. The sun was Mum's enemy: it faded the covers if she wasn't careful, and made the flowers wilt sooner.

The dining room, besides the table, chairs and Dad's sofa, held a wind-up gramophone with a cabinet in which were stored His Master's Voice 78s, including our favourites: 'Tiptoe, through the tulips, through the tulips, through the tulips . . .'; 'The Laughing Policeman', who did nothing but laugh so hard that we did too and once Colin wet his pants; and 'The Cats' Chronicle', which prints all pussy cats' news.

And best of all, Frank Crumit and his bum songs. Bums were rude, we knew that, but Frank's bums were all right. They were Americans and were also called 'hobos' and sang about a land that's far away in the Big Rock Candy Mountains. We sang along with Frank:

In the Big Rock Candy Mountains you never change your socks,
And little streams of alcohol come a'tricklin' down the rocks.
The brake men have to tip their hats and the railroad bulls are blind,
There's a lake of stew and of whiskey too.
You can paddle all around 'em in a big canoe
In the Big Rock Candy Mountains.

And his theme song

> *Alleluia, I'm a bum,*
> *Alleluia, bum again*
> *Alleluia, give us a handout*
> *To revive us again.*

Innocent as a nest of singing birds we sang along with them all, including what I discovered later to be a bowdlerised version of 'Abdul Abulbul Amir'.

Beneath the windows which overlooked the garden stood another bookcase which, besides 'ordinary' books, held dictionaries. These were for looking up words at meal times. 'Knowledge,' said Grandfather Wright, and probably someone else before him, 'is knowing where to look it up.' None of which made any sense for any of us until we could read. Before that was an atlas or two and Brewer's *Dictionary of Phrase and Fable* where I found *Famous Last Words*, the most memorable of which was St Lawrence's, whose martyrdom took the form of being roasted on a gridiron, and ran thus –

> *This side enough is toasted*
> *so turn me, tyrant, eat,*
> *and see whether raw or roasted*
> *I make the better meat.*

Another friend was Fowler's *Modern English Usage,* which was first published the year I was born therefore worth picking up. Dad read me H.W. Fowler's dedication to his brother who 'died, age 47, of tuberculosis contracted during service with the BEF in 1915–16'. He writes, 'I think of it as it should have been, with its prolixities docked, its dullnesses enlivened, its fads eliminated, its truths multiplied.' I liked that, and remember I nagged Dad about 'prolixities', but didn't get far.

When I could read, I discovered that the problem with dictionaries is that you have to know how to spell the word required before you can look it up and find its meaning. There are fair traps in learning.

Beside the dining room ran a long narrow place called the servery, at the far end of which was the smallest space of all, smaller even than the dolls' cupboard. This was called the water safe and projected beyond the outside wall. It opened above a shiny wooden slab which housed three large bins for sacks of sugar, flour, odds and ends.

The safe had fly-proof netting all around the servery. Shelves surrounded the shallow square pond, into which water ran all day and then disappeared out down the plughole. It never stopped; cool water lapped around a damp brick on which sat a blue plate with daisies and on that sat a pound of butter which never melted, not even in the nineties, Mum told us. The safe's shelves were lined with things which might 'go off' if Mum wasn't careful, but she was.

Years later the Frigidaire arrived and there was more excitement as Mr Jones wheeled it in to install this miracle, with its ability to make squares of ice enclosing tiny trapped bubbles, its promise of ice creams on tap. Mum was relieved when the door opened and the fridge swallowed up meat and puddings which sat on shelves. Above was the doughnut-shaped top where the engine was. Periodically its mechanism gave a convulsive shuddering rumble, then calmed down again. The fridge was Mum's friend but the safe was more interesting to me; the coolness of the brick in its square pond, the deep golden butter slab for spreading, the plums cooling and the sound of water falling. When I met the word 'plashing' I thought of the safe.

It was running when we came down each morning and was still running, cool and safe and endless, as we trailed up to bed. It could do this, we were told, because we had an 'Artesian bore'.

'A what?'

'You'll know when you're older.'

Colin loved it too.

On the dining-room side of the servery two huge meat covers hung one beneath the other. They were silvery grey and made of what Mum called pewter, another good word, though Mum says they were too big to be any use and took a lot of cleaning. Near them was a hatch through which food could be handed into the dining room. One of the few games the three of us played together was Slides. When the coast was clear we skidded onto the shelf beneath (with a leg up for Colin), wriggled through the slide, hit ground in the dining room, then ran around for another go. The idea being that someone must be in the wooden hatch at all times. It usually ended with us all singing along with 'The Road to Vicksburg', or one of Frank Crumit's other classics.

We were caught once or twice but the game continued for years.

Beyond the servery was the kitchen, which was of little interest. None of us were ever allowed to help Mum, let alone attempt cooking. Beyond that was a larder, notable for me because it was said I had swallowed a fly there. Another door led to the washhouse with its copper, which was lit from below and boiled its head off every Monday. When the wash was finished the floor was scrubbed with Pearson's sandsoap, which was again of great interest to me. Each slab had two tiny pictures on each of its sloping sides, like those vans which now carry sheets of glass. On one side a tiny lady tended a sick child, saying, 'I WISH I had used Pearson's Sandsoap'. On the other side an equally tiny, but happy lady holds a laughing child, saying, 'I'm GLAD I used Pearson's Sandsoap.'

Sometimes Wrightie came to help Mum on washing days. We all loved Wrightie and she loved us. It was she who translated the Pearson's sandsoap ladies for me before I could read. Near the end of the washing process the cool water was made blue by a little muslin bag containing a lump of solid blue Reckitt's, which made your sheets 'whiter than white'. She also told us sad stories in the kitchen after she had finished in the washhouse. The three of us sat in a row on the kitchen linoleum and watched as Wrightie flopped herself in a wicker chair which crackled with fright as she landed. Then she began her stories, all of which had dreadful endings. One was about a little girl who fell in a boiling copper, which I begged for, then wept each time I heard it.

David would point at me in concerned but scornful tones, 'Look, Bub's crying,' and Wrightie would clutch me to her deep and loving bosom and tell me it was only a story, 'just a story, dear.' Wrightie also read me the messages of advertisements for blue-bags. 'Whiter than White.' And another in which a bubble from a mouth says, 'Don't let Mrs Next Door Sniff at your Whites.'

We all knew Mondays were busy for Mum and Wrightie and we were not welcome in the washhouse. Nevertheless if Wrightie was on duty alone she would let me 'help', until one day a tiny white hand surfaced among swirling soap bubbles. Wrightie and I shrieked together. This time it was her warm wet sacking-apron which caught my terror. Even when she lifted the dripping object from the boiling cauldron with her wooden pole I wouldn't look despite her laugh. 'Look dear, just a poor wee shrunken glove that got in by mistake. It's now no use to man or beast.'

'No, no, no.'

'There, there, love – look, what's Wrightie got in her pocket?'

And out came a soft green jube dusted with damp and slightly hairy sugar.

CHAPTER 3

Like all Roberts Street houses, 609 faced onto Cornwall Park, a public space with gardens, a mini zoo and playing fields where men played cricket and spectators sat under oak trees like their replicas in *Country Life*, which, like *Punch*, Dad 'took for the surgery'.

There were other attractions at the park: trees for climbing (illegal and hotly pursued by Mr Edgar, the custodian) and a faintly murky-looking pond with two white swans, overfed ducks, and ducklings which came and went and were wept over.

'Cats,' said Mr Edgar, 'bloody cats.'

Imagine being eaten.

The so-called zoo was a disappointment. The monkeys were kept in a brick enclosure *en route* to Nana Jackson's house, where she lived after Grandfather Jackson had died. Occasionally one or two inmates of the cage would fling themselves at fierce speed round and round the small cage, up and down and round again, chattering as they flew. They would then lapse into silence or a desultory grooming of one of their fellows. Two of them had most alarming behinds; flaming red, bulbous and swollen. Were they meant to be like that? And who to ask yet again, especially as it was bums?

The cage and its concrete surroundings stank of Jeyes Fluid. One whiff of it now and I am back at the monkey house, as Mr Edgar called their little brick cell.

I was sorry for them, and made up adventures in my head for their release, but not with much conviction. They were too sad, two of them were repellent (the ones the boys liked best) and they smelled to high heaven (according to Nana Jackson).

The rest of the Cornwall Park zoo consisted of birds, who seemed happier. In one cage two sulphur-crested cockatoos delighted Colin and me, snapping their head feathers open/shut, open/shut, flip/flap, flip/flap, thus revealing and hiding the brilliant sharp yellow of their crests. The next cage housed three pink galahs, cheerful looking in their pink and grey feathers, busy and good to watch. Colin and I stood hand in hand admiring the way they ate, their strong beaks, the determined winkling of nuts from shells, their wicked winking eyes. They were *living* for those nuts. You could see.

Next door was the Long Run, which had patchy grass and more space, with ragged shrubs for the peacocks and guinea fowls to hide behind. What satisfactory birds the peacocks were; walking, stalking, haughty miracles of beauty. The clattering of their strong wings would bring Colin and me running, followed, if we were lucky, by the full display, though often there were false alarms. The fanning of peacock feathers dazzled us. We were glued to the whole process, sunk into the glory of the eye in each feather till their owners turned to show off their fluffy backsides and then turned again to us, backing and advancing. Boy, were those peacocks skites.

I also admired the guinea fowl, dressed in the same neat black-and-white patterns favoured by the elderly widows of Hastings for their best silks. Mrs Rochford, Mrs Felkin, Mrs Fannin; all older friends of Mum and excellent women, all as dignified as the male guinea fowl and as suitably dressed; neat but not gaudy, as Dad said.

We heard our peacocks' anguished shrieks each night as we lay tucked in our beds and snuggled deeper. The night before the Big Earthquake, we were told, they had screeched all through the night.

My father rented a cottage at Waimarama Beach near Hastings for three weeks each summer. In 1931 David and I, aged six and four, were stealing Nana Wright's chocolates which she always carried, when all of a sudden, out of nowhere, the Big Earthquake began roaring and rumbling and tossing us to the floor. We scrambled up, were flattened again while the ground heaved and the roar increased. My main memory is of astonishment. Who was doing it? What was happening? David – David would know. He did. Primer one had done earthquake drill just before his school broke up last year. 'Earthquake!' he screamed and hurtled out the door, followed by me on hands and knees. Aunty Lorna, David's godmother, grabbed me as she ran past and the fibreboard cottage began to crack.

Colin's escape was more dramatic. He was only two, playing by himself brrm-brrmming a Dinky Toy car around the rainwater tanks which stood on their wooden stands. The force of the upheaval knocked one of the tanks sideways. It landed within inches, *inches*, of the spot from where Mum had snatched him moments before.

Stealing chocolates and Colin being saved by inches were my strongest memories of the disaster, plus the excitement of sleeping with dozens of others on Mr Barker's tennis court up the hill. The wild sea, he told Mum, was 'moiling and toiling and threshing about', had flung fish around, swallowed islands, and had then disappeared way out beyond Bare Island.

The grown-ups feared a tidal wave, and local farmers from the nearby hills drove down the broken road, collected all the beachcombers and carried us up to the shelter of their farms, where all of us slept outside. The Maori at the local pa decided they would not go to the hills.

The giant wave did not appear but the aftershocks went on for weeks. No one slept inside for some time. All this is legend to me. My memories of that night are of the ripe apricots from the tree at the end of Mr Barker's tennis court where we slept. The fruit were more golden and sweeter than any tasted since. And a field mouse ran over my hand during the night. The delicious skittery flutter of minikin feet remains with me, along with the apricots and Colin's whimperings as he lay in Mum's arms all night.

Dad was in Hastings when the earthquake struck at 11am that morning. The road to Waimarama was blocked and it was some time before any news came through. We learned later that Dad was in the operating theatre at Royston Hospital, removing a patient's gall bladder, when the operating table began waltzing all over the floor, pursued by the operating team. No one panicked, the operation was completed and the patient flourished. The only time Dad had ever had to chase a lady round the room, he told us later when we could appreciate his wit. His wit failed him but the image of Dad, who had never been known to waltz, let alone chase ladies around rooms, pleased us.

A tent hospital was set up in the racecourse and doctors and nurses worked night and day operating on the wounded. Royston Hospital itself, and its equipment, staff and doctors, became the nucleus of Hastings Emergency Hospital. We didn't see Dad for two weeks.

*

Our rival town, Napier, was more devastated than Hastings due to fire damage. The town had burst into flame when, according to legend, a lighted bunsen burner in a chemist's shop was tossed to the floor.

But Napier had the benefit of HMS *Veronica*'s assistance. The sloop was in harbour and her captain and ship's company came to the rescue in true naval fashion. When the ship was decommissioned the ship's bell was given to the city of Napier, where it still hangs 'proudly' on Marine Parade. My Napier friend Jill Waterworth showed it to me immediately it appeared. Skite.

When expatriates of Hawke's Bay of a suitable age meet throughout the world, our talk often turns to the earthquake. Each and every one of us has our tales to tell. Where we were, what we were doing when the Big One struck (earthquakes always 'strike'). We are back there on the morning of 3 February 1931, being thrown off our legs or trikes or whimpering in terror, or alternatively praying and wetting our pants on our first day at school. A country friend outclassed us all by seeing the land open before her eyes, swallow a couple of sheep and then close again. Poor sheep. Spooky.

We repeat the stories we have learned since. We know the numbers. Two hundred and fifty people killed and thirty thousand more in need of food and shelter for weeks and months after the day went mad. How the land lifted at Napier, the inner harbour disappeared, where whole hillsides collapsed and rivers disappeared. And all this at the height of the Big Depression, the time of unemployment and bitter poverty.

Small girls learned of the domestic chaos, how just-filled bottling jars crashed from high shelves and glowing red Beefsteak tomatoes, Black Boy peaches and plump Golden Queens mingled with shattered glass on housewives' kitchen floors, and dear Lord, the mess.

I absorbed this when young and wept for the dead children, like the little flower girl killed in the Beauty Salon where she was 'having her hair done' for a wedding that afternoon. It was too much to believe. Having her hair done one minute and then dead. Another wedding in the district went ahead, but 'it didn't last'.

A few years afterwards my mother and I went to Napier to consult an ear, nose and throat man called Mr Scoular. I had had hay fever since birth, breathed through my mouth, sniffled and snorted, and my eyes streamed, all of which Mum found unattractive in the extreme. Blame was laid at Your Father's door.

The best part of my several visits was a framed picture drawn by someone called Bernard Partridge, which showed a globe with the British Isles in the top left-hand side and New Zealand on the bottom right. In front of the globe a female figure in draping robes sat beside a large shield, resting her sad head on her hand in grief.

'Who's that?' I asked.

'That's Britannia,' said Mum.

'Who's Britannia?'

'Ask your father.'

At the bottom right-hand corner of the globe the artist had sketched some small scratchy black lines and billowing smoke to indicate disaster. A small place being 'rent asunder' at the bottom of the world.

Below the print was a caption: *AN EMPIRE MOURNS. February 3rd 1931.*

I stared at this picture with awe every time we made our hopeless visits to Mr Scoular. How nice of the lady, who was obviously important and British. How noble of the Empire to grieve, and Mr Partridge to draw the picture. Mr Scoular told me it came from a contemporary copy of *Punch*. This made it even better. *Punch*, which I had known from childhood's beginnings, was thinking of us.

The school where David had received his first information on earthquakes was called Mahora, a local primary school in Hastings whose motto is 'Piki haere', which is Maori for 'Keep on climbing'. David loved the place and made friends quickly. Shoes, he told me, were sissy so he hid his in the hedge in the morning and put them on before arriving home. It never occurred to either of us that the reason that many kids wore no shoes was because they had none to wear in the Depression.

David and I were not friends as children. I was a dreamy wet hen with hay fever and he knew it. He was older, more powerful and given to sudden rages and minor bullying. He was often ill as a child, made frustrated and miserable by a juvenile form of coeliac disease, an allergy caused by gluten in wheat flour, which was not diagnosed until many years later. In the meantime he kept Colin and me on our toes with painful twistings of the forearm called Chinese burns and well aimed pinches on our respective bottoms. In between he drove his pedal car into the ground then graduated onto a bike.

Mostly, however, he spent his time mucking about with those who were about to be big kids: the O'Malley boys and the Peaches and the Crutchleys and Bruce Cummings, all of whom spent a lot of time hooning their bikes up and down Roberts Street or the straight avenues of Cornwall Park. Like David they were obsessed with speed; anything that *went*.

As a fractious, sleepless baby, the most effective way to lull him to sleep in the King Street days, Mum told me, had been for Dad to put David in his Moses basket on the back seat of the car and drive round and round the flat, grid-like streets of Hastings until he slept.

Failing which, Mum pushed the pram interminably round and round the block. Motion of any kind was good for David, and the faster the better. His knowledge of the makes of cars followed quickly at an early age. Every car in the district was pointed at, its name lisped in triumph.

The big kids and speed were not for me. The only one who interested me was Bruce Cummings: he was so weirdly tidy, so extraordinarily clean. A snappy dresser in embryo was Bruce, with his snake-clip belt centred neatly above his pleated grey shorts. His shirt never came out of his pants. Ever. He was smooth. One day he asked if he could kiss me. I had no feeling about this, but everyone else seemed to think it would be a good idea so I agreed. Bruce and I stood on the concrete floor of the shed, my behind pressed hard against the bench-vice while he kissed my mouth.

'Now,' said Bruce, 'you're my girl.'

'Oh.'

He pointed upwards. 'Look.' Peering through the high windows, supported by the rickety outdoor table, leering, guffawing, hee-hee-heeing with glee at the peep show below, were David, Colin, Wally and Terry O'Malley and a Crutchley boy from round the corner.

No one had ever kissed me on the mouth before. An interesting trick. I tried it on Colin later but he rebelled.

*

Colin was my best friend. Two years younger with hair like pale silk, blue blue eyes, jug ears too big for his face, and a wide grin, he was young enough for me to both love him and boss him, to train him into becoming a useful operator of the People. Holding them at their solid middles we sparrow-hopped them around on their painted black shoes and Bunty's woolly blue feet as they acted out their adventurous and dramatic lives, which I recorded, once I could write, into small cut-up notebooks. We never thought of them as dolls, let alone called them so. They were our People. When I see a small child clutching a doll by its nonexistent waist and hopping it around I am tempted to ask, 'What's she doing now?' but have learned to keep quiet. The joys of making up can be too vivid, too fierce for interruption. Besides, no one should hijack another's world.

All the participants in our stories were brave and skilful, except for Bunty who tended to lag behind and get lost or fall into tiger traps. They were also athletic, their cheerful daring bordering on recklessness as they forded swift rivers or flagged down the train seconds before disaster. The stories I told myself after lights out were also brave adventures. But now I was the heroine who saved the day, who walked the jungle paths with one arm resting on the head of her faithful lion cub Natee. My dreams were good too. I used to screw my opened eyes shut again in the hope of finishing off a particularly good one. Difficult to achieve but worth a try.

My 'making up' was heavily influenced by comics. *Frolic and Fun with Mustapha Bun* introduced me to camels, sheikhs and beautiful ladies. *Teddy at the Seaside* revealed the curious life of English children at the seaside, with pails and starfish and piers, and never a mention of our proper beaches with their big waves and buckets and pipis and kina.

Best for narrative were David's American comics which starred the G-man, Dick Tracy. My first moment of knowing what was going to happen from indirect evidence provided by the author happened with him. Three strong-jawed men sat side by side in the back of the cop car: Dick himself, his offsider and an even tougher-looking man between.

'But what were the thoughts of the silent third man?' asked the words in the bubble. 'What were Fingers Moroney's thoughts?'

'He did it,' I said, pointing. 'Fingers Moroney shot the defenceless janitor.'

'How'd you know?' said David.

'I just know.'

Fingers did too.

'Let's play People,' I'd say to Colin.

'Where've we got to?'

'Jane's got the baddies stuck on the bridge. She's jumping on their hands. They're hanging on underneath, see.'

'How?'

'Like this.'

Not only were they People, they were people I knew better than anyone in the real world. They were my real world. Jane, Molly, José, Bella and Bunty. We never gave shape to the baddies in our stories. They were faceless, nameless, known only as They.

'Good adventure place,' Colin and I would mutter to each other in the back seat of the Buick as our father drove past the cliffs and stony river beds on Sunday drives up to Kereru or Mangatahi, to see Uncle Harry and his family, who farmed at Craigieburn, or sometimes to Porangahau to see Uncle Freddy and Aunty Elsie and their two little girls, who brushed their teeth in tooth mugs because their water tanks were so low. The sound of the yellow celluloid windows crackling remains, and the sight of the white enamel bowl with the blue rim, in case I felt sick, were all part of the Wright's Sunday drives. How hot it was in summer, how still the country lay as the silent sheep lifted their heads and I scrambled out just in time and an old ewe coughed in disapproval.

CHAPTER 4

My father was a shadowy figure when we were young, a tall, polite man who left home in the morning and came home smelling of ether and Craven As, a friendly combination but without the sweet tang of my mother, whose nicotine mingled with Elizabeth Arden's Blue Grass Toilet Water. Blue Grass? Another puzzle.

Our mother was beautiful, gregarious and well loved. She was good company and entertaining, her arms wide in welcome when her friends arrived, of whom she had many and of all ages. There were younger ones, with gentle names like Esther, Florrie, and Dulcie, who came to her for advice and knitted us woolly animals, which were rejected immediately by David, and by Colin, once he learned they were sissy. I also took little interest in them. They were not People and I liked animals who seemed pleased to see me, like dogs, who were not allowed.

Mum also had more robust younger friends like Barbara Landels, who taught David and me how to ride our bikes. David achieved this in a flash. I took longer, wobbling illegally round and round Cornwall Park cricket field with Barbara L panting behind in case of almost certain collapse. Hastings and bikes went together, and I did learn eventually, which was just as well. Being flat as our hats, Hastings swarmed with bikes and strong legs pumping; high school boys' hairy ones and the trousered ones of office workers whizzing home for lunch, cutting corners, 'going like the clappers'. Women didn't go like the clappers, or not many. They sat up straight and were thankful for string skirtguards and not having to throw a leg over the bar like the men.

The visits of Mum's country friends – Greta, Lorna, her sisters and sisters-in-law – were all precious to her. They would call in on their way home, having been dropped off by their respective husbands, who then retreated to the Club in Market Street. Trips into town from distant farms over unsealed roads could be a challenge in the thirties. Stores of all kinds for farm and home and enough of all to last a month, or even more, had to be collected from the stock and station agent of their husband's choice. The

Farmers' Co-operative Society (the Farmers'), de Pelichet McLeod (which was badly damaged during the earthquake), and Williams and Kettle were all well known. Even the townie children like us knew the names.

The town day was always 'hectic, absolutely hectic', according to the wives, and presumably for the men also, though I heard little about them as I squatted head down amongst the sensible shoes in the sitting room and got on with my colouring-in, a minor talent at which I shone. My coloured crayons hardly ever went over the edge.

I enjoyed the news exchanged over Mum's tea and Fly Away sponge. The country version of chat always seemed more exciting. There was often an update about the neighbour on the telephone party line who eavesdropped on others on the line and was revealed by the chimes of her long-case clock in the background. Which served her right did it not? And what a laugh, except nothing would stop her and really and truly it was too much. But there were much worse things to reveal. Jock's prize bull had had to be put down. Jessie could imagine Jock's reaction. I heard the gloom in her friend's 'Put down', and Mum's sympathy in her 'Oh, my dear'.

Then Uncle Harry, or Freddy or Bill or some other husband, would arrive to carry his wife away and Mum would embrace them fondly, still laughing and saying, 'Come again soon, dear, I'm lost without you.'

I never heard Mum call any of us 'dear', let alone 'darling'. The word seemed excessive to me as a child when I heard endearments between my friends' parents in their own houses.

'Where are you, darling?'

'Here, darling.'

'Where, darling?'

'Here, darling.'

'Oh, *there,* darling.'

Or worse, when used crossly by fathers. 'Isn't lunch ready *yet*, darling.'

It gave me the creeps. Silly sissy kissing stuff was not the norm at 609. I never saw my parents embrace, kiss, or even touch each other intentionally. Obviously they must have done so at some early stage, and Mum must have cuddled us when we were small, but there was no photographic evidence of such *louche* behaviour, which is ridiculous.

She loved us, of course she loved us. She gave us sugar with lettuce leaves for lunch, she took us to the park for swings when we were little and gave us proper Sister Jackson bed-baths when we were sick in bed, an enormous treat. She made us birthday cakes with candles and icing and a lemon/orange cordial called 50/50. Birthdays were special: 'Birthdays,' Mum said, 'come but once a year.'

After our birthdays, the biggest thrill of our early childhood was to wake on a morning after our parents had people for a meal. By each of our beds sat a naked chocolate and beside it a brilliant inch-high chocolate-paper goblet which once had wrapped the said chocolate. It was magic. Not only the chocolate but the goblet, which to me was evidence of true love.

Later we learned the secret of making them. Wrap shiny paper round a forefinger, twist some of remaining paper below for stem, flatten remaining paper for base and stand upright. Quite simple really, considering their importance as evidence.

And yes, Mum was lovingly demonstrative with her women friends and relaxed and friendly with male friends who admired her, including Mr Thompson the butcher, who saved for her the best H-bone corned beef in the Bay.

It was just that for some reason displays of emotion or affection, or (God forbid) praise for her husband and children defeated her.

Nor was our father given to emotional excess. Dry and laconic, he left for the surgery or the operating theatre each weekday morning and came home to read the paper, eat a well-cooked meal with appreciation and go to bed early to read books. He was amiable, but not designed for the *Sturm und Drang* of fatherhood. Tolerant of humanity in general, especially if they were his patients, all of whom he treated with the same courteous attention he paid his wife and her friends.

Mum told me once he had 'surgeon's hands'. 'He could have done anything with those hands. Anything,' she said, staring at me with such intensity I felt uneasy. What was wrong? What should I do? How?

The work he did was well done, she granted, but he was never *friendly*. He said so himself, laughing as he did so that although he might forget the names and faces of his patients, he never forgot the neat little scars he left them.

It was years before I discovered how much his patients loved him.

I see him taking his ease at 609 after his round of golf, or a tennis match which preceded the Sunday roast. Nana Jackson walked across Cornwall Park to join us each week. Mum, we all knew, was best at roasts, as well as nursing.

Understandably, Dad was an expert carver and sharpened the knife with a flourish; swish, swish, swish, he went, then inserted a pellet of rolled-up bread beneath the broken guard of the carving fork and lo, with a flick and a twist of his wrist the crisp brown top slice of the rolled sirloin was divided into three sizzling pieces onto our eager plates, of which Colin's still had a rim for spillage and a picture of Humpty Dumpty before the fall.

Dad had quotations for various moments during meals, so familiar to us I thought all fathers said them and cherished them as he did. 'Soup of the evening, beautiful soup,' he said to greet its arrival; 'Fate cannot touch me. I have dined tonight,' when he had; 'A carver is either a fool or a knave,' at any stage. Fortunately he didn't like the well-done outer slices. The pinker the better for Daddy and his quick-flashing knife on the Sunday joint.

Then there was pudding. Trifle perhaps, or Spanish cream, which I learned years later is an excellent culture for the causative organisms of some types of food poisoning. 'It has been known,' said the textbook, in a burst of confidence, 'to lay many wedding parties low.'

Table manners instruction continued and, no, we couldn't get down, even if we didn't want any more. Not until everyone had finished. After which Nana Jackson had a brief chat with Mum and gave advice over the washing up. 'You should get one of those little rubber scrapers, Jessie,' she said before departing to walk home across the park, her navy blue straw well anchored with hat pins and her small grey gloves clutching a basket with a covered basin containing 'a wee poke which will keep me going for days'.

When the field was clear Dad placed an old copy of *The Hawke's Bay Tribune* at the end of the long sofa in the dining room to avoid his shoes messing it, lay down, sighed deeply and opened his current book from the library, usually a whodunit, except on holidays. Children were shooed out and denied entry. We mauled each other. We distracted him. We made a hellish row. I liked the word *maul*, but knew enough not to ask what it meant when the act of doing it displeased.

He admired and irritated his loved wife. How did I know? How does any child know? An early memory at Roberts Street surfaces. My mother and I were upstairs inspecting the still-wrapped Christmas presents. Mum disliked those messy Christmas trees dropping bits all over the place, and presents always waited in her bedroom until the day. She picked up her husband's gift to her, shook it and said wearily, 'Not another wretched vase.' I snatched her hand. 'It'll be lovely. Mum, you'll love it.' She looked at me bleakly. 'Time I put the meal on,' she said and we trailed downstairs.

As a well-fed middle-class child of five, with my People waiting in the cupboard and Colin at my side, I knew little of the big earthquake of '31 and less about the Depression. I did wonder what was happening when I went with Mum to a soup kitchen in Avenue Road. There in the large bare room were Mum and other men and women handing over food to long queues of men, women and children. The queues worried me. They were not happy and eager like the queues at cinemas we occasionally saw, jostling a bit, laughing. These were the saddest faces I had seen. 'Why are they sad, Mum?' 'They're waiting for food. They'll be happy later on. Go and play, Bub.'

I sat in a corner near Mum and began 'making up' with Molly, a soft stuffed doll with a pink knitted frock. A small girl about my age appeared. I told her where I'd got to and that we could take turns with Molly if she liked. Which we did amicably until Mary's mother appeared and they departed.

'Where's Molly?' asked Mum later.

'I gave her to Mary. They've gone home.'

'Why did you do that?'

'She hasn't got one.'

Whereupon my lovely mother and I caught the Number Ten bus all the way to the Cornwall Park stop and home to 609 Roberts Street and hot cocoa for a treat.

*

'Not in front of the children' was rigidly enforced at home, as was 'Don't contradict', a phrase which dogged our lives. Adults, especially parents, knew best.

When my father mentioned topics like the Depression, or the Slump, he would stress the point that he was a lucky man. Of course he had unpaid bills which would remain unpaid – how could they not? – but at the moment he was lucky.

We were not hungry or cold or miserable and we knew little about anything. In fact it was quite difficult to find out anything about anything at home other than the meaning of words and the necessity of good behaviour. We did notice sometimes men or women who came to the door with offerings of jars of cream or home-killed meat, something which Mum, that true farmer's daughter, always spoke of with reverence. 'There is nothing like farm-killed meat.' She thanked all comers most gratefully, though I did hear her say once after the donor had left that she did prefer meat which was not 'on the hoof', by which she meant unplucked or unskinned or unexcavated.

All children are self-absorbed, and the smaller they are the more so. Newborn babies have to concentrate to find the nipple and plug into sublime contentment. There is much to learn when small. We were told frequently how lucky we were and we believed this, but the contexts remained dim. In our childhood most of the children in the district had holes in their teeth owing to lack of fluoride in the water. We learned this later, when it was far too late. Visits to dentists, let alone for cosmetic reasons, were unknown to many adults and children in the Depression. Teeth often rotted early, and many were pulled and replaced by false ones as soon as possible.

So I knew I was lucky to go to Mr Whyte for my corrective plates to avoid buck teeth, but didn't feel it. They were uncomfortable and sometimes painful to wear, and I spent hours searching for them when they were 'mislaid'.

I also knew I was lucky to 'take things' after school, a privilege known to children whose parents could afford to pay for the pursuit of culture. I 'took' dancing with Miss Grantham and Miss Patterson, wore a short pink tunic and lumbered around accompanied by Miss Patterson's heavy sighs – or was it Miss Grantham's?

I also 'took' piano from Miss Clayton who had the dire task of teaching me. She seemed a sad lady, though presumably not all pupils could have been as hopeless as me. She also had bad breath, an unfair complaint because those who have it are never aware, and those who confront it never forget, no matter how desirable the sufferer's other attributes.

On my first lesson with Miss Clayton she sat beside me on the dark blue velvet piano stool and tried to instill into me a few basic facts about acoustics. 'Which instrument would you hear from the longest distance away, Barbara?'

Anxious to please as ever, I made a stab at it. 'The piano.'

'No,' said Miss Clayton dully. 'The drum.'

'Oh.'

The two things I longed to 'take' were elocution and tap dancing but these were vetoed. Dad said if I could get around with 'How now, brown cow', I should be all right and Mum didn't like patent leather.

At five I went to school at Queenswood, a small school around the corner, 'A hop, skip and a jump', as Nana Jackson said, who had little knowledge of my dreamy progress through life. One pat on my head per visit was enough for both of us.

Queenswood had boarders as well as daygirls. The latter were aware that the boarders were on a higher plane. Also the school was run on strictly hierarchical terms. One of Dad's quoted truths could have been the school motto:

Big fleas have little fleas upon their backs to bite 'em.
And little fleas have lesser fleas and so on ad infinitum.

On my first April Fool's Day at the school one of the big kids, Sheena (NHRN), told me to ask Mr Cameron, the caretaker, for one of his 'loose screws'.

Anyone could see through that one, and although I was aware that Mr Cameron had an alarming looking red face and was known to be ratty, I was more scared of Sheena than him.

I knocked on Mr Cameron's shed door and gave the message. He finished rolling a weedy looking cigarette, lit it and blew smoke at me.

'Shove off,' he snarled, 'and tell that young Sheena she can put that in her pipe and smoke it.'

Puzzled but relieved, I shoved off, returned to Sheena and told her with cunning that Mr Cameron said he was sorry but he had run out of loose screws. Clearly disappointed at my lack of gore or whimpering, Sheena ran off to a tennis match. Which she won.

Popularity was of major importance at Queenswood, so much so there was a prize for it. At the end of the year every girl (and one or two small boys) were invited to name the girl they liked best in the school. We voted in strict order of precedence. I voted for Pat Tiffen who voted for Wendy Whitlock who voted for Ann Stokes who voted for Mary McIntyre who voted for Barbara Herrick who voted for Tiny Groome who won the cup.

Ability in sport was also considered a good thing, from Miss Rixon the headmistress down to my contemporaries. Ability in any form of schoolwork, however, was definitely a bad thing to one's class mates, the majority of whom were practising to be big fleas as soon as possible.

Nevertheless there were many good things at Queenswood. I loved the uniform and the school song, of which I now can't remember a word. I made friends – a new and exciting experience. And I discovered how much I enjoyed finding out about things. The first of which was how to tell my right arm or leg from my left. The mild form of physical education we achieved with Miss Thorpe took place on the wide, white, crushed-limestone drive. It became obvious that everyone else knew this secret. I watched carefully to avoid scorn. Since then left is the climbing roses and right is the walnut trees.

Another good thing was Miss Rixon's art pictures. Once a week we marched into her sitting room and sat cross-legged on her faded carpet while she gave us a brisk run through great paintings of the world. This consisted of her handing around postcards of the works of the Great Masters. She told us where each one had lived, where these treasures could now be seen, and what to look for.

'The colour, girls, see the colour, and the depth, see, on the shoulder there.' The sun shone on our backs as we peered at the little cards and absorbed art, or didn't, as the mood took us. Miss Rixon's fervour for her heroes never lessened; Rembrandt, Leonardo da Vinci, Michelangelo and Titian, I gathered, were the bosses.

I was lucky also with my first teacher. Miss Linsey was gentle, an excellent thing in an infant room. Every morning began with the day's hymn, with Miss Linsey playing the piano and conducting as well, her curls bobbing as we sang.

There is a happy land,
Far, far away.
Where saints in glory stand
Bright, bright as day.

Or better, our version of 'All Things Bright and Beautiful'.

All things bride and bewdyful
All creadures grade an' small.
All things wise an' wondyfull
The Lord God made 'em all.

Miss Linsey also forgave my first go at cheating. When we did good work in our exercise books she awarded us with golden stick-on stars beside the work in question. When my stars were absent for too long I attempted forgery with my gold colouring pencil. She called me to her knee and whispered that this was not a good idea. This was called cheating. Also it didn't work as she could tell her stars from mine. However, she wouldn't mention it to the class. Merciful Miss Linsey.

The best thing of all, however, was learning to read.

The process seemed magical to me. Those little squiggles which we drew with our HB pencils, our tongues sticking out at the effort, were interesting enough, but when we did get them right, and put them in the right order, they could then turn into words, and then all these different words, again in the right order, could turn into sentences and finally stories.

I learned to read quickly and was good at it. So good I was planted in my plain green uniform with green-and-white checked shirt, green tie and polished brown sandals in front of a higher class to demonstrate my skill. Which I did, but not for long.

'She said weepon, Mrs Baxter. It's weapon, isn't it? She said weepon,' said the class.

I stayed away from school pleading sickness at prize-giving one year when I was due to march up and collect the minuscule cup for Best in English. My shame would have been too great; the scorn for swots, skites and those with tickets on themselves was too crippling. There was quite a sophisticated system of bullying at the school and, like most unemphatic children, I wished to belong. If the things I liked doing best in the world – 'making up' and reading – were considered suspect by the big kids, then I would retreat and keep the whole thing under wraps. I would hide them in the dolls' cupboard and get on with my real life.

But not only the big kids thought such activities were a bit odd. My tiny little cup for achievement was considered all right by Dad and Mum. However, there were limits.

'Mum, I'm writing a story.'

'Well, shut your mouth before you start. You don't want to swallow another fly do you?'

'No, but Mum . . .'

'And run outside and play.'

I was a bookworm. I imagined the species as unattractive and slack jawed, munching their way through all the books in the house. The names of many of the best books of childhood have disappeared. Books motored through, devoured at a sitting, wallowed in. Books collected from the library with Dad and returned with speed. Mum didn't read library books. Her fastidious cleanliness got in the way.

Dad handed on his early favourites to me ('Barbara is the reader') – Sir Arthur Conan Doyle, Rudyard Kipling, Robert Louis Stevenson, and R.M. Ballantyne's series of *Adventure Tales for Boys* – but I don't remember our talking about any of them. I do remember having nightmares about *Struwwelpeter*, but that was long ago in King Street. I read *Gulliver's Travels* from the solid bookcase, which was considered laudable. I thought it good, but without the page-turning impact of *Dimsie Intervenes* or *Anne of Green Gables*.

'Take your nose out of a book.' 'Run outside.' To this day I am glad when it rains.

For some reason playing with dolls during the day was not as bad as reading. Besides, Colin and I and the People could decamp outside. Dolls were licensed play; reading, let alone writing, during the day was idleness.

Years later I read an interview given by Ray Lawler's mother when *Summer of the Seventeenth Doll* became a success in London. Kenneth Tynan wrote in his review, 'We have found ourselves a playwright, and it is time to rejoice.' Wow. Mrs Lawler said she was glad now she'd let Ray stay inside and write stories, even if it was sissy, instead of 'nagging him outside to play cricket with the other kids'.

I felt a fierce stab of envy.

In the meantime, friendships progressed. Barbara Herrick was much younger than the rest of her family and Mrs Herrick, another fine woman and good at making problems go away, suggested to my parents I should play with her Barbara every Saturday at their house, which was called Lindisfarne. This delighted me. Mrs Herrick had kept her ballgowns and other discards for the dressing-up cupboard, a large and bounteous space in the corner of a room which opened onto a wide verandah and garden beyond.

Barbara and my greetings were brief – a crisp 'Hello' and we began dressing up. We always had the same frocks, hats and shoes, and homed in on them instantly.

Once dressed, Barbara led the way, straight-backed and head high as she sailed along the shingle path in her black lace gown, the waist round her knees, the rest flowing in a regal train and her toes clenched tight in the effort to keep her mother's ex-ballroom shoes on her feet.

I followed in rust red silk the colour of old shearing sheds, clutching a black beaded evening bag. We were heading for Barbara's playhouse, where we refreshed ourselves with cocoa, sugar and cold water.

The progression over, we would get down to business, with a brief summary, a sort of 'Now Read On', like the comics. 'Where'd we got to?' I'd ask.

'You'd just escaped from the pirates.'

'But I was bound up.'

'Well, get unbound. Here's a knife,' said Barbara handing me a dead plane leaf. Adventure, heroism, making up and dressing up combined.

Glorious.

At lunch with Mr and Mrs Herrick there was often for pudding a white blancmange rabbit with red cherry eyes. Fortunately it had two. More amazing than the rabbit was the mounted head of a moose in the hall, complete with a strange bell pull on its neck. Mr or Mrs Herrick had shot it in the deep bush down on the left-hand side of the South Island where they had been imported for shooting.

Lindisfarne was bathed in gold mist, like Waimarama Beach, or swimming with my friend Wendy in the deep pools in the nearby Ngaruroro River. Especially when there was a floating log to ride on.

Wendy Whitlock was the daughter of the editor of the *Tribune*. She lived across the other side of Cornwall Park, which we treated as our pleasure garden, with a wary eye out for Mr Edgar. We once had a complicated system of signalling by Morse code, which we spent much time perfecting. Wendy and her torch stood on her side of the cricket field, as dusk fell and starlings began to whirl and settle and whirl again in the oak trees, and the street lights flicked on along Tomoana Road, where Wendy lived. There she stood, flashing her message on/off on/off with her torch. At the other side of the field, by the kiosk, I watched for a preliminary volley of short flashes, followed by her message in Morse. To which my torch was meant to reply R for Roger. This could be difficult. Sometimes we met mid-field to consult, sometimes we ran home and rushed to the telephone to clarify. It took great patience from us both but our on/off flashes did improve. Our enthusiasm for Morse code may have come from one of her brothers, Tony or Philip, who were at Hastings High and knew everything. Or had we read stories about the heroic 'Sparks' who continued tapping the code SOS, SOS as his ship was sinking? Only the deepening dusk, the whirling birds and our efforts remain now.

Occasionally we saw Nana Jackson in the park. She seemed to be good friends with Mr Edgar, who lived in the house next door to her in Tomoana Road. She regarded me with puzzlement; I felt from an early stage that I was not what she had in mind.

The worst mistake I made with Nana was to break Bubba Lil's (now Aunty Lily's) china doll. She was called Arabella, and had real hair which smelled. She also had a gaze as blank as the Wild English Rose Fairy. Arabella was not built for action, let alone adventures, and crashed to destruction on the gravel drive when I was speeding her along in the wheelbarrow to save her from baying wolves.

Nana was displeased and said so. To think that dear Lily had had Arabella all her life and I had broken her in six weeks. What would your Aunty Lily say? I didn't know, but could guess.

Nana Jackson was also deeply suspicious of making up which she called romancing. Fairies (now extinct) had been bad enough but this nonsense, this pretending was worse. Romancing, to her, was telling lies.

Years later when she died, my father, having cleared his comment by quoting '*De mortuis nil nisi bonum*' before he said it, told me that Mum's mother had been a hard woman. She had locked the children in their bedrooms all day for misbehaviour, and 'other things of such nature'.

She could relax and have fun sometimes, especially when Harry Lauder sang on her gramophone and tears rolled down her soft downy cheeks and she laughed and laughed.

Stop y' tickling, tick, tick, tickerling,
Stop y' tickerling Jock!

She also had an interesting collection of phrases, many of which were handed on to her daughters. 'Useless as a bandicoot', or sometimes 'Useless as a piece of fixed furniture'. Both of which came into use in 609 Roberts Street.

I began reading my old picture books to myself. The *Flower Fairies* poems, as mentioned, were a disappointment, but not *Chickies' Holiday* when I read it carefully. It was a large flat book, on the cover of which Headmaster Rooster, red jacket and a mortarboard in place (something I had never seen before but recognised as something to do with authority), is handing out reports to anxious chickens who ask him how they have done. '"I see some good, I see some bad" the teacher man replies.' The good chickens, satchels flung around their smug little yellow necks, run off laughing to their holidays. These chickens are smart, brisk, destined to do well in the service. Trailing in their wake, satchels dragging in the dust, come the badly reported on ones, those who haven't tried *hard enough*, their heads downcast in shame, their school caps awry.

The Pearson's sandsoap ladies all over again. It was another warning.

I continued to read anything I could find, including newspapers, especially advertisements, which I have always found interesting. *Is seepage disturbing your loved one?* took me a long time to decipher. As did many things as I read more widely.

I am flat on my stomach in front of the fire reading the newspaper. 'Dad, what's w–r–y mean.'

'What are you reading?'

'It says, "The convicted murderer left the dock with a wry smile."'

'Give me that paper at once.'

'But . . .'

'*Now.*'

CHAPTER 5

When I was about seven Mum decided that something must be done about my shyness with strangers. My horizons must be widened, preferably on the farms of her country friends, where the wind would blow away the cobwebs which, in all probability, had been caused by repeated burying of noses in books. David wasn't shy after all, he was friendly and outgoing, and not interested in books.

I liked the idea of farms. They were the nearest I was likely to get to any ranches and prairies and cowpokes – the world of our Saturday morning flicks at the Cosy Cinema. David was now considered old enough to bike down alone but he declined to look after Colin and me. Once again Barbara Landels came to our rescue and the three of us sank back into pure bliss. The prairies, those wide, wide prairies, and the galloping horses with streaming manes, who were often called ponies, and the cowboys who wore white hats and the baddies who wore black. Not only that, but the singing cowboys were liable to burst into song which was even better.

Ole Faithful, we rode the range together
Ole Faithful, in every kinda weather
When y'round-up days are over
There'll be pastures white with clover,
For you Ole Faithful, pal of mine.

I longed for the ponies, the round-ups, the pals.

However, my first horizon widening was more gentle.
I had known Jill in Napier since I was born, we were never shy together and there was not a stranger in sight. Uncle George was my godfather, a large and jokey man, who made merry with continuing jokes about teaching me my catechism.

He also called me Barbarossa which, he told me, meant Red Beard. He would intone Red Beard jokes and the catechism, which extracted delighted giggles.

'What is your name? N or M? Nigella or Merilyn?'

'Merilyn.'

'Then where's Nigella?'

That was easy. 'She's been eaten by a crocodile.'

'How many?'

'Um.' Numbers always reduced me to pulp. My last school report was definite on the point. *Barbara Wright. Arithmetic 18/100. Very Poor. Failed.*

Jill was good at sums, in fact she was good at most things, and lived in an exciting house with a verandah on the top storey as well as the bottom. It was also close to the centre of town yet had survived the fire of the earthquake. The Napier cathedral had been reduced to rubble and Dr George Waterworth had crawled into the quaking wreckage when the nearness of the fire and its smell of burning was increasing every minute. He did it to inject morphine into an impossibly trapped lady to put her out of her agony. No wonder we were all proud of him.

I loved Aunty Mina. She was kind and gentle, and raised money for the orphanage on Bluff Hill. While I was on my anti-shyness visit she had a bridge party for the cause. Jill and I both approved of this; the tea table was 'groaning with goodies' like in a book, and we were allowed to both help and eat. At one table I heard something so rude that I told no one, not even Jill. One of the ladies was powdering her nose with a little pink puff from a compact with shiny red poppies on its lid. As I was watching this, in mid-bite, one of the other ladies at the table said to the powderer, 'I would as soon wipe my bum in public as powder my nose.'

Crikey Dick. The shock. Heck.

During this visit Jill spent quite a lot of time climbing over the wooden gate at the back of the house. This, she told me, was because the whole family were soon going to England for a visit and there would be lots of wooden gates to climb over there, so she was practising.

My next horizon-broadening trip was to Mum's great friend Greta and her family who lived in the country. She too was generous and friendly and arrangements were made. The Wrights would drive out *en masse*, have lunch with their friends, then depart while I had fun with Ella and Patsy and Helen for a whole week. What was more, they would ride horses and so would I. This was true excitement, not only because of my keen interest in cowboys who loved their old pals, but also because one of my favourite heroines, *Norah of Billabong* by Mary Grant Bruce, often spent all day in the saddle. Quite often. It was nothing to her or her brother Jim, or their friend Wally, who was a hard worker like all of them. Also there would be lambs to feed with bottles, their tails wagging so hard you'd think they'd fall off. All these treats, and for a whole week.

My first surprise on arrival was to be confronted by the yellowing pelt of a polar bear hanging from a wall in the sitting room. Supported by a stool in front sat its great head, with snarling yellow teeth and monstrous fangs. The fangs, Ella told me, were for chewing up people and her dad had shot the bear in the plantation out the back. I knew this was a merry joke but gave the excavated bear a wide berth.

The first disappointment next morning was the lack of tail-wagging lambs, or indeed any lambs at all.

'It isn't the season,' said Patsy.

'Oh.'

'Mum, she doesn't even know about lambing.' There was no mention of the word 'townie' but it hung in the air.

Children in town and country led very different lives in my youth. Every farm had at least one house cow to be milked, and the resultant milk had to be separated and the cream made into butter. Every farmer 'killed for the house'. No H-bone corned beef from Mr Thompson for Greta – just a casual comment to her husband, 'Will you be killing today, Ronnie?' to be overheard in the kitchen.

Country children knew the facts of life at an early age. They knew lambs came out of ewes' bottoms, they knew the roles of bulls, that animals mated and died or were sent to the works, and that old ewes were killed for dog tucker. They knew about the seasons, that different things happened at different times of the year and it was important to put the rams out at the right time.

Families were much more isolated, schools were far apart and the Correspondence School was vital for families who couldn't afford or didn't wish to engage a governess.

Radio reception on back country farms in Hawke's Bay was erratic. Telephone lines could, and often did, come down in storms, and were liable to be down for some time.

Greta and her family's road had a paper delivery which David and I found exciting, but not Colin. Papers were collected at the *Tribune* office at the break of day, piled into cars, vans, or trucks and driven along shingle roads at high speed and with skill. The best bit was to see the actual 'delivery'. At each farm gate an arm would shoot out the driver's window, then with a flick and a twist of his muscular wrist, out shot a rolled-up newspaper to land plonk in the middle of the subscriber's drive. It was beautiful to watch. David would be purring with pleasure staring through the swirling dust for the next drop off.

Country children knew a great deal that townies didn't know. Until they came to town, when our country cousins behaved like cowboys let loose in the Big Smoke. David refused flatly to take one of them to see the Saturday morning flicks at the Cosy.

'Last time I took him he wouldn't shut up,' he said. 'He kept saying, "What's he doing? Who's that one? Where's he going?" I tell you Mum, he's daft. Other kids were snarling.'

But not on the farm. At the farm locals were king. The next morning Greta saddled up a brown horse called Belle who was so gentle you could hardly get her to move. Not this time. Belle set off at speed across the paddock with me clinging hard until I fell off. Greta and the girls said I must get on immediately as otherwise Belle would think she had won. I saw their point, climbed on, and Belle took off again. After three goes Greta said Belle was obviously in a bad mood and we would try again tomorrow. Also she knew that I was scared.

'But I'm not scared.'

'Oh yes you are. She can smell it.' This seemed to me a dirty trick of Belle's, and difficult to defeat.

We tried next day with the same results.

But then the problem, the crippling one, set in. I had never heard of homesickness. All I knew was that I longed for Mum. I had to be with Mum. The first night had been all right. I said my prayers –

Gentle Jesus meek and mild
Look upon a little child.
Pity my simplicity
Suffer me to come to Thee.

– and God Bless Mum and Dad and David and Colin and please

don't let me fall off tomorrow. Amen.

But now I was snivelling into my pillow, wailing, 'I wanna go home.' Greta knew when she was beaten and Mum drove out that very day. She and Greta had a good chat then we went home. It was too late to see the flick-of-a-wrist paper-run man.

Mum, a strong woman (though never hard), persevered. This time I would go further afield, 'right past Tikokino, up near Ashley Clinton and near the mountains, you lucky girl'. There I would meet and play with Ann Pigott, who was younger than me and would be thrilled to have a big girl to play with. And yes, the horses wouldn't bolt, not near Ashley Clinton they wouldn't.

Ann Pigott was undoubtedly younger and looked satisfactorily shy when she and her much older brother arrived to pick me up. The brother was not shy at all. I was to sit in the front, he said. Annie would go in the back with the stores and Mrs Wright could bet her bottom dollar that he would drive carefully with two kids on board. Farewells were said, I smiled at Ann in the back, she smiled shyly in return. Things were looking up. Near the mountains would be a real adventure, and kindly horses.

'Know any cowboy songs?' said the brother as we left the tarsealed road and bucketed onto the shingle in a cloud of dust.

What a bit of luck. 'Yes,' I said, 'lots.'

'Sing one.'

I sang 'Ole Faithful'.

'Never heard of it,' he said, flicking a cigarette out the window and lighting another one. There was silence.

I sang a classic.

Home, home on the range
Where the deer and the antelope play,
Where seldom is heard a discouraging word
And the skies are not cloudy all day.
Home, home on . . .

'Never heard of it,' he said

'I know "Big Rock Candy Mountain",' I said, wondering how I could avoid reference to bums.

'Never heard of it,' he said again, blowing smoke out his nose.

'Annie knows lots of cowboys, don't you Annie?'

'Yes.'

More silence. I began to feel the sneaky rise of nausea as the bends and corners tightened, and the cigarettes continued.

'You don't talk much, do you?' he said flicking the second butt out onto the bumpy road.

'No.'

'Can you drive?'

'Me?'

'You.'

'Course I can't.'

'Annie can. Can't you, Annie?'

'Yes,' said Annie, suddenly unshy.

I looked at him warily. He was leaning back in his seat, arms stretched to the wheel, smiling sideways at me with David's Chinese-burn-coming-up look.

'You'd better learn then. We'll be home soon.' He pulled over to the grass verge and put me in the driver's seat, how I can't imagine. There is no memory of my screams or kicks or bites. Annie sat leaning over the back seat with interest. The brother left the engine running, told me which was the accelerator. 'Steer straight ahead till I tell you to stop,' he said climbing into the front passenger's seat. I pushed the accelerator with outstretched leg. Paralysed with fright at the sudden lurch forward, I kept pushing and the car swung straight into a ditch on the left-hand side. Where we stayed for some time until a truck arrived with a man with a cheerful grin and a rope.

After which amnesia descended until my father arrived at the house of the confused and unhappy senior Pigotts at Ashley Clinton. Dad took me in his arms, wrapped me in a rug and drove home. He also gave me a horse rub with a special rough towel after my bath and tucked me up snug as a bug in a rug as well as Mum who hugged me too. I had a vague pleasant feeling that it wasn't my fault, and snuggled deep in the bed, with no regrets except for the loss of those days in the saddle. Which I have never achieved.

Nor have I ever had a bags-I-drive attitude to motorcars. Blame it not on the Bossa Nova, but on the Bossy Brother.

*

Life at Queenswood widened. I was chosen (*chosen*) for a part in the school play, which was called *Cabbages and Kings*. Nothing of which remains except a small photograph of me and Mary McIntyre drawing swords in anger and Tiny Groome looking suitably concerned with her hands folded. Mary and I both wore large and puffy cotton wool crowns, modelled on a royal crown. Presumably we are in conflict for the hand of the princess (Barbara Herrick), and may the best man win. Mary, a good-looking child, appears intent and serious; I dim with giggles.

One of the few photographs which survive the move from King Street is one taken by my father. He had decided there were too few of me compared with the numbers of David and set about rectifying the situation. He straightened the rug on which he sat me, but not my bonnet. The resultant cock-eyed image is typical of many of Barbara's childhood photographs, and not only photographs. Passive yet anxious to please, but just not getting the hang of things, somehow. Bumble-footed, according to David, who wasn't, and also had the Jackson charm. Known to him and his friends as 'tarts', girls liked him from an early age.

Jessie McDonald being one of the first. Jessie lived with her parents at the corner store opposite Queenswood, its display of sweets (chews) at eye level, its bulk goods out the back in sacks. 'It's out the back, I'll have to get Dad,' was a cry heard from Jessie. I suppose she was about fourteen, a dark-haired, dark-eyed girl with a certain amount of pull. Broken biscuits were within her province and she distributed them with care.

Girls got nothing. Nix. Some of the rest of the speedy bikers gang won sometimes, but David . . . David was granted a bagful every time he stepped on the doormat, with its bell which rang to stop us pinching when all the McDonalds were out the back.

By this time I was getting myself to and from school, still with a bow in my hair tied tightly by Mum so it never fell out. Long hair was my dream, but long hair was messy. In a similar way I couldn't possibly have a dog. Not only were dogs messy but what about my hay fever?

I enjoyed the route to and from school. At the join of Roberts Street and Fitzroy Avenue I turned left, which was familiar. The Peach boys lived on the left-hand side and opposite were the Crutchleys, whose father ran his bakery out the back.

At the next corner I turned right and there, within sight, were

Queenswood and McDonald's store waiting for me. A hop, a skip and a jump, but not before I admired the Dyson's house on the corner, which was two storeyed and surrounded by a large, if sparse, garden with no fence. David said this was because Mr Dyson sold cars so he needed lots of room for them round his house. I thought there was something a bit odd about this statement but kept hoping to see this garden filled up with new cars.

There were only eight houses in Roberts Street and I knew every house and most of the inhabitants. They were my people, not as interesting or as brave or as well loved as my People but definitely part of the landscape.

At the far end next to the empty paddock were the Dunns. Mr Dunn, and Mrs Dunn, who was good at golf and had beautiful grey hair, and Nancy, who was about my age and was dark and pretty and 'took dancing', though not with Grantham or Patterson. She was good at it, and had two older brothers like Wendy's, but more alarming.

Next were the O'Malleys. I didn't know Mr and Mrs, but Wally and Terry were part of my life. Wally had red hair and was nice to me. I made up my first poem for him.

Wally O'Malley
has a cast iron belly.

Terry was smaller and darker and quieter. I tried hard to think of a poem for him but failed, which seemed unfair. David and I had a highly developed sense of fairness. 'S'not *fair*' was a constant cry from one or other of us. Mum's reply, '*Life* isn't fair', seemed unfair too. Though not as bad as her other crisp comment when I complained about mouldy big kids.

Sticks and stones can break my bones
But words will never hurt me.

Lies, all lies, they made the wound worse.

Next to the O'Malleys were the Foster Brooks, who lived behind a large hedge and were unknown to us except that the inhabitants owned the best bookshop in town.

Next to us were Mr and Mrs Harry Davies and their two

children. They appeared later than the other neighbours and became good friends. Harry had had to 'walk off his farm', like many farmers during the Depression, and had become a surveyor, a profession which puzzled me. What did he *do*? Didn't the word mean looking? Then what at?

Next came us. Our house had two shingle paths, the one next to the Davies' curving up from the big side gate which was never shut, with the letterbox and the space beneath where the milk billy waited for the early morning milkman's slam, bang, speedy fill up each morning before his van clanged on. Below that were the shrubs in which David hid his shoes before biking off to Mahora barefoot.

It was a matter of honour to have tough soles on our feet. At the height of summer we had races from the cherry tree down the shingle drive (which Colin called 'springle dive') to the big gate. Not to be able to was the mark of a sissy, a loss of caste to be avoided at all costs.

The shingle path from the fibrolite garage to the front door was of little interest except for a pomegranate tree and being my exit gate for school.

Mrs Powdrell and her daughter Miss Powdrell lived on my gate side. Mrs Powdrell was old and dressed like ladies in old, old photographs. She was small, all in black and neat as a pin; her frocks came right up to her neck and ended in a little frill, beneath which she wore an ivory brooch. I liked Mrs Powdrell and her pictures. They were not like Miss Rixon's at all. They belonged to the 'every picture tells a story' school of painting, which appealed to me greatly, especially as Mrs Powdrell was happy to tell me their stories whenever I asked. One of my favourites was *The Old Shepherd's Chief Mourner* by Sir Edwin Landseer. In the centre of an empty shadowy room a plain coffin stands on an equally plain and simple stand. The only living creature there is a large black and tan sheepdog, one of the breed dog trialists call huntaways, so David told Mrs Powdrell.

It made me sad every time I saw it, as Wrightie's sad stories did, but they were tears I learned to hide, because Mrs Powdrell, like Wrightie, thought that grief was too much for Barbara.

A more cheerful one by Sir John Everett Millais was called *Ticket of Leave*. A proud Scottish lady holds a child in one arm;

with the other she hands the guard the ticket of leave which will free her husband. The lady's head is high; she hates the guard, you can see that. And also that the husband is broken, as Mrs Powdrell says. 'Look how his head slumps on her chest, Barbara.' *Slumps.*

Another I remember was a sad lady called Hope sitting on top of the world looking decidedly unhopeful. She reminded me of Britannia and her world at Dr Scouler's surgery.

Mrs Powdrell was a friend. I was not so sure about Miss Powdrell, though even I could see she kept the Powdrell show on the road. She was obsessed with cleanliness, cleaner even than Mum. She polished her garden taps, she raked her shingle paths daily, she kept house and cooked. On Saturday she marked the tennis court for weekly tennis parties with her sister and her family.

She also made it clear to Colin and me that we were only welcome when asked, having found us in her back garden one day. We had hopped over the fence to explore. She suggested we hop back immediately, which we did, careful not to tread on Mum's difficult treasure, a Himalayan blue poppy which struggled for survival beside the lily of the valley. Mum said Miss Powdrell was a wonderful little worker, her highest praise of all.

Next to the Powdrells was Mr and Mrs Burr's house. It was tucked away, Mum said, and she was right. No signs of life could be seen, peer as I would.

Then there were the Cummings and Bruce. Again, the rest of the family were invisible.

And then came the corner house, the most mysterious house of all. Never ever did I see evidence of life, but the thing that interested me was the placing of the concrete path. It went straight from the gate to the house like any other boring old path, but this one was on an angle. It was on the diagonal, Dad told me when I told him of my problem. It opened at the exact corner of Roberts Street and Fitzroy Avenue and the unseen occupants had to walk to the door, also on the diagonal, then down the diagonal path. This worried me but no one else. David told me I was potty. A preview of my next concern which was about why we were not falling off the edge of the world.

The last term at Queenswood was always the best; the fiercer big kids had calmed down and things were quiet. There was a chance of a role for me in the end of year play (the viewing of which made my father pale). And I was getting less bumble-footed, both at skipping and answering when spoken to. Especially skipping.

Apple, jelly, jam tart
Tell me the name of your sweetheart
A, B, C . . .

we sang, as the turners turned and the skipper tripped, and we noted the letter of the alphabet. Interest was taken in boys' names and their place in the alphabet. I would have been ashamed to have tripped on B. Too early, for one thing, and Bruce's fires seemed to have cooled.

Another achievement I learned at this time was pinching from McKenzie's chain store. David and his mates were practised at pinching things, and after some time I was promoted from being the lookout for the gang, to being allowed to have a go myself. Wally O'Malley, I remember, was on my side. Besides, he said, I might squeal if they didn't let me. The thought of such wicked betrayal alarmed me but I took to the game with delight. It left Giant Steps hands down for drama. Like most of us I didn't pinch things I would like to own, like chews. Perhaps I felt that would have been tempting the gods; I can think of no other reason. Women's lingerie was my field; heart pumping wildly, face innocent and fingers light as air, I nicked vast bloomers or strange pink elastic belts of unknown use.

I showed a friend of mine at school called Mary (not McIntyre) my new skill and she enjoyed the thrill. However, her family moved and I returned to be the gang's moll until the game palled. It was more of a winter's game. Also it was difficult to get rid of the loot.

And now it was summer. I was again in the school play and my report was as usual.

Arithmetic. 13/100. Very Poor. Failed.

English. 89/100. Good.

And soon it would be Christmas, and then Waimarama.

The families in the other baches were friends. We mucked about together, the boundaries between grown-ups and children loosened at the beach as they taught us things. Watch out for the dumper waves, for jellyfish, for rips. If the waves are too big, dive under. Never go out too far or swim by yourself. Don't take lilos into the sea; remember the boy who drifted out and was ever seen again. There was hesitancy here though – could it really be true?

Nights were good too. Parents and children occasionally swam together naked, when nights were black. There was added excitement when phosphorus shone in the dark and stuck on people, sometimes on bottoms, or more alarming, on ladies' busts.

Afterwards, families played charades together, after a reviving shot of whisky for the fathers. Pat Barker was one of them, and he and David excelled, everyone agreed. Decades apart in age, and both natural actors. 'They made us howl,' said Mum, 'absolutely howl with laughter.' Free, free as birds we were there; life was best at the beach.

CHAPTER 6

The big excitement at the beginning of next year was Colin's arrival at Queenswood. Why he didn't go to Mahora none of us knew or asked. David was pleased not to be stuck with a little kid to look after and I was happy to show him off. Colin was as much a part of me as Mum was. Also, he made our People adventures nearly as good as mine. However, since he was going to school now, he would be a big boy, news with which he heartily agreed and which every child in Hastings knew. They also knew that big boys don't play with dolls. The sissy quotient in doing so would be explosive and I would have to warn him. We were lucky David hadn't done so already. I decided it would be best at the beach, where we seldom took the People out of the pillowcase with ducks on it which was their temporary home from home.

Sitting barefoot, brushing sand off the soles of our bare feet as we sat side by side on my sagging camp bed on the verandah, I explained things. I told him he had better stop mucking about with the People now he was going to school.

There was a long pause. He watched me carefully, said he could see what I meant but he . . . but . . . he wouldn't tell anyone. Please.

I told him they would find out.

When I was little I had told Mum Colin's eyes were so blue the whites were blue as well as the yolks. The blue whites were getting watery. 'I'll see them, though, when I get home, can't I?'

'Yes, of course.'

'And have Bunty at night?'

His eyes were worse by the moment.

'Um. Well. OK.'

Colin was looking forward to school. He liked the idea of green pants, green and white checked shirt, green tie and well-polished brown sandals. But most of all he loved his wooden pencil box. It was the most beautiful pencil case we had ever seen, made of shiny wood with three red-coated soldiers with busby hats marching up and down. You, or rather Colin, could swing the top open and there were two layers for pencils and crayons and a specially rounded space on the top layer, just the right size for his brand new white rubber, stamped 'Rabbit' in black on the other side.

Fortunately Colin's expertise in sparrow-hopping the People about was no longer as necessary to me as it had been. Formerly he had been required to provide locomotion for half the team, but now things were different. Thanks to the gentle Miss Linsey I could write at reasonable speed, the tongue-biting slow days had passed. Also I was a lovely little speller, which simplified things. I could write down their ongoing sagas with some sort of ease. The People had to be there, but not as much whizzing of them about was required.

As soon as the new term began I headed for McKenzie's and I made my last and only useful theft, a bright blue shiny penny notebook for adventures. I kept it under my pillow at nights in case of particularly good dreams.

I had been known to lose things. Many things. 'Barbara would lose her head if it weren't sewn on' (Nana Jackson). Mum made a few test runs to school and back with us both to make sure I didn't forget Colin altogether or lose him on the way. Having comforted herself with the fact that Colin had a great deal more sense than I had, she left us to it.

We enjoyed our ambling walks to school and back when we exchanged the sorrows and triumphs of the day. He made friends with the other little green-panted boys and all the girls at Queenswood thought he was cute as a newt. I tried him out with Jessie McDonald and her broken biscuits but he failed that one. After a while he decided it was more fun running home with Dicky Davies and we parted amiably.

One afternoon I was wading among the fallen leaves of the plane trees of Cornwall Park Avenue. I was Robert Falcon Scott trekking through the trackless snow beneath as he slogged his way back from the South Pole with the cruel knowledge that his rival Amundsen had got there first.

I stopped to consider. There was not much time to continue being Scott; the leaves would be removed soon by Mr Edgar and his rakers.

Having made the decision I started off again to discover a man and his bike standing in the gutter in front of me. He seemed friendly, very friendly. 'Hello, girlie,' he said. I never liked 'girlie' any more than David liked 'sonny', but I admired his red and black BSA and its bright gleaming bell.

'Hullo.'

'Like a dub?' He looked quite excited at the idea.

'Yes, please.'

I climbed up onto his bar to ride side-saddle. He was giving me a double, more usually called a dub – a lift. Robert Falcon Scott would wait.

'Like some chutty?'

'Yes, please.'

Off we went, me chewing spearmint. 'You're a pretty girl aren't you?' he said.

'No.'

'Got any brothers?'

'Yes.'

'Seen their willies?'

'Yes.'

He stopped his bike, grinning wildly and unzipping and revealing. At one appalled glance I saw it, its colour, its length, its rampant upness.

'No,' I squeaked, sliding off the bar and charging down Roberts Street.

'Where y'going?'

I pointed at Mr and Mrs Burr's house. 'I live there.' I lied.

He made a grab at me, tried again, swore and rode away.

'You're early Bub,' said Mum. 'Did you run all the way?'

There obviously must be some reason for such unlikely behaviour on my part. 'Yes,' I gasped. 'I thought you might be worried about me.'

She smiled, dropped a kiss on the top of my head. 'You are the funniest little girl I ever met,' she said.

I never thought of telling Mum about the man and his dub. I knew the man was nasty, very nasty, and I sensed that having taken his dub and his chutty I was nasty too, and that was worse than rude.

*

Colin now came with Dad and me on our trips to the library. He chose flat colourful books for me to read to him, so many that the lady behind the desk said to him, 'There is a limit, you know, Sonny.'

'Ah,' said Dad, 'but Colin likes to be read to in depth you see, Miss Bancroft.'

Miss Bancroft laughed at Dad and said, 'Well, just this once, shall we?'

Once again grown-ups had different rules.

Colin Frederick Romaine thrived in the infant room. Mrs Linsey told Mum he had settled down beautifully. And then it was end of year and prizegiving and Colin shone. I heard Mum telling Greta the news on the party line. Then came school reports. Mine was the same as ever and I think David's was also, but Colin's said, 'Made a splendid start in all subjects. Well done, Colin.'

And then the beach, better each year. There were new people in the Campbells' cottage this year. English people with a daughter my age. Mum placed a plateful of Mr Morley's white-fleshed peaches onto their green leaves and told me to run next door with them, as she would have done to any new arrival.

'Can't Colin go?'

'No, off you go.'

Off I went. A thin, cigarette-smoking woman appeared. 'This is from Mum,' I said and turned to depart when I heard a male voice booming, 'Are the natives being friendly?' I ran home with speed.

Next day the daughter arrived 'to see Barbara'. With a gentle shove between the shoulders from Mum, I went. Obviously Cristabella had been sent to find if I had heard the booming father.

'Why did you run away?' she said.

'I heard your father and I'm going for a swim and pooh to you,' I said. A great leap forward in unpleasantness. Otherwise the tides rolled on.

The Glazebrooks had brought their portable gramophone and new records. The Western Brothers were different. They hardly sang at all, just let their English flutings drift through songs saying things like 'Let's do some things which we'd hardly like to mention / Such as scalping the odd young man.'

I knew about or had heard of scalping from cowboys and Indians at the Cosy so their songs worried me until David told me the Western Brothers were 'being funny, y' twit'. Oh.

I liked Jeannette MacDonald and Nelson Eddy, though I preferred seeing them at the Cosy where they were always singing up each other's noses. Like in 'Indian Love Call': 'When I'm calling you, ooo ooo ooo.' And another hero bellowing, but not for love 'Give me some men who are stout-hearted men . . . and I'll soon give you ten thousand MORE!'

Three weeks of wonderful swimming at Waimarama, the taste of salt on our brown arms, the 'washerwoman fingers' all wrinkled and white. All these we loved as we got better at dodging the dumper waves and treating each breaker with respect and avoiding the rips. All these things we learned at our parents' knees, especially *Never Swim Alone*. It was a splendid time. The earthquake was ages ago.

We learned to love the night sea too, even when we weren't swimming in it. So different from the day: the dark sea rolling in in deep solemn thuds and the sky filled with bright stars we seldom saw at home.

Charades got better each year also and David won every night, usually with Pat Barker. But the most coveted thing for me at the beach that year was Josephine Glazebrook's pair of shorts with bright flowers on them, the most glamorous, dashing garment I had ever seen and all wasted on a little kid like Jo. Not only were they beautiful, they would be *useful* I told Mum. It would stop David and his friends being rude and shouting 'poppy show' when girls were upside down climbing in trees and their bloomers showed.

It seems odd that neither David nor I remember being told about Mum and Dad going to England.

Were the three of us assembled before them? Told how they would be back before we had even noticed they'd gone? Explained to gently that it was not possible for us to go with them, we wouldn't like it at all, we would be much better and far happier at 609 Roberts Street with Nana Jackson and Aunty Lily with her beautiful auburn hair, who would move in while they were away?

Or did Mum tell us one by one, giving individual attention to each child according to age and temperament?

The news was undoubtedly big, though less so than the fact that one of the boys in David's class was so sick with infantile paralysis that his parents laid truckloads of sawdust in front of their house so that poor Jamie would not be made worse by the roar of the traffic.

Dad's news, though big, had no drama. He had been elected to attend a medical conference in Brighton, England. The fact itself was of little interest to any of us, although I did know the fairies in all my books came from there, and that Britannia had cared about the earthquake.

We must surely have been concerned. Mum was the centre of all our lives. As Nana Jackson said, 'Barbara would give the top brick off the chimney to Jessie.' A statement I understood was not a good thing.

Mum presumably reassured us. We would have a lovely time with Nana and Aunty Lily. She and Dad would be home in a flash and she knew all of us would be good when she was away.

I knew Nana and Aunty Lily preferred boys, especially manly Jackson types like David and Colin. I had always known this and was not concerned. I was not interested in either of them. But to be without Mum . . . how could that be?

Even practical things loomed. Mum was the only person in the world who could tie the bow in my hair so tightly it could stay on all day. She was the best cook, the best nurse, the one who insisted on iodine in spirits, which stung our grazed knees, because the one made up in water was useless, whatever Dad said. She was also the one who could cure any wound with a foment, a strange treatment consisting of a bit of dark green, scratchy material surrounding a cloth which was boiled until its innards were red hot, then removed with forceps from the little steel pan shaped like a giant kidney, tested for temperature against Mum's forearm and slapped onto our affected area till we yelped and Mum's lips clamped tight in concentration. But we knew she was making us better. It was no good unless it hurt.

And who would take Colin and me to the library?

The only speck of good news was that Dorothy was coming back to help Nana and Aunty Lily. Dorothy had helped Mum years ago when Colin was still in his pram. She loved us dearly, like Wrightie, who would also come back to help Nana.

Nor can I remember much about Mum and Dad's departure. I do know that their friend, Ewen Campbell, drove them down to Wellington to catch the boat, but only because David was ecstatic as Mr Campbell's car was a Humber Super Snipe and he would have one one day.

Life became even better organised at 609. Aunty Lily delivered Colin and me to Queenswood on her way to Royston Hospital where she nursed. Dorothy, small, dark, smiling and glad to see us, stood waiting at the gate to walk home with us, play with us, feed us, say goodnight to the water safe with us, then bed us down with kisses.

We saw little of David. He was ten now and busy with his speedy friends, and declined to be bedded down, even by Dorothy.

Postcards arrived from Mum and Dad; the statue of Peter Pan in Kensington Palace Gardens for me, the front of Buckingham Palace, with two soldiers standing in boxes wearing red jackets and furry hats, for Colin, and for David a Rolls-Royce car with a winged lady on the front, and another for all of us of a policeman holding up the traffic so that a mother duck could get her ducklings across the pedestrian crossing. I thought it was kind of the 'bobby', which was what the English called policemen. David said it was dopey and even old Edgar in Cornwall Park wouldn't be so dopey and Colin said yes he would.

On the whole they were of little interest to any of us. They had little of Mum about them and nothing at all of her smell. I returned briefly to *The Rainbow* and *Frolic and Fun with Mustapha Bun*. 'Nose in a book, nose in a book. Can't even bother to read your mother's card all the way from Britain,' sighed Nana.

Barbara Landels rallied, as did Mum's other younger friends. Barbara continued to take us to the Cosy on Saturdays, which was life blood for us all. David would peel off to join the O'Malleys the moment we arrived at the door. He didn't mind being seen with us, he explained, as long as we kept eight steps behind.

Esther Niblock came to see us at home. She gave me a small silver thimble which had been hers as a child and said she wanted me to have it as she knew I would be missing my lovely mother. I said thank you very much and within minutes the present had disappeared off the face of the world and I have never seen it since.

*

David came back from Mahora one day and flopped onto Dad's sofa in the dining room. Colin and I were playing 'The Gay Caballero', another Frank Crumit favourite. David told us to stop playing the thing for heck's sake. We said we wouldn't. He said we were stinks, and he was sick and his throat hurt and so did his teeth. For the first time I looked at him. He certainly looked weird. I put my hand on his forehead like Mum did. To my surprise heat leapt upwards. Colin ran for Nana who rang for Aunty Lily at the hospital who said to put him to bed and keep him warm and she would get home as soon as she could.

David had measles. Aunty Lily moved him into the other bed in the room in which she slept. She had had measles years ago and she must try and quarantine David from the other two. The doctor came next morning, saw the appropriate rash on David's throat and agreed. He said we should be kept home from school – there was no sense in spreading the thing – and Dorothy must keep us away from David at all costs.

Which was easy.

I asked who would get the comics from Foster Brook's, which was David's task on Friday.

Aunty Lily gave me a strong look and said I was beyond everything.

I said I'd be happy to go for them on my bike.

Aunt Lily said not till I had more sense.

I sulked.

About ten days later David was better and I had spots and a temperature. Aunt Lily flicked the thermometer on her wrist and said, 'Colin will be the next.' Which he was.

I was still in bed with a new cache of David's comics I had discovered, when Aunty came to tell me the situation. David was better and he was back in his room but Colin was now ill and sleeping in the room with her, and I must on no account go and see him.

Doctors came, sometimes twice a day. Aunty Lily never went to Royston. Colin had pneumonia, Dorothy told me, looking worried. Then double pneumonia. Which was worse.

After that things blur. I hear Colin's reedy voice calling all through the day and night, 'Aunty, Aunty, Aunty.'

No, I still couldn't see him, nor could David.

Then came the day when we could. David was up and dressed

and me in my blue knitted dressing gown. We stood at the end of Colin's bed in silence. I stared at the strange hot-looking worried face. Where was his grin? He couldn't see me, not at all, I could tell. 'Mum. Mum.' I whispered in tears.

'Say hullo to him,' said Nana.

'Hullo, Colly.'

'Hullo, Colin.'

He said nothing.

'That's enough now,' said Aunty. 'He's tired. Off you go.'

I went back to bed and stared at the ceiling. Slow puzzled tears leaked. Something was wrong. Horribly wrong. 'Mum. Mum.'

I went to sleep and woke to find Aunty sitting on my bed in tears. I jumped up in fright. She told me Colin had died and I must be brave. I cried. She kissed me and told me I was a good girl and she must go and tell David.

I put my head under the blankets and wept for my good, my dear, my best friend Colin, and for me, for me, for me. Then went to sleep again.

It was still light when I woke, and lay staring at the ceiling.

After some time I remembered there were still unread copies of David's comics. I jumped out, grabbed one and hid it under the pillow. Holding my breath, I pulled it out and unfolded it at *Betcha Barnes and His One Wheel Wonder* and tried to read. It didn't work. The tears ran and swamped the paper. It didn't work. Not at all.

David told me later we didn't go to Colin's funeral. Children didn't then. He and I went to be minded by friends of Nana who lived over the back fence. Which consisted of sitting on prickly black horsehair-covered chairs for hours and thinking about dear little Colin who had gone to Heaven. We were not allowed to read, do jigsaws, do anything, though David thought we did have a bun with currants in it. Other than that we sat with Mr and Mrs Alan until Uncle Freddy came to collect us with tears in his eyes.

Uncle Freddy did the telephoning between Hastings, Hawke's Bay, and London, which was not a simple process in the thirties. Relatives sat silent, willing Freddy to get through, to hear above the static, to be heard. To me it was confusion and noise and Uncle Freddy crying every time he put down the receiver.

People came and went. Were kind. David and I hung around and listened and heard Nana and Aunt Lily and other aunts repeat again that Colin was the bright one. He was the one they had their hopes on. Yes, yes, tragic. Poor Jessie, so far away too. Tragic.

I have few other memories of that time except unhappiness which can stay and spread like an infection. I do remember being puzzled by Nana telling me I must always wash apples before eating them because the Chinese greengrocer in Heretaunga Street spat on his apples before he polished them. Why? I wondered. Though for once I had had the sense not to ask. Not now. Not ever. It didn't matter. It was a muddled time.

It took six weeks for the Port Line boat with Mum and Dad to arrive. It had gone round the Horn and Mum had been so seasick she nearly died. The thing which saved her was the advice given her by the engineer, a Scot, who recommended pork chops and whisky.

The other information David gathered during this time was that Captain Egbert St Bede Kirkley, Carabiniers (retired) was sweet on Aunty Lily. He had come to New Zealand to visit his brother, Mr Cedric Kirkley, who had married a beautiful Maori lady and was a friend of Mum and Dad. Captain Kirkley was a nice man. He smiled a lot and introduced us to the practice of tipping, or rather of being tipped, of which we approved. David and I discovered that he was happy to tip us if we would go outside and 'play' rather than hide behind the sofa when he and Aunty were sitting. 'Smooching' was David's word. In time Captain Kirkley asked Aunty Lily to marry him and their photographs appeared in the *New Zealand Free Lance* 'Soon to be Wedded' pages. This impressed me greatly. Next week Aunty pointed out to Nana another lucky lady's photograph which was headed 'Titian southerner to wed'. 'Look Mother,' said Aunty, 'another Titian bride.'

'What's this Titian she's so mad about?' asked David.

Miss Rixon's postcards came to my aid. 'Red hair,' I said. 'He did paintings.'

Eventually Mum and Dad did arrive. We stood on the front porch waiting for Ewen Campbell's Humber Super Snipe to arrive at my front gate. Not David's.

The moment we saw Mum by the pomegranate tree we leaped

forward to run. Aunty Lily clamped a hand on both our shoulders. 'No. Remember this is a very sad homecoming for your mother.' We wriggled free and raced to the gate.

Mum was home. And Dad. And Mum was smiling and crying.

We went to the Havelock North Cemetery next day to put flowers in a brown vase on Colin's grave. There was a small cross at one end of the plot with three stone steps up to the cross. On the top one was written:

> *Suffer the little children to come unto me*
> *for theirs is the Kingdom of Heaven.*

I walked down the path to the car with Mum afterwards. She was crying. I clutched her hand, 'You've still got me, Mum.'

'Yes,' said Mum. 'Yes.'

Aunty Lily went to England and married Uncle Egbert straight after Mum and Dad came home. She wrote to her family and said from now on she was to be called Lillias because Egbert said Lily was a maid's name. And drop the 'y' on Aunty. Aunt, please, from now on.

'And please Mother,' she wrote later, 'never put a stamp on upside down on your letters. It is an insult to the King, even when done by mistake.'

School began again. Everyone was kind. Miss Rixon said a prayer for Colin at assembly which engulfed me in self-conscious shame and sobbing tears. I knew she was being kind. I longed for her to shut up.

She went on to say that she and all the school wished to plant a rose in memory of our dear Colin and things were being arranged.

The day came. To my horror I was offered a bright silver spade for planting the tribute. I panicked, dropped the spade and buried my face in Mrs Linsey's skirts. 'No. No. No.' Miss Rixon said kindly, 'Don't worry, Barbara. Perhaps Barbara Herrick – you'll begin the planting for us, won't you?'

Which, thank goodness, she did.

CHAPTER 7

Aunt Lillias was in England with Uncle Egbert and Nana had retreated home across the park and Mum and Dad were home, but little mention was made of Colin or his death. I wanted to talk about him, to know more about things and why it all happened. I missed him sadly, his wobbly grin and his white hair and mad blue eyes. I knew he had gone to heaven; Mum said so as well as Nana. And was happy, very happy – everyone was happy in heaven, the hymns at school said so too.

There is a happy land,
far, far away.

I remained puzzled. If heaven was so good, why didn't we all go there straight off? And why did it say 'Suffer little children to come unto me' on Colin's cross on his grave at Havelock cemetery, when everyone said he was so happy? I asked Mum, who said 'Ask your father', who told me it was difficult to explain but that was how people used to talk in the olden days. By saying 'suffer' they really meant 'allow'.

Occasionally I found Mum crying by herself. She would sit up straight, hug me and say perhaps Wendy might like to come over and stay the night for a treat. I knew she was being kind and it was unfair to ask her things which would make her cry worse.

At this time David and I became aware of Mrs Felkin and her daughter Miss Mary Felkin, who lived in Havelock North in a house called Whare Ra, which we knew meant 'house of the sun' in Maori. I also knew it was one of the of darkest houses I had ever seen. Made of stone and covered with ivy, the high point of the house for me was a large stone frog which crouched by the front steps, half hidden by ivy. The other thing I liked about the house was its name. The idea of words sounding different yet meaning the same thing in different languages interested me and I asked David to get his Maori friends at Mahora to give him some more Maori words. But he declined.

Mrs Felkin and Miss Felkin were followers of some esoteric branch of Christianity. Mum had known and liked them both for some time, and Miss Felkin had been Colin's godmother. Their faith and ceremonies were, I now think, a comfort to Mum after he died. The only one I knew about took place in 609 Robert Street. Mrs and Miss Mary Felkin arrived with a censer, incense and an air of gentle authority.

Mum and Dad and David and I stood in the hall and Mrs Felkin sat because of her legs which were alarmingly swollen. There was not much room in the hall except for a table where a telephone sat and its chair which Mrs Felkin now occupied. Beside her stood a gong stand with its gong for bonging in the olden days to tell people meals were ready but which now was never used except when David practised his version of 'Come to the Cookhouse Door, Boys'. Above us all was an old painting of St Sebastian on a cross with arrows sticking out of him, which Colin used to call the Funny Jesus.

Miss Felkin stood halfway up the stairs, said prayers, then swung the censer strongly in three directions, murmuring as she did so. David and I knew about censers and incense because every Christmas the Felkins of Whare Ra invited their friends to do Poojah to Baby Jesus. All present, including children, however young, were invited to take turns in making this rite of worship. We knelt before a crowded Nativity scene with animals of all sizes and colours; a camel with a nodding head stood shoulder to shoulder with a pink cow twice its size, three Wise Men trekked their way through the shambolic crowd from the left, the shepherds from the right. The Christ child was minute. We were then asked to take the censer from Miss Felkin, swing it to the front, to the left, then the right and say, 'Happy Christmas, Baby Jesus'. David did this with well co-ordinated grace. To me it was torture, words became scrambled, legs collapsed as I mumbled on.

The ceremony at 609 was solemn and reverent but I never discovered what it was about.

For reasons unknown Wendy's and my parents decided that the time had come for us to leave Queenswood and attend a little school five miles away in the village of Havelock North.

Neither of us queried this startling decision. Change meant

drama and both of us were all for that. At first Wendy and Mr Whitlock, a kind and endearing man who had lost two middle fingers in the war, collected me at the Cornwall Memorial Gates in his car and drove us into town where we caught the Nimon's bus to Havelock.

St Luke's School was indeed small. Our teacher, Miss Granville, taught classes from standard one to standard six, in what had once been the original Church of St Luke's and still had its steep wooden roof and lancet windows. Miss Gardiner, her assistant, operated in a shed-like building nearby, where she taught us singing, put on our annual play, and presumably taught 'the little kids', though I have no memory of this. They have sunk without trace.

St Luke's, being a church school, had its own vicar, the Reverend Stephen Weymouth, who lived with his family at the top of the paddock where we played and made huts among the highly scented and prickly hawthorns. Our part of St Luke's was a typical one-teacher country school which had been put down in a village about four miles from Hastings, which was concentrating on becoming a city.

It was also where we played team games, including a basic form of basketball, and once again I heard the cry, 'Aw, do we have to have *her*, we had her *last* time.'

I have no idea how many boys and girls were taught by Miss Granville in that desanctified old church. Forty? Sixty? All at different stages and different abilities and a wide variation of curriculum. Miss Granville's task seems impossible to me now, but in those days hundreds of solo teachers taught with similar numbers in country schools. Also the unmarried teachers boarded with the parents of their students in turn, which cannot have been much fun, though occasionally a young woman 'caught a bachelor farmer' in the district, which was thought to be a coup.

Miss Granville told us she had eyes in the back of her head and thus knew who was misbehaving. We knew this was a joke and laughed but froze into stillness. It is only now I wonder how she achieved her control, her discipline and her firm hand, all the arts so necessary in the educating trade.

Added to these achievements, she mastered the ill-tempered little black stove in the middle of the room, which she kept glowing throughout the winters. Even Mum was impressed, as was the

Reverend Stephen Waymouth. Neither of them knew how she did it.

The Anglican faith was part of our curriculum. Our instructor was an impressive sight striding down the paddock on his way to the church in the mornings. Tall, thin and possessed of that flair which some but by no means all clerics achieve when they put on their vestments, Mr Waymouth was our friend, our handsome, nimble friend. Sometimes, to our delight, he would have a few goes at skipping, his face laughing, his robes flying wide. Though he never skipped before our morning service. Once a week the entire school filed ('No talking please') into the Lady Chapel of St Luke's for our morning service. Mr Waymouth was there already. He stood up, framed by the stained glass behind him, and cried loudly, 'This is the day which the Lord hath made.'

'Let us rejoice and be glad in it,' we squealed back.

Then Miss Gardiner played the organ, Mr Waymouth and Miss Granville sang loudly and we gave the hymn a go, even if it was a new one, though the old ones we knew by heart were much more popular.

Then Mr Waymouth gave us a short 'address'. The only one I remember was about the Lord God being a comforter. 'Not in the sense that a scarf is a comforter to keep us warm in winter, good gracious me no, but in a spiritual sense.'

When we were unhappy, he said, deeply unhappy about something that had happened to us, we could pray to the Lord and he would help us. I sat up straight. I hadn't thought of doing that. However, there were two puzzles. First, I didn't know a scarf could be called a 'comforter' and second, what was 'spiritual'?

I asked Miss Granville how to spell it. She told me with a smile and no query and I wrote it down. Later, when I had put my bike in the shed, and said hullo to Mum, I looked up 'spiritual' in the dictionary. 'Spiritual: of or concerning the spirit, as opposed to matter,' it said. Useless. I did try Mr Waymouth's advice but not until Mum had heard my usual prayers, in case she cried. I tried the comforting prayer for some time, but the spirit was lacking and we drifted apart. As did the sharpness of the grief of Colin's death, but that took many many years.

Occasionally, when I knew no one was around to find me, I opened the left-hand top drawer of the chest of drawers on the upstairs landing. It was in fact one deep drawer, pretending from the outside to be two, with two wooden knobs to fool you. I had discovered some relics of Colin inside. His shiny pencil case with its place for the rubber, which had gone with the pencils and crayons. His spelling and writing exercise books studded with gold stars from gentle Miss Linsey. And his only report.

'Colin has made a splendid start in all subjects. Well done, Colin.'

Then I would put them back again and slide the drawer shut with care.

One of the few dispiriting things about St Luke's School was that Mum decreed I must have a 'proper lunch' because I was so thin. To do this I had to join another school at lunch time, one even smaller than ours, which produced this item. This school was run by a widow called Mrs D'Oyly who provided education for her three young daughters and also several daughters of local farmers, whose mothers picked them up each Friday and carried them home to 'the old pine tree, to Bunkhouse Billy and the Boss'. Lucky pigs. No other child from St Luke's ran up and back to Mrs D'Oyly's house at lunch time. There was not much bullying at our little school but secrets prevailed. Betty Nimon had tons of secrets, most of which appeared at lunch time and all of which I missed.

How pathetic to care! How searingly real to care!

Apart from secrets, life at St Luke's was a breeze. Like nuns in a well-run convent, we were expected to be good and kind to each other, and we were, more or less. Perhaps it was the feeling of sanctity which pervaded the surroundings, or the goodness of Miss Granville, Miss Gardner and Mr Waymouth. It was a good place.

The only problem, I now realise, was that I learned nothing whatsoever during the years I was there. Surely there must have been some useful facts I could have picked up in those years, other than sharpening my spelling, but I can remember none. Miss Granville realised I was beyond aid in arithmetic, but after all I couldn't be faulted in my tables. This, however, was not enough, a fact which I proved later.

Our headmistress and I had the same rhythm. Nice and slow and easy suited us both. She was pleased with my reading and writing and my ability to learn poetry by heart. I have a faint memory of us using slates sometimes, which seems archaic. She was certainly still an advocate of spelling bees. Two classes would join up in a random line at the end of the room for this exercise and wherever I began I would always whizz up to the front. I had never met a form of competition where any skill of mine had been made visible and I was smug. I told Mum, who from then on would ask me each week who had won the spelling bee and I was forced to admit it was me again and she would nod. Dad would smile and say he would expect nothing else.

There was one extra task Miss Granville devised for girls only – we were to make a baby's cotton petticoat under her tuition. At the end of each year every garment was grimy, black, and unfinished.

I did make contact with the *New Zealand School Journal* at St Luke's, a new discovery to be devoured with speed, but still there was little mention of a New Zealand tree, bird or bush. I was back to primroses and wild roses, though not, I think, burdock.

Another treat at St Luke's was the annual school play, produced with dedication by Miss Gardiner. In my favourite one, whose name is now lost, I not only had the star part, but also wore a wig of riotous gold curls which fell about my shoulders. So improved was I by this prop that Mum took me next door to show Mrs and Miss Powdrell the transformation. Both thought it was lovely, quite lovely.

St Luke's parish hall was packed on the night, including my long suffering father. At the end, I and my wig stood alone on the stage and 'projected to the back' as instructed by Miss Gardiner.

'Those whom the world call mad,' I cried, 'are really fey, and can believe in fairies.'

Wendy's and my best friend at St Luke's was Elizabeth Simpson, an attractive, bright-eyed girl who lived in Havelock North with her younger sister and her friendly parents. Mrs Simpson, small, dark and bright-eyed, once called her umbrella her 'bumpty-reller', which I thought very witty.

One day Elizabeth came to school bursting with astonishing news. She told us her father, who was Maori, had decided that he no longer wanted to be Mr Simpson, he wanted to be Mr Karaitiana, which was his true and right name. When his own father died, his mother married a Pakeha called Mr Simpson who had 'given his name to his stepson'. But Elizabeth's father was Maori, not Pakeha, and proud of his heritage, and had decided to begin by changing his name back to his rightful one.

This was true excitement, better than any book story. From now on Elizabeth Simpson would be Elizabeth Karaitiana, as would the whole family. Better than any play for surprise and drama, and a happy ending – all were there. We were happy with the news and Elizabeth delighted.

Many years later, when my book *Long Hot Summer* was published, a New Zealand reviewer pointed out that one of Anderson's characters had made the decision to return to his Maori name and heritage far too early. Decisions such as this among part-Maori, according to the reviewer, did not occur until several decades later. I had committed an anachronism, a mistake eagerly to be pounced on by any reviewer. Criticism of criticism by reviewers is puerile. A private snarl from the writer to herself should be enough. However, if the reviewer in question was present at St Luke's School in the thirties when Mr Karaitiana made his decision and Elizabeth broke her news, I didn't see him. And nor did Wendy.

About this time I had my tonsils removed after several attacks of bronchitis, and possibly also in an attempt to stop my mouth hanging open in that vacant way.

Anyone who experienced anaesthesia sixty or seventy years ago will remember the hideous stench of gas and rubber which preceded sleep, and the nausea which followed waking. For me, however, there was another benefit from my term in hospital, beyond living on ice cream. A nurse handed me my brush to tidy my hair. I explained that my mother did my hair as she was the only one who could make the bow stay in.

She looked at me sternly. 'But you're nine, aren't you?'

'Yes.'

'Well,' she sniffed, 'tell your mother it's ridiculous for a child of nine to have her hair done by her mother.' Another true nurse.

I told Mum a censored version of the comment and the bow disappeared. I was lucky not to be wearing it when I arrived at Hastings High School.

*

I was present at two landslides in the 1930s. First the earthquake in '31 and second the election in '35 when the Labour Party swept into office for the first time, with a majority of fifty seats.

My parents had voted for National or its equivalent since time began. They were conservative by nature, as were all their farmer friends. On the night of the election the Wright family drove to nearby Otane to listen to the results with their friends on the Barker's new wireless. There was a festive feeling about as we ate home-killed lamb, accompanied as always by Mum's enthusiastic reception. Pat Barker said the Depression was getting better day by day. Dad agreed, and the unemployed figures were dropping. 'National Political Federation should sail in.'

I remember all this but also the festive air sinking. Things became more and more gloomy as the figures rolled in. I went to sleep from boredom. David gave manly support to the adults and stuck it out.

Next morning Betty Barker rang Mum. Their young son had come to her with a plate of Queen Anne chocolates his mother had meant to serve with the celebratory coffee and drinks. My memories of the landslides, both '31 and '35, contain memories of wasted Queen Anne chocolates.

Nineteen thirty-eight was Wendy's and my last year at St Luke's. We said goodbye to our friends, to Miss Granville, Miss Gardiner and Mr Waymouth, then climbed into Mr Nimon's bus filled with cheer at the thought of our long hot summer.

Mr Nimon clipped our tickets with his usual sigh and we rushed to the back to laugh and shout and behave like loud rude girls. We began with a song I had never liked much:

No more Latin, no more French,
No more sitting on a hard board bench.

And went on with one of our favourites:

There was a man called Michael Finnegan
He grew whiskers on his chin-egan,
The wind came along and blew them in again
Poor old Michael Finnegan. Begin again.

An old lady in a straw hat turned in her seat to watch us. We looked in return expecting a reproach for loud behaviour, and in school uniform too.

'Ah, girls,' she said, 'so you are off for your holidays?'

'Yes.'

She sighed deeply, much more deeply than Mr Nimon. 'The state of the world, the state of the world. Poor, poor girls. You will be left over from this war as my generation of women were left over from the last.'

We giggled, rolled around, behaved worse, poked tongues out at her back when she turned to gaze at the road ahead. We were still laughing as we pedalled home against the headwind blowing into our faces as it always did.

Just before Christmas I had a card from Elizabeth. 'I watered your garden but it is all dead and dying. Tell Wendy her garden is all dead and dying too. Happy Christmas, Love and kisses, Elizabeth Karaitiana.'

CHAPTER 8

In 1939 I became a real Hastings schoolgirl. Five days a week I hopped on my BSA bicycle (British Small Arms, according to David) with its skirtguard of purple and green netting and pedalled with speed and style across town to Hastings High School. Despite my failure in arithmetic I landed up in 3A where we did Latin and mathematics. I knew Dad would be pleased about Latin and I could only hope for the best regarding maths. Elizabeth Karaitiana and others from St Luke's were there, including Maxine Phillips who was so well liked she had been asked to every birthday party throughout the year. Such enviable feats are not forgotten.

Wendy had gone to board at Woodford House in Havelock North. She was now 'Way up on the hill / where the wind bloweth free', as the school song sang. I was envious of her, mainly because of her interesting new wardrobe, which was large and varied and available only from Mr Blackmore of The House of Blackmore in Heretaunga Street, opposite the Queen Anne chocolate shop.

Wendy showed me all. I picked up a small pair of white cotton pants. 'What's these?'

'They're linings.'

'What for?'

'To go under our bloomers.'

'For when you wet your pants,' I giggled. Not a witty comment, and treated accordingly by Wendy, but I had done my best not to be impressed.

Once again neither of us knew why our parents made the decision they did for us. Parents were like the centurion in Mr Waymouth's Bible. The one who said 'I say unto this man "Go" and he goeth, and unto this man "Come" and he cometh.' There was little explaining or consulting with one's children in the class of '39.

Hastings High School was an impressive-looking place after Queenswood and St Luke's. The main block consisted of a two-storeyed brick building with a bell tower which would not have disgraced Greyfriars, Billy Bunter's *alma mater*.

The bell tower was the focus of a daring escapade unlikely to be attempted by the Fat Owl of the Remove. The story was still being told and retold by all at the 100th reunion in 2004, of how Priest and Comrie of the Sixth climbed up the steep tiled roof to the bell tower, then on up the vertical tower, to attach a pair of ladies' panties to the top spike, where they flew high and proud above the astonished school next morning.

Hastings High was founded in 1904, a school with history, spacious grounds and enormous playing fields. But most convincing to me was the fact that all the staff wore academic gowns, just like in books. It also had a motto, 'Akina', which means 'strike harder' in Maori. The school emblem on our blazer pockets was the now extinct Huia, of which a rather battered pair of male and female birds still perched in a glass case in the main building a hundred years later.

The headmaster when I arrived was Mr W.A.G. Penlington, known irremediably as Wag. He held assembly every morning, assisted by the first assistant, Mr (Jonah) Jones – in charge of boys – and an alarmingly red-haired Miss Steele, who played the piano and was in charge of girls. She was a power in the school and known to be so from the day one arrived.

At the end of each assembly, when the brief prayers, the hymn and the notices had had their turn, there came the piece of classical music. The school, especially Miss Steele, was very proud of its latest record player, a handsome gift from the American philanthropist Mr Carnegie. Each morning a different piece filled the hall. I had not heard classical music at home, nor with Miss Clayton, and at first I sat waiting for things to finish so we could file out and get on with proper school, but after a time I loved the noise, the sheer wonder of the sound: Verdi's Overture to *La Traviata*, Liszt's *La Campanella*, Bach's *Jesu, Joy of Man's Desiring*. This was good stuff, even I could tell. And what about the composers? The men who made them? Here was something even more astonishing than the process of people who write books. How could these men do it? How did they invent it, keep the sounds in their heads, then put down the required symbols in the required order so that musicians hundreds of years later could decipher them and continue to make the same noise? Not only that, how could different instruments make different sounds from the same symbols? It was beyond me;

better just to sit (with my mouth no longer hanging open) in the assembly hall and be grateful.

For the first time I became a priggish and hard-working student. I loved Latin, wallowed in it, couldn't get enough. I still have my ancient *Latin for Today – First Year Course* by Mason D. Gray and Thornton Jenkins, edited by Cuthbert McEvoy MA, and stamped 'Foster Brook, Bookseller' who lived in our street.

On the back page I have written in pencil in fat round letters, 'The English Noun clause introduced by that is expressed in Latin by the infinitive and the subject of the noun clause is put in the Acc case.' I suppose I may have understood that at some stage.

I also noted that the essential in Latin is endings. You wouldn't get anywhere if your endings were wrong.

I loved the difference, the stories, the fact that so many of our words had Latin roots as Dad told me. That until recently medical students had to take Latin so they could understand so many medical terms. I also liked the smudgy black-and-white illustrations: *Faustalus finds Romulus and Remus*, *Mettus Curtus sacrifices himself for Rome.* Everything in Latin was so sure, so brave, so certain.

In 1939 Latin was the only subject in which the sexes mingled at Hastings High. Or rather the girls sat in the front desks and hairy-legged heroes in black shorts and black socks crashed their way towards the back. Our teacher, 'Jonah' Jones, was a seemingly amiable man but a stern disciplinarian. He liked boys, tolerated girls and loved Latin.

The teachers I met at Hastings High were all good at their jobs. They were practical, hard working and interested in their subjects. One or two used *aide-mémoires* as useful adjuncts to learning. I know the French *grave* accent slopes from the left and the *acute* from the right because our teacher explained it to us. If, she said, someone came into the room from the left they would have to climb through the window with guilty stealth, that is *gravely*. On the other hand, if they came through the door on the right they would come in briskly, with nothing to hide, that is *acutely*.

Even maths seemed more possible with Mrs Hilyard, a motherly older woman with spectacles and a mind like a steel trap. Elementary geometry had a certain appeal for me which was exciting, though algebra remained beyond me; once more I was at sea in a sieve, like the Jumblies.

The best of our teachers for me was Miss Avery. She was tall and rangy with straight black hair clamped to her scalp with black hairpins, which for some reason were called bobby pins. There was nothing bobby-like about Miss Avery. Bobby pins smacked of later; of Deanna Durbin, pedal pushers, teenagers, white ankle socks and flatties – culminating in one lucky beauty being crowned the most popular girl in the sophomore year.

Not so Miss Avery, nor us. She taught English to us with inspiration and devotion. In the long summers of Hastings, she took us outside to the big front lawn where we sat beneath the shade of the silver birches and learned about poetry. There are many types, she told us: sonnets, narrative poems, lyrics. Could any of us think of any other type?

I thought of Wally O'Malley and his cast iron belly but kept quiet.

The poet we were going to talk about today was a man called William Shakespeare who lived four hundred years ago. How many of us had heard of him?

A few hands lifted, one or two waved. Our father told David and me occasionally that Shakespeare knew everything about parenthood: 'How sharper than a serpent's tooth it is / to have a thankless child.'

I was interrupted from waving my hand by a girl sitting behind me dropping a daisy down the back of my neck.

Miss Avery began reading from *The Merchant of Venice*:

The quality of mercy is not strain'd
It droppeth as the gentle rain from heaven
Upon the place beneath: it is twice bless'd;
It blesseth him that gives and him that takes;
'Tis mightiest in the mightiest; it becomes
The throned monarch better than his crown . . .

Wonderful and more wonderful.

The bell rang. Miss Avery became brisk. 'Quickly, Barbara.'

'Yes but . . .'

'Come along.'

'Can we have him next time?'

'I think it could be arranged. Run.'

And we did have him, often. Great wallops of good words read aloud.

'Always read poetry aloud to yourself, girls. Essential.'

David was now boarding at Wanganui Collegiate and loving his second school. As always he made friends quickly and kept them forever. Perhaps my parents thought that things would be even more lonely for me without David as well as Colin, but one day Dad told me we were getting a dog. This was good news, I had been begging for one for years. All the Wrights were pro-dog, but Mum was decidedly anti. To her they were only one step up from cats, who made a feline beeline towards her whenever she appeared.

The chosen dog was a wirehaired fox terrier called Tip which was short for his pedigree name, 'Tiptoe through the tulips'. Regrettably, after so much excitement, friendship did not bloom between us. He was as haughty as his pedigree suggested, and occasionally ill-tempered and snappy. We enjoyed our walks together but we were by no means 'pals' – one of the few cowboy words I didn't like the sound of.

The thing Tip liked best was the dog shows where he won many prizes. Dad, who never walked except when following a ball round a golf course, pursued Tip and his lead round and round the ring at a strange skittery trot – Dad that is, not Tip who was obviously enjoying himself. In charge with his proud jaw jutting he reminded me of Grandfather Wright, with his General Smut's beard.

Our next dog was friendlier. Our silky black dachshund, who Dad christened Schweppes, had a heart of gold and a gregarious nature. Everyone loved him, including, eventually, Mum. Schweppes's basket sat first in the washhouse, then migrated to the kitchen, and finally infiltrated and settled into Mum's bedroom. No eye in the world is more melting and loving than that of a black daschund. He won us all and we were his devoted friends.

The problem with Schweppes was unexpected. He loved not only us, but like Browning's *My Last Duchess*, made the mistake of loving the whole world. He strayed into the park, scratched his way under 609's now closed gates and strayed further and further until he was seen in town, for goodness' sake. He had discovered a kindly butcher who tossed him an occasional saveloy. Things went from bad to worse, until Mum met him trotting home along Roberts Street with his head stretched high and a string of stolen sausages in his jaws trailing behind his hind legs.

He was too reckless, too careless, and died too soon after the episode of the sausages. He was run over by a van in Fitzroy Avenue and most sadly mourned by us all. His basket and blanket went back to the washhouse, later out into the shed, then disappeared.

In 1938 Dad had bought a large console model Gulbransen radio. This outstanding object stood in the sitting room between the padded window seats and Grandfather Wright's bookcase. It was almost my height, made of dark shining wood with heavy green silk criss-crossed in front where the sound came out.

It must have been school holidays when it arrived, as David was home. He was undoubtedly more informed about the Gulbransen than any of us. Dad said airily that he knew nothing about technical things, nothing at all, in the same casual tone of voice in which he said he was a terrible business man. Terrible. Which left problems either hanging in the air or put to one side to be 'looked at later'. He and Mum and I stood in awe in front of the monster. Presumably there had been large radios around for years but none had impressed me as much as our upstanding console Gulbransen.

The reason Dad had bought it was so we could keep in touch with what he called The World Situation. One must know what was going on. How could Hitler think he could annex Austria? Mad. Completely mad. Yes, the BBC was essential.

The Gulbransen and the fluting male tones of the BBC had much to announce. In September we heard the British Navy was mobilised, and the following day the Munich Agreement was signed between Chamberlain, Daladier, Hitler and Mussolini. Chamberlain returned claiming 'peace with honour'. Oh, the relief in 609. Bertha and Harry Davies from next door came over for a 'spot' to celebrate.

Bertha was also celebrating her acquisition of a new electric heater. 'It is a wonder, Cecil,' she said. 'I can put it on when I am kneeling saying my prayers at night.' 'Ah,' said Dad, 'you would be getting the best of both worlds?' 'Exactly, Cecil. Exactly.'

I took little interest in the news though I was aware of Mussolini. He had featured in a playground chant at both Mahora and St Luke's:

There's a war in Abyssinia, won't y' come,
There's a war in Abyssinia, won't y' come,
Mussolini will be there, shooting peanuts through the air
There's a war in Abyssinia won't y' come'.

Though not of course at Hastings High. Primary playground stuff like chants had been left behind.

Dad began coming home to listen to the BBC at lunch time. Germany invaded Poland on 1 September and New Zealand declared war on Germany on 3 September. Michael Joseph Savage spoke to the nation on 5 September 1939:

With gratitude for the past and confidence in the future we range ourselves without fear beside Britain. Where she goes, we go. Where she stands, we stand. We are only a small and young nation, but we march forward with union of hearts and wills to a common destiny.

'Excellent,' said Dad. 'Grand. Well done.'

Tui Reid was dark-haired and good at games and later became the mother of Susan Devoy, New Zealand's world champion squash player. We were hurrying back from the silver birches after one of Miss Avery's sessions when Tui said '*Night Nurse* tonight. Good oh.'

'What?'

'Don't you listen? You're mad. Six o'clock tonight,' she said, sprinting ahead.

I found the number of the station from Tui and whizzed home – 'went like the clappers' – to tell Mum the good news. No luck. *Night Nurse* clashed with the BBC News, and besides, I had my homework. And anyway, Tui would tell me what happened. Which she did.

About this age I began to hear voices. The first time it happened I was standing near Mrs Powdrell's fence and our pomegranate tree. I was not in any way concerned, let alone alarmed. There were voices, perfectly amiable, sometimes male, sometimes female, never children. I was not sure what they were talking about; there seemed to be just a flow of other people's voices like a stream in the distance. No alarming commands came from them, thank goodness. Just unknown people talking in the back of my mind. I didn't tell anyone. There didn't seem much point. I was not unhappy about the situation and 'my voices' disappeared after about a year or so.

Another odd sensation was more lasting. I would stand staring in the bathroom mirror, telling myself firmly, 'Your name is Barbara Wright, you are twelve years old, you live in 609 Roberts Street with your nice kind mother and father, and your brother David in the holidays.'

This oddity was much more alarming. To stand and stare into a glass at a mirror image of yourself, wondering who, or even what, is staring back at you, is not a good experience.

Years later, long after the 'Who am I?' stage had ended, I mentioned this odd activity to our son Jeremy, who was studying psychiatry. 'Existential angst, Mum. Fear of not being. Quite common.'

'Oh.'

Now the end of the year was coming. The silver birches' catkins were shedding pollen and I was sneezing and Miss Avery would be striding out with Form 3A for the last day on the big lawn.

'Cross-legged please girls, don't sprawl. Now, how many of you know Alfred Tennyson's poem 'The Lady of Shalott'?'

Total blank.

She read:

On either side the river lie
Long fields of barley and of rye . . .

Willows whiten, aspens quiver,
Little breezes dusk and shiver . . .

Soon it would be break up and David would be home. Then Christmas, which was no good now because of the sadness of Colin's birthday on 28 December. And then, at last, came the day we set off for Waimarama, which is Maori and means 'moonlight'.

The road was unsealed, dusty and winding and my enamel basin was near at hand as ever. Then came the moment when incipient nausea disappeared and Dad pulled the stuffy, laden car off to the side of the road at the same place on the hill he stopped every year, to give us our first view of the beach. The beautiful beach with its long white surf creaming in for miles, and beyond lay Bare Island, and then the Pacific Ocean and the World.

This year I had something special to check. Miss Avery had told us aspens were another name for poplars and I wanted to see if our poplars quivered, were 'tremulous' as Alfred Tennyson's poem said.

Silver poplars grew thickly by the bridge near the entrance to Waimarama where there they shielded and sheltered the Catholic seminarians' camp each year. We seldom saw the young men except when they went fishing, usually on Thursday or Friday mornings. Lots of them stood milling around on the beach in their black neck-to-knee bathing togs, laughing and calling and fooling around. Then the two strongest swimmers would swim away out beyond the breakers, dragging a great net behind them, then swimming wide and strong for a while before heading back for the shore, just like the picture of fishermen flinging their nets in my *Bible Designed to Read as Literature*, which Dad had brought home from the surgery because there was a man down on his luck selling them. Under one black-and-white picture stood Jesus saying, 'I will make you fishers of men.' Dad agreed with me there was some story to that effect and yes this was similar.

The beachcombers, especially the children, ran to watch when the swimmers reached the shore dragging the wet net with its cargo of fish jumping: snapper and terakihi, all panting, falling and flapping about, and big crabs, which no one ate, that were tossed back into the sea with the tiddlers.

I had other things to check.

I was glad to see the silver poplars did quiver in the breeze, their leaves flicking from silver to grey, green to silver grey, silver to grey.

That was also the year I learned the facts of life. One of the girls and I were hanging out her family's bathing suits. She pointed to a smear of white slime on the crotch of one of her older brother's togs. 'Yuck', she said, 'he might've rinsed that off.'

'What is it?'

'Spunk.'

A new word. 'What's it mean?'

'Don't you know! Spunk's what men have in their cocks and they shove it up you and then you get a baby.'

What a very nasty thought. So much so that it seemed a good idea to forget the information, but this was not possible. Especially when we returned to Hastings and I saw husbands and wives pushing prams the length of Heretaunga Street. 'They've done *that*,' I thought. 'All of them.' I never thought of my parents having done so. There are some things beyond imagination.

It was also the year David and Gary Glazebrook learned to drive, by the simple method of driving Mrs Glazebrook's borrowed car on the unsealed roads behind the beach. Both David and Gary had understood the workings of motor cars from infancy. All they had to do was sit in the driver's seat, turn on the switch and set off. It was also the time of the smoking picnic. The boys, Tommy Couper, David and Gary pinched a few cigarettes from their parents and we retreated to the sand hills where we sat puffing, and no one felt sick. That night I told Mum. Disgrace from fellow puffers followed. The shame of being a sneak and traitor was swamped by the agony of deceiving her.

'You still haven't told me you're sorry,' she said sadly after the confession.

CHAPTER 9

I am sitting at the kitchen table peeling Mum's early peaches. Her favourite for bottling, Golden Queens, are not ready yet. I know this because when biking home from school I heard one woman shout across the road to another.

'Done your Queens?'

'Naah,' cried her friend. 'Too soon.'

I also know that Golden Queens are not a freestone variety, and thus are 'devils to put down'. However, help is to hand, in the form of a small kitchen tool designed for levering out recalcitrant stones.

We have just done Gerard Manley Hopkins with Miss Avery this afternoon. I liked him, especially 'Pied Beauty' with the unexpected bit where he writes of his pleasure in 'all trades, their gear and tackle and trim'. I hadn't met trades in poems before and decided that the little wooden-handled tool was part of the gear and tackle and trim of bottling. Like any keen candidate for teacher's pet I decided I would mention this to Miss Avery at her next lesson.

Bottling is a hot trade in Hawke's Bay. Later the province will be called The Fruit Bowl of New Zealand, with a Blossom Parade to match, but now it is just hot. Temperatures reach ninety degrees Fahrenheit in high summer, the time when fruits swell and ripen and, according to another new poet, Andrew Marvell, the 'curious peach / into my hands themselves do reach'.

This line seems to me an image of plenty, abundance in the Bay's long hot summer, especially when Miss Avery explains that 'curious' in the seventeenth century meant 'curiously wrought'. And didn't we like his 'stumbling on melons'. The poet, though, was English like all the others and his nectarines and peaches would have reached themselves into his hands in July–August. *Flower Fairies* had revealed to me long ago the mess the Northern Hemisphere makes of seasons. It would be autumn there now, and squirrels would be putting down nuts for winter.

'Do I have to go to Woodford?' I say. Mum looks at me in damp-cheeked surprise. I have chosen a bad moment to bring up the topic.

'You've always wanted to go to boarding school. Look at the fuss you made when Wendy went to Woodford.'

'I like High.' I have no words to explain that I don't want to lose Miss Avery, no words at all. I realise there could be someone like Miss Avery at Woodford but I don't want to risk it. On the other hand, I have wanted to go to boarding school since the days of *Dimsie Pulls Through*. In the meantime I drop the subject.

The People now lay undisturbed in their cupboard but I continued messing about in notebooks of bigger size than the one pinched from McKenzie's.

Dad and I continued our regular raids on the library. He also handed on his treasures such as *Alice in Wonderland* which, to his disgust, was not a winner for me. However, we shared enthusiasm for Edward Lear. Excitement ran high when I discovered we had somewhere in New Zealand where one of this characters from Nonsense Songs lived.

On the Coast of Coromandel
Where the early pumpkins blow,
In the middle of the woods
Lived the Yonghy-Bonghy-Bò.

'It's the "early" that makes it,' said Dad. 'Remember the "early".'

And I have, when I see a Green Triumble, an early species.

Occasionally Mum and Dad and I went to an evening session at the Regent Cinema – newer than the Cosy, with more blue velvet about, hence grander. The film this night was *Mr Smith Goes to Washington*; honourable young man fights corruption, takes his case to Washington, wins.

Evening sessions followed a well-trod routine. We stand up for 'God Save the King', we sit for the *News of the World*, we laugh at the cartoon *Donald Duck and Huey, Dewey, and Louie*, we gaze at the beauties of foreign parts in the *Travelogues* and hear once more the rich American voice intone farewell: 'And now, as the sun sinks slowly in the west, we say farewell to Cuba, Land of the

Rumba.' Every week there is a different scenic wonderland, and every time the boys in the front shout 'Boat!' at the appropriate moment so the boat sinks slowly in the west and we laugh again. Then we wait for the lights to come on and the usherette to whizz up and down the aisles with her tray of Eskimo Pies and licker ice creams in cones. Licker for me, nothing for Mum and Dad.

A man across the aisle from us looks bored, yawns, tries to swallow it, and yawns again.

'Look Dad, that man's stifling a yawn.'

'Stifling, child, stifling. *Sty* not *stiff*. Good try though.'

Dad and Miss Avery taught me that words can be a lifelong interest, as rewarding as that of any other harmless passion: fossil hunting, for example, or bird watching. Words also have their species; their rare birds, their flyblown lousy ones, their damaged and their newly hatched. Words can migrate, hibernate, reappear. They can conjugate and breed new versions of themselves, like any other living thing. They may be talismans revered for their beauty, or slang loved for their crassness.

Now I am on my way to Woodford House, where the wind still bloweth free, and am happy at the prospect. Wendy speaks of boarding school in the highest possible terms. It is super, absolutely super. It was also explained to me by Dad that it would be a financial strain for him to have two children at fee-paying schools and he would be delighted if I would rather stay at Hastings High. I understood his point immediately.

Mum's last task for me was to demonstrate the fun way to deal with menstruation. 'Why does it happen?' I asked. For once Mum didn't recommend Dad for information. 'So you can have babies later.' Worse and worse. What on earth would you want with a baby?

I have my wardrobe packed in a trunk like David's, but filled with my white cotton linings, my maroon bloomers, my tunics and blazer, my grey velvet frocks for evenings in winter and my flowered Liberty cotton frocks for summer evenings. Most exciting of all is my woven grey cloak which swirls around me most satisfactorily.

The day before I went to boarding school I biked down on my BSA to King Street for a check-up with Mr Whyte. As usual there was something, a tricky little molar lower right. A shameful tear leaked as Mr Whyte drilled. He stopped for a brisk mop, muttering, 'Mopping up operations round Tobruk.' That was witty, nevertheless I was surprised. Not only that a grown-up would be flippant about the sacred BBC News, but also that Mr Whyte would play with words, comfort with jokes. As I was leaving he put an arm on a young nun's shoulder and murmured, 'And which is your night off, my dear?' Happy confusion, shy smiles and laughs from both charge and chaperon while I worked out what the joke was. I liked jokes and was pleased when he told me that I could go into a sideshow as the girl with the smallest gold filling in the world.

As we drive up the hill I am wearing my unbecoming grey woollen walking-out uniform, with the cloak flung over it. It is cumbersome, the cloak, and not easy to manage, but I have begged to be allowed to wear it despite the heat. Dad tells me I look like a Carmelite nun and he hopes I will not get carried away by extreme ascetism. I am used to his inexplicable jokes but this time am too excited to ask for an explanation. I am on my way.

There has been no rain for months in Hawke's Bay and as usual the Havelock hills are silver grey. 'Poor parched hills,' says Mum as she does every summer. Normally I would wonder how she knows the hills *mind* being parched, but this time I don't bother.

We cruise along the Havelock road in the Vauxhall and then I remember I haven't any toothpaste. Normally this would engender pained sighs, but not today. Dad will stop opposite the chemist in Havelock and I will run in. Clutching my Colgate in its little brown bag I bang into Judy Masterton as she enters the door. Judy has just left Woodford and is now an Old Girl. Panting with heat I am obviously on my way up and Judy gives me a word of advice. 'Don't be a bumptious new bug,' she says. More exciting than ever. Advice from *Dimsie's First Term*. I thank her for an Old Girl's advice and run.

I was not concerned for a moment that I would be a 'bumptious new bug'; that would have required enterprise and daring. I recognised the phrase immediately as one from overseas. Words more suitable to girls whose seaside holidays had piers and pails and spades and starfish, and never have they seen a dumper. Also they had packed their school trunks with Mummy – never Mum. Or sometimes Nanny came in to do the task.

*

Before the war and for some time afterwards, Woodford House regularly recruited teachers from Britain. I can only assume this was because the Board of Governors thought the applicants would be better in every way. Similarly, when I enrolled at Otago University in 1944, there were few New Zealand-born university professors teaching New Zealanders. Those who studied in British universities and were offered teaching positions there usually took them. Anglophilia in the colonies was alive and well when I was growing up. My father was by no means the only man in Hawke's Bay who called Britain 'Home', though he enjoyed living in New Zealand. 'Wonderful little country, wonderful,' he would murmur occasionally.

At Woodford enthusiasm for all things bright and beautiful came from the old country which led to an odd renaming of parts. At home I came *inside* or went *outside*, accompanied by the same pair of shoes. At Woodford, they became anglicised into *indoor* shoes and *outdoor* shoes, and must be worn accordingly. We learned never to speak of our unattractive grey walking-out uniform as 'costume' or 'suit'. Miss Hamber, our English matron, transmogrified them into 'coats and skirts'. She knew, and handed on her knowledge to us.

We studied nothing of our New Zealand history at Woodford, neither Pakeha nor Maori, any more than I had at Queensword or St Luke's or in my year at Hastings High. Bearing in mind that I went to Woodford over sixty years ago it still seems odd, very odd.

I also had great gaps in my education. I left Hastings High with a fair knowledge of the Phoenician trade routes and landed up in Woodford's fourth form where I found Gladstone building a good cabinet.

The school was riddled with rules, none of which worried me in the slightest. No talking until after morning chapel, no running up steps two at a time, no talking as we walked past the chapel. If we were found in each other's rooms, ever, under any circumstances, our one and only exeat for the term would be cancelled. It was years after that I discovered this edict was to avoid any temptation towards lesbianism, rather like the policy of draining swamps before the malarial mosquitoes appeared. Surely someone with some sort of sense must have queried this rule, but not to my knowledge.

Home had had many rules and I was used to them. I was also used to being well cared for. I knew I was lucky, but I did wonder sometimes why I felt I had missed the point, had been a bit slow on the uptake. For twelve years reports sang the same tune:

Conduct: *Satisfactory, but often inattentive in class.*

As I had hugged Dad and my precious Mum goodbye she handed me a notebook which she had used as a journal when she was 'with your Father in England'. There were pages left, she said, why waste them? I opened the book sitting on my narrow bed after they left.

Mum was writing about their visit to Kew Gardens. 'And the flowers, oh the flowers were wonderful. I longed for my little Barbara.' My mouth dropped. Mum, beautiful sweet-scented Mum, had longed for me. I was filled with the sweet stinging warmth of unexpected joy. Mum loved me, she longed for me. She had written it down in a book.

A bell rang. There is something both imperative and alarming about the sound of a large hand bell, especially when rung by a hefty prefect such as Head of Nelson, second in command to Head Prefect.

My next door neighbour seemed to have disappeared.

I sprang up, slipped Mum's book in a drawer and ran out the door. Nelson House was on the move. 'What is it?' I whispered to a fat girl who looked as though she knew a thing or two. 'Supper bell,' she hissed.

Supper? 'Supper' was the tea and buns after St Matthew's parish concert, where Wendy's and my recitation about a little dog who died, but who laughed because he'd had his day, had been greeted with total silence. Rupert Brooke's poem had been a sad flop.

Fortunately I had changed from my woolly bear walking-out uniform plus Carmelite cloak into my flowered Liberty cotton summer evening wear.

Off I went, joining the Liberty-flowered stream as it surged down the stairs from Upper to Lower Nelson, through the cloisters then on down the steps, past the Chapel of St Francis of Assisi in silence and on down through the original Woodford House where the seniors slept, then past the matron's sick room, which I found later was popular with the unathletic who hoped to avoid exercise of any sort.

On that first night we walked straight into the dining room. Normally there was a much more complicated way of marshalling the troops. We stood in a straight line in the hall, staring at the prefects who stared back at us. A prefect spoke, lines filed in from the left. All of this in complete silence. There was a lot of silence at Woodford in my time. The headmistress, Miss Holland, believed that it engendered self-control, a belief which would be hard to prove or disprove.

Three things stay with me from supper that summer evening sixty-five years ago. I noticed on the left-hand wall as we passed a machine-made tapestry of Robert Herrick's message to young women, with a few fat cherubs rolling about.

Gather ye rosebuds while ye may,
Old Time is still a'flying.

I didn't do Herrick with Miss Avery but I often looked at Dad's *Palgrave's Golden Treasury*. There I found a poem called 'Counsel to Girls', whose correct title I found later is 'To the Virgins, to Make Much of Time', which would have been much more interesting. I liked the poem but was interested by the last stanza – which was not on the tapestry.

Then be not coy, but use your time,
And while you may, go marry:
For having lost but once your prime,
You may forever tarry.

Perhaps someone had donated Robert Herrick's first stanza tapestry to the school, thinking it might reiterate the sentiments expressed in the school motto, *Nunc Acceptabile Tempus*, which I translated as 'Now is the Right Time'. Miss Holland and Herrick were in agreement in some ways. When a girl made the excuse to Miss Holland that she hadn't had time to finish her homework or some other task, the reply was a cool look and the words 'You have all the time there is'. Unanswerable.

Now I was at a faraway table. An older girl stood at one end and the rest of us, mainly new bugs, grabbed a chair, stood behind it and hoped for the best. The mistress on duty and those who knew the drill about grace before meals bowed their heads and mumbled. *Bless this food to our mouths and us to thy service, Oh Lord*, which was followed by a cacophony of wooden chairs being scratched and slammed about on the floor of the dining room.

Safely seated, I stared at the white plate in front of me. On it sat one large red tomato, which I recognised as being of the Beefsteak variety. Nothing else. Large plates of bread were present, likewise butter, neither of which helped me much. I glanced at the older girl, who presumably was a prefect. She was plump, with two long plaits and a wide smile. 'This is what we do,' she said gently, and, picking up her knife and fork, began cutting her Beefsteak into bite-sized pieces.

'I'm Norma Shelton,' she said. 'What's your name?'

My three other memories of that late afternoon were the sun pouring through the windows onto my lonely tomato and Norma's generous smile.

There were no daygirls at Woodford then and we boarders led a cloistered existence, but there was freedom for me in many ways. The friendships I made were mine and mine alone; and there was the beauty of the surroundings. I also learned another useful fact of life, one induced by proximity of others. You don't have to like someone to work alongside them effectively. Tolerance is a gift worth learning early.

I don't know what Dad hoped I would obtain from my time at Woodford. I think Mum hoped I would come out of my shell, behave nicely and marry a Hawke's Bay sheep farmer, preferably of Scottish extraction. A hope doomed from the start.

It is embarrassing to admit but I had no aspirations at all, academic or of any other sort, other than a wish to write books someday, an ambition so far away there was little point in thinking about it. A friend told me she was determined to come top of everything at Woodford, an ambition which astounded me. She also told me how unhappy she had been when she arrived, having come from a remote farm in the Bay of Islands where she had been driving her elderly invalid father about in a truck since she was twelve years old. She had grown up into a self-assured and responsible adult when she arrived to face the nit-picking minutiae of Woodford House rules. She survived happily but some girls from farming backgrounds, with their beloved horses and their great outdoors, seemed barely to survive from one holiday to the next.

The worst thing you could be at Woodford was a skite. You were allowed to praise someone else, anything from the top of their hair to their smashing serve to their pretty little toes. But never, ever, think of admitting you could do anything well, if, by any chance, you could. A friend of mine was the Junior Champion in athletics. I have a photograph of her holding all her cups looking absolutely enraged. You couldn't even *look* as if you were pleased. Odd behaviour, but deeply ingrained at Woodford. It was also fashionable when I was there to say you hated your time there. I loved every minute.

The headmistress, Miss Mary Holland, was a wise, admirable woman, a good teacher with a love of learning. She also had determination to hand on these delights to her senior forms. She was a devout woman with great presence and insisted the chapel must be the centre of the school. She instilled in us the knowledge that we were fortunate and therefore owed something in return. A sentiment which most of us agreed with at school, and some throughout their lives. A sentiment sometimes considered patronising but which made sense from Miss Holland. Unfortunately she taught English only to the sixth form and retired when I was in the fifth form.

Break up at the end of my first year was excellent. All the right things were there: good music in the chapel, the yearly carol service in the hall and Miss Hamber's flowers, which never altered—huge vases filled with Christmas lilies, small bright red roses and deep blue delphiniums. Colours of the Union Jack, perhaps, in case we had forgotten.

Promises to write were made and forgotten. And then the last chapel service and the bellowing of the final verse:

Those returning, those re–turn–ing
Make more faithful than before.

Then Mum and Dad and I climbed into the laden Vauxhall to head for home, and David was coming soon and Wendy just across the park. I raced up the stairs to say hello to the People, to be stopped in my tracks by shock. They had gone. Nothing, nothing was left. All that remained were the empty shelves which had housed the whole gang, the notebooks and the neatly labelled shoeboxes of clothes. Mum had given them all away.

'But how could you, Mum?'

Mum said she was sorry, and she was too. It had simply not occurred to her to check with me. I was a big girl, she explained, and no longer required dolls, so she had handed them on.

'Besides, you wouldn't want to play with them now would you? At fourteen?'

I was even more shocked. 'No, no. Of course not.'

'Well, then.'

CHAPTER 10

The first blow to my pursuit of knowledge at Woodford was the news I would not be learning Latin. I wrote home in horror (telephone calls were only for emergencies): Why? Why? They knew I was mad about Latin. My father wrote a firm letter back. Surely I had realised from the curriculum that if one took Latin one had to take mathematics and, considering my record, I would be more sensible to take the arithmetic and geography option. Besides which, Latin became a great deal more difficult after the first year.

From that moment I disliked geography and floundered around in Miss Dolores Padbury's arithmetic class. As usual I flaunted my ability at tables but gentle grey-haired Miss Padbury indicated that this was not enough.

She had other attributes, Miss Padbury. She taught mathematics to those with the ability to understand and, like Miss Kathleen Rixon at Queenswood, she had postcards of the works of great painters and showed them to us with a similar loving enthusiasm. She was also a devout Catholic, which was useful for the school as she drove the one or two of the girls of her faith to their church in Havelock on Sunday. Meanwhile the rest of us thundered down the hill in a grey woollen crocodile then thundered up again like the grand old Duke of York in reverse.

As the term progressed I discovered a friend who took Latin but not maths.

'How could you?'

'Dad insisted.'

I wrote again, but with a sinking heart. Dad was not one to fight any headmistress's stern dictum. Mum answered my letter. My father said it would be too late to change and besides Latin becomes more difficult after the first year. So bang went *Circus Maximus*, *Quintus Fabius Maximus* and *Pastor et Grex. The pastor of a church is so called because he, like the shepherd, looks after his flock*, was the last I learned.

In geography we 'did' capitals of the world, we 'did' imports and exports, we gazed at black-and-white pictures of the USA wheat belts, corn belts, cotton belts, we drew maps of various continents, we coloured blue crayon rims around the edges to indicate blue oceans of continents lucky enough to have a strip of sea. My years of colouring in had come into their own, but to little purpose.

New Zealand, of course, had blue rims all around which made us an island, a fact we had learned in our each and every infant rooms. The whole thing was a disaster. The only good thing about it was the strong smell of nicotine on our returned homework which reminded me of home, be it Craven A, De Reske or any other brand, though I missed the sting of Mum's Blue Grass Toilet Water.

Practically all the members of the staff smoked, including Miss French (NHRN), who was sharp tempered and quick off the mark. She and I maintained a pact. I would not bother her and she would ignore me. I missed French at Hastings High with the *grave* and *acute* mnemonics and the exciting bright yellow paperbacks entitled *Le Mystère de la Chambre Jaune* which we translated with the speed of a stalled glacier, but with great interest. All through the year we had laboured, but never reached *le dénouement*.

Woodford staff must have felt isolated during the war. Hardly any of them had cars, there was very little petrol, and, being from England, many had no local friends. The art mistress, Miss Edgar, made a staff coat of arms depicting a worn-looking teacher slogging uphill to the staff house with arms laden with books. The motto beneath read *Dulce et decorum est scola labore*.

Miss Lucy Hogg, second in command and a redoubtable woman, taught us history in the fourth form. Honourable, hard working and kind, with cropped hair and wide about the ankles, she strode about the school with purpose and intent. She could spot mischief from afar, be it a rogue banana skin dumped in a lavender bush, a child sighted where no child should be, or a senior girl reading an unsuitable magazine when she should be practising the pianoforte. All these errors would induce a characteristic explosion about her face ending in a pout of disapproval. Her highest praise for a girl was, 'She is sensible, and means well.'

As was her unique method of teaching. Presumably devised by herself, it was both sensible and meant well, but tedious beyond words for anyone who wanted to know *why?* I had always wanted more of the 'human interest' side of history as well as the 'what happened next'. Mum's answer to questions from early childhood had been 'Ask your father'. Dad usually tried but became puzzled, or bored, retreated into 'Look it up child, look it up'. Where did you look up what the Phoenicians looked like? Who decided which were the Seven Wonders of the Ancient World? Both of which we chanted together in current events at St Luke's.

Hastings High had been good for people who asked questions. Woodford less so, especially in Miss Hogg's history classes. She would stand before us, shipshape and Bristol fashion, a piece of chalk in her hand and her expression stern, as she taught us about nineteenth-century British politics – how, for example, Gladstone's Home Rule Bill for Ireland had passed its third reading in the Commons on September 1st, but was rejected by the House of Lords eight days later. Miss Hogg would then turn to the blackboard and write in exquisitely straight lines and in the clearest handwriting ever seen –

Heading. *Gladstone's Home Rule for Ireland.*

Followed by Salient Points: 1 / 2 / 3 / 4.

We wrote it down word for word in our notebooks. 'Tabulate, girls,' she cried, 'tabulate.'

We tabulated. Practically all the sense of which has now sunk into oblivion. However, for anyone with a visual memory it was simple to churn back facts at exam times. My history marks soared but all I can remember of two years' history with Miss Hogg was Betsy Reed's drawing of *Gladstone building a Good Cabinet.*

The juxtaposition of her surname and given name, Lucy Hogg, also worried me. The Lucy didn't go with the Hogg. Lucy is a Victorian child with an Alice-in-Wonderland headband. Hogg is Hogg.

I have no memory as to who taught us English in our fourth and fifth years, which indicates a lack of enthusiasm from both pupil and teacher. The teacher (let me call her Miss Popper) demonstrated once more that books were written only by brilliant English men, preferably extinct. My main memory of her was her enthusiasm for parsing. 'Parsing girls, and analysis.' The difference between her teaching and Miss Avery's being that Miss Avery loved her work and taught with passion whereas Miss Popper didn't give a hoot, or not one I heard.

Much emphasis was placed on the works of the Romantic poets. They thought nothing, we were told, of walking seventeen miles to post a letter. A good thing in itself, we gathered. 'We walked,' Dorothy Wordsworth writes in her journal. 'William composed.'

That was how you did it, then. You sat, or preferably walked, inspiration came in shafts, you composed and wrote the words down later.

Miss Holland's grief at the outbreak of the war was deep; she had bleak memories of the last one. Her decision as to Woodford's contribution to the war effort was typical of her: unusual, well thought out and deeply welcomed by the recipients. Honey for the navy was within the scope of the youngest pupil and the most ancient of Old Girls. It involved raising money for the fund by any legal means, and handing it over to the school, who bought large tins of local honey and sent it to the League's Seafarers Comfort Supply Depot in England, who then forwarded it to the men in small ships of the 'wavy navy'. By the end of 1941, over 6,000 pounds in weight had been shipped and received with great enthusiasm, according to letters which the school received. Letters of thanks, many of them very moving, poured in to the school. One of the saddest came from a lieutenant on the HMS *Enchantress*: 'Good luck to you, your school and all the old girls. Keep smiling, because that's what we are doing over here.' It arrived with a note attached: 'We regret that the HMS *Enchantress* was lost in the Battle of the Java Sea.'

During the holidays I headed for the Hastings library. On the shelf with the Angela Brazils and other schoolgirl romps such as *The Fourth Was Fun for Philippa*, I came across a non-fiction book published in Britain which made the point that the spirit and attitudes of the girls' boarding schools there were based upon the hope that their students, within the impossible bounds of gender, would grow into the female equivalent of fine, upstanding young men; girls who obeyed orders yet had a sense of leadership, who did their duty and never moaned. Certainly this unlikely ethos was maintained at Woodford. A high standard of rigour was expected: going for long runs (unusual for girls at that time), having cold baths, and not being allowed hot water bottles. The place was freezing in winter. My father told me later that he knew Woodford girls whose hands had been scarred by chilblains.

Ruth Nathan, an enterprising, petite sybarite, attempted to defeat the chill blasts of early morning chapel by smuggling a child-sized pig-shaped blue hot water bottle to her bosom beneath her winter uniform. The drama was intense when the pig burst outside the chapel in front of the *List of Fathers and Brothers Serving Overseas.*

Like boys we learned about heroes, from Ulysses to Robert Falcon Scott and modern war heroes. I don't remember any heroines held up for our admiration except Joan of Arc. I had always been greatly relieved that my eleven-year-old Words within the Head had not been compulsive, alarming and sacrificial. In the same way, at Queenswood, when we were invited to make contributions to support missionaries in Africa, I gave my pocket money willingly, but prayed silently, 'Please God, don't send me a Call.'

My new friend Jan Poulton asked me to stay with her in the real country and with a real family. Father, mother, two girls, two boys, united in amiability and work. Mr Poulton was old but knew Banjo Paterson's classics, the first poems I had met which weren't British.

There was movement at the station, for the word had passed around
That the colt from old Regret had got away,
And had joined the wild bush horses – he was worth a thousand pound,
So all the cracks had gathered to the fray.
All the tried and noted riders from the stations near and far
Had mustered at the homestead overnight,
For the bushmen love hard riding where the wild bush horses are,
And the stock-horse snuffs the battle with delight.

It was like being with Norah of Billabong.

They also sang round the piano in the evenings, with Janet and Rachel taking turns to play.

Jan and I learned by heart the snatches of Wordsworth Miss Popper read to us. We two, 'one another's best', would chant them to each other when no one else was around as we stared at the distant view of snow on the mountains:

Earth has not anything to show more fair:
Dull would he be of soul who could pass by
A sight so touching in its majesty.

Or, with less reverence and more fun, the wedding-guest's reaction to the Ancient Mariner:

Hold off! Unhand me, grey-beard loon!

We found the novels of Thomas Hardy in the classics section in the dim-panelled empty library at school, but not his poetry. I remember only two contemporary novels. One was *Absalom, My Son*, which fell open at the part which begins, 'Her hair fell forward in a soundless bell of gold.' And another one, by an American woman, where 'the green peas slipped through her slim brown fingers into the yellow bowl', which I thought was beautiful, in concept and execution.

Weekly essays were to me the highlight of the week despite the fact they often came back marked 'C+ Watch your commas'.

But all the time I knew that the next two years with Miss Holland would be different. Even when we were in the fourth form we heard of Holly's regular readings with senior girls. How they sat on hard chairs while she read aloud from Shakespeare or Milton or Ancient Greeks and Romans. Girls came down from her upstairs sitting room in trances, some of them.

It was an exciting prospect.

I and Nora Bayly, the one who drove the farm truck at twelve, spent most tennis sessions at the volley boards. The physical education instructor, Miss Wright (no relation, any more than our beloved Wrightie had been) strode about the place in a short green gym tunic striking terror in the hearts of slobs who were Not Trying. Nothing was done to make us any better at tennis or any other sport, although there was probably little anyone could do. Perhaps Miss Wright assumed that our ineptitude would wreck the game for others.

Nora and I were delighted by our exclusion. We lobbed the ball over the board, slid down the slope past the blackberries, pocketed the ball, then lay back relaxed and hidden as we 'tired the sun with talking', which Dad had told me once. I was learning initiative and Nora already had it. Once we surprised a possum in the fork of a nearby tree. It glared at us and skidded higher. 'Pity we haven't a gun,' said my pigtailed friend.

I don't know how Miss Wright got rid of us during basketball. We were, however, excellent spectators when our A Teams played other A Teams from far and wide. One day Miss Avery arrived in her position as coach with the Hastings High A Team. There was no one in the team I knew, but greatly daring, I jumped to my feet when the game ended and ran down the steps to greet her.

'Hullo, Miss Avery!'

'Barbara, hullo. How are you?'

'Well, thank you.' I stood there oozing with devotion, gazing at the straight black hair clamped to the head, the bobby pins, the rangy figure, the smile. I longed to say something which explained it all.

'I liked the Shakespeare,' I said eventually.

'Good. So do I.'

Miss Wright was hovering with intent. 'I'm sorry to interrupt . . .'

'Goodbye, Miss Avery.'

'Goodbye, Barbara. Nice to see you. Thank you, Miss Wright, tea would be good.' She smiled at me again. 'Don't forget to say him aloud.'

I think Mum would have been pleased at my daring. I was 'coming out of myself', no longer crippled with shyness. The school itself suited me, not necessarily for academic reasons but for many others. The war caused shortages of women teachers as well as men. During the forties Woodford was not a smart school. Most of the big names were farmers' daughters from the North and South Islands. The admired ones' parents rolled up in muddy old cars with plenty of room for a sick dog in the back. Girls from Auckland city were few, and considered shiny and glamorous. They knew about boys and had photographs of themselves with misty bits of tulle drifting about their shoulders. There was thought to be a whiff of skite about them.

Also we were in the country, surrounded by beauty. 'Way up on the hill' meant just that. We looked down over the Heretaunga Plain across to the Kaimanawa Ranges, beautiful at any time but spectacular in winter, when Hastings was covered by fog with only church spires visible, the mountains were covered in snow and Havelock beneath us clear as a bell. Mr Ebbett and his staff made the whole place beautiful, and his triumph was the garden of the Chapel of St Francis of Assisi.

My favourite place was the wisteria-draped cloisters which connected Nelson to the chapel. The smell of their blossom in springtime was unforgettable. We stood in pepper-scented silence each morning before filing in. The headmistress waited in silence, then lifted her head and said, 'This is the day which the Lord hath made.'

'Let us rejoice and be glad in it.'

Miss Holland announced her retirement at the end of 1941. The farewells from her admirers were many and various, culminating with the final farewell in the hall. The chairman of the board and his committee sat on the side of the stage staring at Miss Holland who gazed back at them. The staff sat behind, anywhere they could get a glimpse reflecting their respect and affection. Rows of pupils crammed the hall below, a few tearful but the rest of us tougher, and younger, and bored more easily. The chairman of the board went on interminably. The tedium was saved for me and Wendy by his last sentence. 'Miss Holland and I,' he boomed, 'sat together on a board for twenty-five years, and I never heard her complain.' Tough bums.

An announcement as to her successor was made. Miss Kathleen Moseley would take over the position of headmistress next year. She had an honours degree in English from Oxford and had returned to her old school, Wycombe Abbey, to teach.

Miss Holland read to the school an extract of a letter from her successor, in which she had mentioned she had been supervising prep and had to reprimand a girl who had said 'Blast' when an air raid warning had interrupted her work. I found this impressive, but was more concerned about Miss Holland's absence next year.

Miss Moseley continued to be impressive on arrival. Everybody was wild about her. She had great style and elegance and was dramatic. I see her taking communion at St Luke's church, going up to the communion rail with clasped hands and bent head as though she were Mary, Queen of Scots, going to the block.

The Reverend Stephen Waymouth was also dramatic in his worship. He would leave the unleavened bread and wine on the altar, take three steps backwards down the steps without looking, raise his arms high and fling himself before the altar.

I don't doubt both worshippers were genuine, but they were certainly interesting to watch.

With so much glamour and her First from Oxford, Miss Moseley could have led us by the hand through the raptures of English literature, but unfortunately my main memory of her is that she often missed classes, or much of them. She would come rushing in at the end saying 'Oh, girls, I do apologise. A crisis on the pig farm.' Or the laundry. Or the sanitorium. And we all laughed politely for poor Miss Moseley, but after about the seventeenth time even the most worshipping of her admirers were beginning to think, 'Bother this.' Miss Hogg must have been running like a pie woman (Mum) doing two people's jobs. By my last year I was getting disillusioned with Miss Moseley. She was a confusing sort of person.

When she did appear she was an excellent teacher and told us esoteric things, such as Aristotle's six parts of a tragedy, which could be once more tabulated in order of importance:

1. Plot.
2. Character.
3. Thought (theme, idea).
4. Diction (language).
5. Music (sound).
6. Spectacle, which nowadays I suppose would include 'special effects'.

We then moved on to the three unities of a play – action, place and time – and a brief glimpse of true tragedy: 'A tragedy is the initiation of an action that is serious and also, as having magnitude, complete in itself . . . with incidents arousing pity and fear to accomplish purgation of such emotions.' Heady stuff in a classroom of New Zealand girls overlooking the pig farm, across the Heretaunga Plains and on to the Kaimanawas. There we were hearing the wisdom of a Greek living over three thousand years ago.

Miss Moseley also introduced us to T.S. Eliot. Jan and I were enchanted. 'Lonely men in shirtsleeves, leaning out of windows.' We knew these men, had seen them in Woodville or Hastings. And John Donne, which gave us different pleasures. 'Busy old fool, unruly Sun.' Wow.

She also encouraged us to keep what she called commonplace books, in which we copied down favourite poems, bits of prose, quotations from the wise and less wise. Mine started then and is still going.

The worst aspect of Miss Moseley's crisis-in-the-pig-farm problems was that Miss Hogg now taught English to the sixth form. Which, bless her soul, was a disaster.

Again she wrote headings on the blackboard, followed by neatly numbered dates and names of poems. We read Shakespeare's plays, including *As You Like It*, which we stumbled in reading around the class, girl by girl. Once again we wrote in our notebooks and regurgitated at exams. I think Miss Hogg disliked teaching English. It was too messy to tabulate.

We had two types of essay. In one of them Miss Hogg read us a piece of English prose. We listened like sprinters on their blocks, so that the moment she stopped reading we could 'get the last sentence'. There was a rumour that any girl who had the last sentence down received five extra marks. Presumably in recognition of the fact that she was still awake.

The more usual type of essay continued to be greeted along the lines of 'Watch your commas'. I had become used to this, but one week I rebelled in a minor way. Essays that week were to take the form of fiction. Mine had been a war story, so sad, so brave that my eyes were wet as I wrote the ending. A boy in France had come upon an unexploded bomb, had hidden it beneath his meagre jacket, run to the nearby German Barracks and flung it over the fence, whereupon it exploded, killing several German soldiers and himself. It was marked 'Highly unlikely. C+'.

I put up my hand. Miss Hogg blinked; she was not used to questions.

'Yes, Barbara?'

'If we write in our story that something happened, then don't you sort of have to believe it did?'

Immediately there were cries of 'swot', 'crawler'. I didn't care in the slightest. 'Don't you, Miss Hogg?'

As I have said, Miss Hogg was a kind woman. 'I see what you mean, Barbara, but I think in this case your story was a little . . . extreme.'

It wasn't until I read *Biographia Literaria* many years later that Samuel Coleridge seemed to know what I meant, more or less. He asks readers for 'That willing suspension of disbelief for the moment, which constitutes poetic faith.'

How wise. But it took a long time coming.

In my last years a young woman called Miss Priddle taught science. She was enthusiastic and amiable and managed to make even nutrition vaguely interesting; lettuce, for example, consists of 99.9% water.

She also taught a little chemistry. She led us down to a small crypt-like room opposite the chapel. There were benches, bunsen burners, pipettes, test tubes and little else. We melted down iodine, we did obscure things with mercury, she told us about the Periodic Table. She didn't attempt more elaborate experiments in this chilly, ill-equipped space, but one day she described the process of electrolysis of water. You immerse two electrodes in water, turn on the switch and collect the gases from each electrode. And lo, the amount of hydrogen in one flask is twice the amount of the oxygen in the other flask. H_2O, the symbol for the compound, was shown to be true. Miss Priddle in her little white coat and her curly brown hair might just as well have described the breaking of the atom. The only disappointment was not seeing the result.

She also taught us some rudimentary zoology. Animals came in families. Not only that, but the first division was into invertebrates and vertebrates. I agree it seems strange I should not have worked this out for myself before the age of sixteen, but so it was.

One achievement in 1942 was my winning the Maori Essay Prize. Our book of reference was *The Maori As He Was* by Elsdon Best. I knew nothing about the Maori as he had been and little more about how he was now. I liked David's Maori friends at Mahora, Elizabeth was one of my best friends at St Luke's and there were other Maori girls at Hastings High in 3A, though not many had a chance to get to secondary school. If David and his friends were lucky, Maori boys at Waimarama Beach would let them gallop their ponies along the beach, but never girls.

Elsdon Best has fallen from favour now. I enjoyed his book immensely.

Miss Holland had decreed that no money would be given for prizes during the duration of the war. Instead the money would be given to the Honey for the Navy Fund and the winners given a card indicating the achievement. This did not apply to cups and other donated prizes. My prize, Herbert Guthrie-Smith's *Birds of the Water, Wood and Waste*, was donated by the former Governor General, Sir Charles Fergusson, and his wife Alice, who were both friends and admirers of Maori.

In my last year I made it into the school's choir. Music was important at Woodford, and the choir was well trained, though I still missed Mr Carnegie's largesse in assembly at Hastings High.

Another skin-of-the-teeth achievement was becoming a prefect. One of the big kids at last – and with good friends. The sweetest and the most musical year.

The only comment I remember from my final school report was Miss Moseley's: 'Barbara has been a far better prefect than she realises.'

Enigmatic to the end.

The prospect of studying English literature no longer appealed to me. Science was the thing. Great big beautiful science, particularly the natural sciences, and best of all zoology.

I talked to Miss Priddle. Physics, she said gently, would probably be beyond me and Chemistry a challenge, but yes, it could be done. I could have kissed her. I knew nothing would stop me reading, and one day inspiration would come from on high and I would write books as well.

CHAPTER 11

'We're headin' for the last break up,' I crooned to the only friend who shared my enthusiasm for 'cowboy songs', which superseded 'Westerns' which are different. For one thing, no cowgirls sang in the thirties, if indeed they existed. Also cowboys sang with more enthusiasm to their 'ponies' than their girls. In fact the only female I can remember being mentioned was 'My gal Lily', who shared a line with 'Buckhouse Billy and the Boss' in 'Ole Faithful'. Both cowboy songs and Westerns preceded Weepies, a genre in which David and I specialised later.

This time we would be the ones who were not returning, the ones whom we ask the Lord to dismiss with His blessing, in that most evocative of all sung school hymns.

Lord, dismiss us with Thy blessing,
Thanks for mercies past receive;
Pardon all, their faults confessing;
Time that's lost may all retrieve;
May Thy children, may Thy children
Ne'er again Thy Spirit grieve.
Ne'er again Thy Spirit grieve.

Now we would be the Old Girls. One or two were damp eyed at the thought, but not many. It was time to get down from the hills. The war still dragged on. The list opposite the chapel doors of fathers and brothers serving in the forces had grown longer. The shock when Singapore fell to the Japanese in 1942 had been enormous to the adults. Yet few of us discussed the war, though we had been kept well informed at school. Now we were in the real world, with radios everywhere and the BBC still regulating life. We saw the casualty lists, which woke us up, and heard the messages from 'our boys overseas' (never 'men'). It was the first time we heard proper New Zealand voices on the air as cheerful voices called 'Hullo, Mum and Dad and all the friends at Eketahuna'. Radio announcers then were chosen most carefully, to avoid 'the accent', or 'the twang', as much as possible. Standard English was desired to avoid wincing from Ngaio Marsh and her followers, of whom there were many.

After four years Hastings seemed unchanged; the main railway line naturally enough continued to run through the main street, the clocktower towered, but still not very far. The streets were no wider, the itinerant photographer still hovered by the intersections to snap. Mainly women, who were most prepared to buy his results to see themselves hatted, gloved and dressed for Town.

Hastings citizens were proud of their town. There was a rumour that it had only just avoided being Hicksville after Mr Hicks had sold the land to the railway company, having presumably acquired it from local Maori at an earlier date and at a greatly less sum. Now the thought of Hicksville was lost and buried.

Hastings, Napier, Havelock North, and the settlement between them, Clive, were all named after heroes of the Indian Mutiny. All the Hastings shops remained in their correct positions on the long length of Heretaunga Street, all the same proud names above each window: Noel Wilson, chemist; J.S. Thompson, butcher; Elizabeth, ladies' apparel; Villa d'Este, hairdresser. All the shops had the same employers and employees except for the boys who had gone overseas, and those who never came home. Also the girls who were in the forces and loving every minute after their jobs behind the counters.

Now the town was bustling, positively bustling. Wars put the wool prices up, so we were told, and our farmer friends did not deny it. Their wives continued to lunch at the Farmers' Co-op, on the second floor. You stepped out of the lift to be faced by a tiled wall topped with what Miss Moseley had told us was the Grecian Key pattern. Facing you were two doors; one with a black stencilled profile of a woman powdering her nose like a well-conducted person (unlike the disgraceful behaviour threatened by Aunty Mina's bridge player). The other door wore a black stencil of a top hat. We knew we were home in the Farmers' Tea Rooms, a large space in the classic tea room style, with starched white linen, trim smiling waitresses, three-layered stainless steel racks bearing sandwiches below, then biscuits and finally small iced cakes, which David and I had fought over until Mum devised the system of 'you cut, I choose'. The Farmers' had been a treat but now the only revival of interest was when the Rotarians, discreetly hidden by wooden screens for their weekly lunch, burst into song. Years later they were still at it.

> *I love to go a-wandering along the mountain track*
> *And as I go, I love to sing, my knapsack on my back*
> *Val-deri,Val-dera*
> *Val-deri, Val-dera-ha-ha-ha-ha-ha*
> *Val-deri,Val-dera*
> *My knapsack on my back . . .*

The Rotarians never let us down.

Having discussed with Miss Priddle the possibility of a bachelor of science, I had written to Dad in the last term. Please could I do science, preferably at Otago University where my Napier friend Jill was already ensconced?

I was aware that Dad would be supporting David at medical school in Dunedin for many years. I tried to lessen the impact of my request. A bachelor of science would take only three years, and I wouldn't expect any more.

He wrote back immediately. He would be happy to help me but there was to be no slacking. As I must be aware chemistry would be a challenge. He would pay my fees and board at St Margaret's Christian College for Young Women Students if he could get me in, and a modest extra amount for Bluff oysters and wool-lined underwear. It could be cold in Dunedin. And, of course, I would work in the holidays like David.

Wonderful noble Dad. I wrote back and told him so.

Mum's first action on my leaving school was to frogmarch me off to the Villa d'Este hairdressing salon to Gloria, who gave her a nice strong rub in the weekly wash. Mum also enjoyed what she called 'a good sit', as though it was precious to her. She had beautiful silver hair which seemed to be Gloria's crowning glory as well, so proud was she of dealing with the best-groomed head of hair in Hastings, Mrs Dr Wright's, who was to be seen at the Villa d'Este weekly.

David inherited Mum's dark curly hair but mine was straight so the 'perm' was the only solution. I avoided the antique type of permanent wave where the client's hair was wrapped for hours around steel rods attached to an alarming looking machine, but not by long. A perm was still a tedious and lengthy procedure and results could be variable. The tight curls took months to calm down. We used to greet our newly permed fellows and speak kindly, 'Don't worry about the frizz, Betty. It's only the first month.'

Why did we do it? In Mum's case the reason was obvious. It wouldn't blow about and be messy.

Her next sortie was to introduce me to another of her good friends, Miss Gishard, the Hastings corsetière, who welcomed me cordially. All her clientele, like Mum, stiffened themselves in whale bone, or its substitute; corseted themselves in the cause of decency. None of Robert Herrick's admiration of 'sweet disorder in the dress' for Miss Gishard or her clients.

I made a stand and refused corsets. I was thin, so much so that in my last year Mum suggested to Miss Hamber, as one true nurse to another, that Barbara should have a daily eggnog, without the alcohol of course.

Miss Hamber leapt at the idea. A more disgusting beverage I have never met, and one which produced no effect at all, whereupon Mum wheeled me off to a doctor of her choice. She suspected tuberculosis, he suggested an X-ray. All was well. She decided she would just have to feed me up.

My next session with Miss Gishard was for a brassiere or two. Breasts, those important features of her trade, were never mentioned. Bust was the word she used, as though fusion had taken place between two breasts to make one bust. Mum had a different word. She was generous, well stacked in the right area, and disliked so being. She always called it 'my front', in that irritated tone of voice with which a keen gardener might describe a problem area in the garden, such as 'that wretched dry bank where nothing will grow'.

I had some saggy cotton numbers left over from school but now we were into what Miss Gishard called uplift. This was the era of 'pin-up girls', of busty film stars whose photos were pinned above thousands of bunks of men from the army, navy or air force all over the world. The breasts inside these bras were so uplifted, so reinforced, they looked as if they were a secret weapon, which could impale any hot-blooded serviceman who planned to pin their beauty against the wall. The uplifted pin-up girls were always photographed with their heads flung back and mouths open to indicate sexual rapture. It was all very confusing, when met in Miss Gishard's.

I had nothing against uplift, quite liked the idea, but the embarrassing part of my sessions with Miss Gishard was the keen interest she took in the fitting and filling. Berlei was her favourite brand. I stripped to the waist in deep embarrassment with Miss Gishard beside me in her curtained cubicle. She told me to drop my bust forward into the Berlei, to get the right fullness. I did so and stood up quickly. 'Now Barbara,' she cried 'flick your fingers inside like this' and demonstrated with her fingers in my Berlei. 'Uplift, Barbara. That's what we're after, Uplift!' She patted my uplifted nipples. 'And always make sure these two are even. If I see a lady who's uneven it's all I can do not to flick them right. Quite a few are uneven. You wouldn't believe. That's where Berlei and me comes in.'

My third reluctant visit was to Miss Grant, dressmaker, who had made Mum's clothes forever. The best thing in her front room was a painted cut-out wooden Ancient Egyptian figure proffering a tray on which sat a brass ashtray, a brass-covered box of matches and another box which presumably had once held a packet of cigarettes. Neither Miss Grant nor her husband smoked. 'It would get into the materials,' said Miss Grant. 'Besides I've never felt the urge, and nor has he.' Miss Grant was her *nom de guerre*, behind which she created garments of quality, finesse and detail.

I needed one or two things for Dunedin. Miss Grant would make them and Blythes in Napier would provide the material, as their range was better.

Mum chose everything I wore until I was twenty and was earning real money. Why, I can't remember. Inertia on my part, I suppose. Also I loved my mother and wished to please this strong-minded woman with good clothes sense.

The one thing I bought in the three years I was in Dunedin was an off-the-shoulder blouse designed for a tempestuous tango dancer. I was enraptured with it and showed it to Mum with pride. She gave it a pained look. 'Well,' she sighed, 'I can't do anything about it now but for heaven's sake don't wear it here.'

I didn't.

One thing she and Dad were calm and cheerful about was my

height. The last time Miss Wright took our weight and height at school I was shocked to find I was six feet tall. However, I remain grateful to the school for its emphasis on such an Edwardian pursuit as good deportment. We could achieve a blue button, a red button, or, if one achieved ramrod stance and a thrusting bust, a red badge for deportment. Miss Wright hid, or pretended to hide, as we marched into the dining room, as we walked up to Nelson House, as we drifted up to the classroom with its armless statue of the Wingless Victory. I did achieve a red button, my only whiff of athletic endeavour. And I avoided the round-shouldered slouch.

There is of course, tall and tall. A six-foot young woman was unknown in Hastings and therefore liable to be considered odd, if not weird.

This was proved when Mum and I were at Westerman's, waiting for her change to come whizzing back in its little brass container on the overhead line from the unseen office. One of Mum's fellow members of the Red Cross committee appeared. During the war Mum and other retired nurses went once a week to the headquarters to brush up their techniques in First Aid. When the siren screamed Mum leapt onto her BSA and rode to the Presbyterian Hall with two layers of tissue paper over her lights. Mum said the most alarming part was avoiding wobbly little boys on bikes, hoping for a Zeke or two.

Mum introduced her fellow Red Cross member to her daughter. The woman stared in amazement. 'But she's *enormous*,' she gasped. Mum stared straight ahead as the little brass container clanged above, bringing her change which was proffered by the sales woman. 'Thank you,' said Mum and we sailed out the side door of the shop, extinguishing the Red Cross member with great glorious gales of laughter. We reeled down the street to the Women's Rest Room, a one-storeyed, white stucco place providing *clean* lavatories (one glance and Mum knew) and several curtained cubicles for mothers to breastfeed their infants out of sight. After all they had to go somewhere unseen by the world.

Dad's reaction was different when told. 'Winsom she was, as is a merry colt / Tall as a mast, and straight as a bolt,' he said. 'Chaucer.'

The next thing for Mum to deal with was dances. I couldn't dance. I had parted with Misses Grantham and Patterson years ago but now I became attached to Miss Brody, another dancing teacher in Hastings. She greeted me coolly and put on a record designed for the purpose. Towering above her, I watched her dead-bored face. 'I am your male partner,' she said. 'One and two and three and back,' she sighed to the empty walls. It was worse than my visit to Busts.

David had inherited Dad's bad eyesight; both of them were declared unfit for service and both had been at medical school in Dunedin during wartime. My friends met his friends; girls met boys in states of thundering innocence. I knew more about Bing Crosby than I did about these young men; I knew Bing had a toupé but was not sure about the rumour he had a wart on his vocal cords.

Mum told me at this awkward time that she and her friend Beryl realised how lucky they were to have had their daughters safe and sound at Woodford, not hanging around street corners on Fridays on late nights.

'But what do they *do*?' I said.

'Hang around street corners. With boys.'

'Oh.'

In the meantime we swam at Waimarama and the Tukituki River. We sang vaguely indecent songs. We played tennis. Not such a good idea, but bearable if boys were there.

And obviously boys met girls at school dances.

The dances, ah the dances. The dances weren't so bad. They were at the assembly hall at the municipal buildings, where you could see flicks, recitals and theatre, and where I had my glorious first experience of musical comedies, *At the Balalaika*. We sat in the front of the circle and I could smell the blue velvet beneath my nose. For school dances we decked the assembly hall with flax and toetoe provided by farmer parents. We ran errands for parents. We helped, we hung around, we talked to boys. All quite fun in a shy sort of way.

On the night of my first dance I wore a long pink organdy frock and pink lace-up dancing shoes. I turned nervously from Mum's long glass. 'Do I look all right?'

'Of course you look all right. You've got two arms, two legs, a nose. Off you go, Cecil, it's time you went.'

David gave me a friendly hint. The important trick was to grab a partner for the Supper Waltz, otherwise I'd be hanging around on the edge of the food. I thanked him but could think of no method to achieve this desired escort; this character in black trousers with white cotton gloves to avoid staining our pastels: our pale pinks, our blues, our occasional heliotropes.

The boys asked me to dance, which was a relief, but most of them could not dance either. If this was dancing it was not much fun. It was also a surprise that there were so many six-foot boys in the Bay. I was taller than David and always had been, but here *en masse* within the assembly hall of the municipal buildings there were dozens of candidates to nobble for the Supper Waltz. My first dance was agreeable if not triumphant.

After the Supper Waltz and the supper had been achieved satisfactorily there came an announcement: 'Ladies and Gentlemen, clear the floor please for the Exhibition'. The orchestra began 'When they Begin the Beguine'. From behind one towering clump of flax slipped Nancy Dunn from Roberts Street, and from behind another across the room slid another ace dancer called Brenda, both Miss Brody-trained. They met in the centre, they swooped, they leapt, they flung their arms about in unison, they writhed, presumably to indicate those nights of tropical splendour which the song promised. They even managed to smile as they whirled. Misses Grantham and Patterson had tried to put emphasis on smiling. At our long lost recitals in this municipal buildings they had large placards behind the stage which said SMILE to remind us to do so when we were on stage. Few of us did. Remembering our steps took up most of our time.

Nancy and Beryl's exhibition faded to the end, one to the right and one to the left. The applause continued and after several deep curtsies Nancy and Brenda swept (there is no other word) behind their appropriate stacks of flax.

'Once more into the breach, dear friend,' I thought as the last waltz began. Soon Mum would be coming to pick me up and what if I wasn't dancing? But then, not from the flax, but just as nimbly, came Gary Glazebrook, half a head shorter than me, immaculate in tails and confident, smiling and opening out his arms, 'Barbara,' he said.

He danced well, I relaxed and followed like a graceful lamb.

This obviously was real dancing. A small group of parents appeared by the entrance to collect their offspring. I had a glimpse of my mother. She stood gazing in delighted astonishment as we whirled by.

Gary bowed in smiling acknowledgement.

'Hullo, Mrs Wright.'

I smiled benignly.

PART II

CHAPTER 12

Brisk and smiling, Jill from Napier leaned out the window as the train slid into Hastings. 'Hurry up, I've kept seats,' she called as we shoved our hand luggage on board. I hugged Dad goodbye, followed by David with his sports jacket, green pork-pie hat and manly handshake. Mum never came to wave goodbyes. She hated farewells, and trains were dirty things, black as your hat if not worse. John Cashmore, a friend of David's, and also of poor sight, was even better at the laconic farewells. Like all of us he had left his heavy luggage at the station the day before, and sauntered along Railway Road the next morning without a parent in sight.

Two boarding establishments only were available in Dunedin for young male students. Selwyn College was newer and nearer the main campus and its small trickling stream which rejoiced in the name of the Leith River. The older of the two, Knox College, where Dad had been and intended to enrol David, was further away from both the university and the medical school. Knox sat beyond the botanical gardens which drifted up a small hill towards a nearby cemetery, a good place for friends of either sex to meet, where neither the quick nor the dead would disturb them.

Knox College was considered by some to be a more sombre and hard-working place than Selwyn, possibly because of the Calvinistic nature of its namesake. No other man than John Knox in 1558 had named his pamphlet *The First Blast of the Trumpet Against the Monstrous Regiment of Women*. Sentiments rejected by the College's inhabitants, but still a good title.

Unfortunately Dad had not enrolled his son in either establishment in time. This error meant that David had to hunt for board every year. He soon discovered student digs vary enormously both in comfort and landladies; however, he did have more freedom which he used to advantage. Also, he said, you met more interesting people in digs. His few trappings moved with him: a large armchair with big ears that remained useful against many draughts and a square of blood-coloured Feltex carpet with a sinister-looking yellow patch which he blamed on the infant of a former landlady.

Warned by his error, Dad enrolled me early for St Margaret's Christian College for Young Women Students. Jill had already been in Dunedin for a year; both our fathers had studied medicine at Otago and David was now doing so. No other campus than Otago had ever been considered.

Unlike Woodford, St Margaret's was warm in the winter, nevertheless Jill had advised woolly bloomers and and at least one hot water bottle. After all you did have to go outside, and it could snow. *Snow.* I had just read *War and Peace* and knew about it. Natasha, war, snow.

Jill also advocated the importance of ingratiating yourself with whichever girl occupied the only room on the ground floor. Innocent to the bone, even I guessed correctly. This girl was the only one who could let you into St Margaret's after the evening curfew of eleven o'clock. Or not, if she chose. Miscreants banged on her window, and if given entrance and assisted by a heave up from your current boyfriend, you were inside. Jill knew several who had used this entry frequently last year. It sounded to me like 'When they begin the beguine with nights of tropical splendour' in woolly underwear. The word which seeped deepest into my mind was 'current'. 'My current boyfriend.' What resonance. What finesse.

The journey to Dunedin took two long days by train plus one night in the ferry, in which I inevitably threw up, even when assured by the unfortunate stewardess attending our cabin that the sea was as smooth as a millpond and would I like a plain biscuit stamped WINE. I groaned.

'I'll have hers too thanks,' said Jill lying back in her bunk in pink winceyette and reading to me 'It Pays to Increase Your Word Power' from the *The Reader's Digest.*

'What's "sycophant" mean?'

'Oh, do shut up.'

The anti-sick pills appeared after I needed them, and flying home and back by students was unheard of, despite the threat of an occasional U-boat scare. We crawled off the boat into Lyttelton to be greeted by a man behind a tannoy bellowing interminably, 'There are eight carriages round the corner, eight carriages around the corner, eight carriages, eight . . .' The voice sounded so outraged I waited for it to roar 'Don't just stand there y' no hopers! Eight effing carriages round the effing corner like I said!' We then had to manhandle all our luggage round the corner before it could be loaded onto the southern train, where we dug ourselves in for another day of fug. I complained to David about the situation. 'Stop whinging,' he said. 'You'll never get anywhere unless you shove things along a bit. Push hard.' A comment I have found invaluable ever since.

David and most men in the carriage smoked all day. I didn't mind the smell; it reminded me of home, and back then smoking was considered manly for men and sophisticated for women. The deep inhalation and the measured exhalation of the plume of smoke were useful adjuncts for film stars, especially when the slick-haired hero lit a cigarette and handed it to his inamorata before lighting his own. The whole thing was quite a performance; evidence that the gent knew his business, that passion was nigh, if not yet high. Even better, the couple were leaning over the rail of a luxury liner gazing at the darkening sea and then the cigarettes disappeared, the moon rose above the horizon and the clinch began in earnest. CUT.

Hints like these were useful in the high days of the Hays Office and were picked up easily by film fans in the days when even married couples had to be filmed in separate beds. The best visual euphemism I remember went something like this. Lady and gent indoors. Fall into passionate embrace. Camera swings off, pans onto windows, or better, French doors. Sudden blast of wind flings doors open, followed by streaming, billowing curtains.

I get it. You get it. They get it. Lust has been fulfilled and the Hays Office are happy.

Otago was the first university established in New Zealand and those of us lucky enough to have been there remember our time with affection. Or, if unlucky enough to have hated it, to keep quiet about the matter.

There was plenty of space for students in 1944. The city and place had been made for growth, there were handsome trees and verdant grass around the clocktower and campus. The majority of these imposing buildings were made of Oamaru stone, pale rock which lasts forever. The majesty of Hastings High dwindled before my eyes.

I was looking forward to the natural sciences, especially zoology, plus botany, geology, and as little chemistry as possible. 'No physics for God's sake,' said David in agreement with Miss Priddle. She had also told me of openings for women in science. You could work in laboratories, including medical ones. If you were lucky you might eventually do research. I was not sure how this was achieved, but I knew it was out there somewhere. Science, I knew, began in Dunedin.

For a child of the thirties, jobs were known to be precious things. There was emphasis on 'getting your letters', on working hard to ensure a steady job in the future. Any job could fold, we knew that, but a tertiary education gave you a better chance. To achieve the latter in the forties you had either to be intelligent enough to win a university scholarship, or have parents who could afford to help with fees. Equally important was to find a holiday job. More difficult for women, but casual work was more available to females in wartime.

The battle for tertiary education for women had been won long ago, but a faint feeling that it was a luxury for us still lingered. I did know one girl whose mother told her to be careful: 'Boys don't like clever girls.' After all, with any luck we would get married, in which case hard-earned money might be considered to have gone down the drain, an unattractive thought which fortunately did not occur to my father. Education to him was 'a good thing for all'. Also he was of the 'educate a woman and you educate a generation' school of thought.

'How do I enrol?' I asked David as we finally fell out of the train into the large and imposing-looking Dunedin Railway Station. He looked at me once again with doubtful concern. 'You have to use your common sense. It's hell. I spent the whole time last year barging into Dolly Flower.'

I had never heard or seen Dolly Flower which somehow made things worse.

He gave me a friendly punch on the upper arm. 'It's hell, but you'll make it,' he said again, and disappeared behind a Victorian pillar.

'Come on,' said Jill. 'What are you standing around for? This way.'

Next morning no one at St Margaret's Christian College for Young Women Students seemed to be enrolling in the natural sciences. After signing up at the registrar's office, the next task was to find the different departments. Chemistry and geology were comparatively easy, but it took me some time to track down botany and zoology. They were some distance away from the main campus, tucked in behind the Otago Museum in Great King Street.

New students were instructed to present themselves to the professors in charge of the relevant departments and check their enrolment. This turned out to be easier said than done.

The botany department was in disarray owing to the ill health of the Professor who had been forced to retire during the vacation. Two respected young postgraduate women had been employed to take over the labs and lectures until a new professor was appointed. I didn't know this and spent a long time knocking on doors hunting for a professor who had suddenly become emeritus.

The head of the zoology department was also elusive. There was no sign of anyone in the two lecture rooms or the formalin-scented dissecting labs. Once again, I knocked on doors to be told by their occupants they were not professors of zoology any more than they had been professors of botany half an hour before. I tried a new door and went in. A very tall thin man stood staring at a small bone in his hand. 'I'm looking for the professor of zoology,' I said.

'Yes?' I moved my eyes from the dry cleaner's ticket on the hem of his jacket and told him I wanted to enrol in Zoology 1.

'Fossil penguin,' he said, handing me the bone. 'I don't think that would be too much of a problem. What's your name?'

Brian Marples, the professor, became a good friend. The first time I went to his house there were a couple of dead sparrows on the hall table. 'Ah, good,' he said. 'The boys are trained to bring home anything dead.'

The zoology and botany departments were a short distance from St Margaret's and the campus. Both of the departments looked run down, but the museum behind which they lurked was by no means so. Here you could find acres of interesting things: shelves of bones, eggs large and small, scarabs, delicate dead arachnids, buffalo horns, all methodically labelled beneath locked glass, for experts to explain to us about the things on these shelves of knowledge.

Other pleasures stood around the walls in the form of dioramas, one of which held stuffed native birds looking much more cheerful than the huias at Hastings High. Another portrayed Maori warriors with spears raised in endless pursuit of now extinct moas. Dioramas have lost respect in modern museums, as have glass-topped shelves, but even skeletons have their charm once you know which bone is which and what its function is, and how the different species differ. Some things take time to reveal their joys, and museums then tended to hide their treats.

Animals without Backbones by Ralph Buchsbaum was our first textbook in zoology, the science of life. The first chapter begins 'Anyone can tell the difference between a tree and a cow', which sounded encouraging, but turned out to be of little help. Microscope work was more interesting and became even more so when we studied invertebrata. The amoeba was described by R. Buchsbaum as 'a one-celled animal that displays a minimum of differentiation'. We agreed with this as they flowed beneath our lens, met a minuscule piece of food and flowed around it. If an amoeba is cut in half it becomes two amoebae – asexual reproduction at a glance. Whoever first saw this wonderful beast? Whoever had the wit to look for it in muddy pools?

A paramecium (a complex protozoan, or first animal) is even more fun to watch. When your paramecium is not quietly feeding on bacteria it roams about, occasionally bumping its front end into obstacles. If it does it backs off and tries a different route. Their method of locomotion is identical to that of the dodgem cars which had recently appeared at the sideshows of the Hawke's Bay Agricultural and Pastoral Show, the highlight of the year for every child in the Bay. 'Bang, crash, back off and try again,' go the dodgems, and so does the paramecium, the only difference being that the dodgem drivers seek collision, unlike the protozoan who is looking for food to keep body and soul together.

Prof Marples was a good lecturer but his enthusiasm was seen best in the laboratory, first with microscope work, then later in the year with various animals preserved in the reeking formalin tanks waiting for dissection.

Dogfish came first. I gave a momentary sniff, thought this was no place for my mother's daughter, grabbed my scalpel and began.

Another textbook was G.R. de Beer's *Vertebrate Zoology*, which made itself clear in its subtitle: *An Introduction to the Comparative Anatomy, Embryology and Evolution of Chordates.* Comparative anatomy is a fascinating subject but de Beer's book was not easy. His prose was dense and there were no photographs like in our American textbooks, just information in every line, and meticulous black-and-white drawings, such as Fig. 91 –'View of the blastoderm of a hen's egg after 24 hours'. Nevertheless we came to prize the author. He knew it all and seemed determined we should too. He had taught Prof Marples and his prospective wife, Molly, when they were in England. Prof told me later he had mentioned to them that they had spent very little time dissecting their respective dogfish when they were getting to know each other. I have always respected good noticers.

Young men and women drifted around the zoology labs in short white lab coats like Miss Priddle's. These were demonstrators, who I thought must be brilliant students until I discovered they had passed Zoology 1 with reasonable marks, were chosen by Prof Marples and were paid a small but useful pittance. I was a demonstrator for zoology for my last two years, was proud of my short white coat, learned a lot and bought a small yellow Bakelite radio the shape of a Walt Disney cloud, rounded at both ends.

High days in zoology were field days when we crashed about under various species of beech forests and flung ourselves down on mossy wooded hollows to hear the Prof hold forth on various subjects. The first one was called ecology. I had never heard the word nor seen Nothofagus (New Zealand beech trees). I tossed a small green pebble against a covered rock and exposed beetles, slaters and unknown invertebrates as they skidded, scuttled or slid for other shelter. 'You realise you've upset the ecological succession of that rock for a hundred years' said Prof. For a moment I was back with Miss Avery and my attempts at being teacher's pet. I had no idea what he meant but I did know that South Island beech forest with the sun shining through is one of the most beautiful sights in the world. Also at that moment a reasonable-looking medical student brushed my hand with intent. To hell with teacher's pets.

*

Botany, oh dear. Botany was not a joy for me, although another science of life it may be. The two young postgraduate students, Miss M and Miss N, did their best but their lectures were tedious beyond words. Whatever the topic, both of them read the lecture notes they had taken down from the professor emeritus. For the first time I met true boredom, the bone-grinding, pulverising kind which numbs the brain.

There were other moments in botany which were not so bad. In the lab we sat with flower stems held tightly between dried pith, cut the thinnest slices possible with our razors, stained our specimens and put the results under the microscope, where we saw different coloured rings called xylem, cambium and phloem, and other essentials for healthy stems, the names of which elude me. I do remember the abscission layer: 'the area of natural detachment of leaves' (the reason leaves fall off).

Another matter of botanic interest was the carbon cycle. Here I learned how vital plants are for the existence of humans, owing to photosynthesis. News I had not known before. Plants are able, by the process of photosynthesis and exposure to light, to convert carbon dioxide and water into carbohydrates. I had noticed, who couldn't, that plants are eaten by animals which in their turn are eaten by humans, all of whom die at some stage. Having done so their bodies rot, or (as Miss M or N delicately said) 'break down', during which they give off carbon dioxide gas – a process assisted by denitrifying bacteria. Then the cycle begins again. I found this process a very sensible tidy business and extremely well worked out. We drew diagrams to illustrate the cycle. Mine were drawn with care, so strong was my enthusiasm for the procedure.

We heard nothing of such things as 'carbon reservoir' or 'net ocean uptake', or even 'carbons'. There was no concern about climate change, or the need to understand the impact of carbon emissions on climate change. The carbon cycle has suffered a sea change. We were too soon.

Another postgraduate student taught us elementary genetics, which, again, were interesting and new. We began with Gregor Mendel, the Austrian monk known as the father of genetics for his experiments with 'common garden peas'. He was also the only scientist of his time who had got the process of heredity more or less right. Others in the nineteenth century all accepted the 'blending theory' but Mendel with his 'common garden peas' discovered that traits show up in offspring with no blending of parental characteristics. The mechanics of heredity, we learned, are essentially the same for all complex life. We knew most flowers have female sex organs (pistils) and male sex organs (stamens) in one plant. Some, like common garden peas, are able to self-pollinate as well as cross-pollinate. Humans, that peak of complex life forms, need the opposite sex to breed.

I knew this of course, had known since I'd seen those fathers and mothers thundering along behind prams up and down the length and breadth of Heretaunga Street, but was surprised to find that the less complex life forms were at it too, with the assistance of both bees and breeze.

The new professor of botany arrived in my third year – from England, as did any other professors I met at Otago University. This one was passionate about his subject but it was too late to imbue me with his enthusiasm. A well-dressed man, he wore a tweed hat on field days, which seemed most suitable for the occasion. He was also courteous and assisted female students, holding the lower strands of the wire fences down with a well-shod foot. This was thought hilarious by the male students and embarrassing to us, who were used to scrambling through wire fences since we were small.

Interesting males were not to be found in the botany class of '42. These were to be picked up easily near the central buildings of the campus: chemistry, physics, geology and the mining school. And most important of all, in the nearby cafeteria.

Chemistry lectures were a nightmare, or would have been if I had expected anything else. I failed my first year and passed reasonably well on my second attempt but with little more enthusiasm.

The professor of chemistry also came from Britain, but he must have come from a different part than the others. He pronounced the letter 'o' to rhyme with 'bong' and I found myself waiting for it, 'one' being a word that crops up frequently in chemistry. 'Take WON gram of X plus WON gram of Y', etc.

There was little human interest during chemistry, except occasionally when a pretty girl arrived late. (Women were still called 'girls' and men 'boys'.) The boys drummed their heels in mock disapproval as, with a mixture of coy shame and pleasure, they watched her scuttle in and fall into a seat.

The Prof paid no attention, just continued 'won'-ing away beside a thin impassive assistant who helped with his experiments. They were pretty to watch – nothing ever went wrong, fell off, dropped down or blew up. Sometimes, when a more dramatic result was achieved, they were rewarded by a casual stamping, but not often.

The experiment I waited for in first year was Miss Priddle's electrolysis of water. The apparatus was set up, the electrodes charged, and the amount of hydrogen collected in its flask was twice that in the oxygen one. The symbol H_2O was true. The only sorrow was that the demonstration lacked the drama I had hoped for.

At the end of chemistry lectures we milled around by the steps in what David called a Hawke's Bay Picnic (no mingling between the sexes). Boys stood pork-pied, smoking and yarning in groups. Several women smoked, but for women to smoke in the streets was considered not much better than walking them. Brothers and sisters could exchange greetings and those who 'were going out' immediately claimed each other. If the pair had a row and ceased to 'be going out' then both were free to play with some one else. However, very few boys made a pass at a girl who was known to be attached. It was as though she was 'bagsed', like some favourite little friend who had been nabbed to play with someone else at primary school.

English lectures nearby in the opposite building ended at the same time. They were aloof to us in their humanities as we were to them in our science. I did notice one young man among them with an unusually large head who I now realise was the poet James K. Baxter, an eighteen-year-old about to have his first book of poems published by the Caxton Press.

Listen to this:

High Country Weather

Alone we are born
And die alone;
Yet see the red-gold cirrus
Over snow-mountain shine.

Upon the upland road
Ride easy, stranger;
Surrender to the sky
Your heart of anger.

The geology department plus mining school had large wide steps which enabled the men to to sit on them overlooking what was known as 'talent'. For some reason I did not think of geology students as boys. They were amiable men and much more relaxed. I enjoyed geology, both geomorpholgy and crystallography, though the former more so. Again we had a good textbook, this time by a New Zealander – *Geomorphology: An introduction to the study of landforms*, by Professor C.A. Cotton. In his introduction he writes 'Geomorphology makes its appeal not only to geologists and geographers but also to those who love Nature and have eyes for the natural landscape.'

Me, I thought smugly. Like me.

Geomorphology men also had bad jokes:

'Where's the Hog's Back?'

'Didn't know he'd been away.'

The study of crystallography involved gazing down a microscope to see the structure of particular crystals and how they could be distinguished from others, often with the assistance of a large hairy man draping himself over your shoulder as far as possible while he explained what you should be seeing. Very friendly, the geology department, possibly because the sex ratio was unbalanced. Few women were making a career of the subject in the forties.

It was good to see David around, smoking cigarettes furiously beneath his green hat. He greeted me amiably whenever we met, 'How's it going, Bub?' He was also reassuring about romantic snubs. 'Aw, don't worry about him. The man's a drongo and his new girl's worse.' We became good friends, which was one of the pleasures of our years in Dunedin. He always found good digs after the usual searching. In my first year he shared them with two other boarders who were fifth-year Meds and thus on a higher plane. Morrie and Ralph, said David, had been decent to him, very decent. I was not surprised. Most people who met D.G.R. Wright did like him; he was quick, cheerful, and, ever since the days of charades at Waimarama, could make people laugh. What surprised, in fact astonished him, was that Morrie and Ralph liked me. They spoiled me, took an interest in my affairs, both in my daily concerns and in what they called my love life. 'And then what?' featured frequently in their questions. I was flattered, especially when Morrie, who was not tall, measured my femur from hip to knee and told me the good news. If I had six inches removed surgically on both legs we could get somewhere. Then, he promised me, we would be Away to the Races.

Dear friends, Morrie and Ralph – always named in that order, as they are in memory. My store of confidence grew larger by the day in Dunedin.

It was then that I realised that this attribute of confidence is virtually all you need in life. One of the less ravishing-looking girls at the Freshers' Dance had asked the captain of the university rugby team to be her partner. Being of amiable disposition he came. She grappled him to her soul with hoops of steel and off they went, waltzing through the night with her head high. 'One two three, one two three,' round and round they went. Presumably all dances were not waltzes. And nor was this one. It was not waltzing, but it seemed like that to me as I watched them.

The flicks were another popular entertainment for obvious reasons, especially in the winter term. Boy met girl, shared a couple of dozen Bluff oysters at two and six a dozen, then moved into the warmth and dark of a cinema for a reasonably inexpensive and enjoyable evening. The back seats were best, being the darkest for writhing together, embracing with hands groping higher and lower and lipstick all over the place. Where else could you find such felicity on a bleak and stormy Dunedin night? Very few students had cars, the back seats of which could come in useful for exploration. Occasionally men were able to borrow a parent's car but not often. Another refuge, but by no means so comfortable, were huge concrete edifices which were said to be found all over Dunedin. They were enormous drain pipes which, we were told, were a form of air-raid shelter in case the city was attacked by enemy aircraft. The one I knew sat on the grass square behind the museum, where returning couples often called in to to say goodnight on the way back to hostels or digs. There were hazards however: pairs were liable to bang into other pairs in this chilly bolt hole. This could be irritating in the pitch dark, but did not diminish the usefulness of this gift from the Dunedin city fathers. Nor did other drawbacks such as the sour smell of damp concrete. Or at least I hoped that was what it was.

*

There were several older men seen about the campus in my years. These were returned servicemen who had been wounded and returned home to recuperate and, if they wished, take up university grants awarded from the government.

Most of the ones I knew were studying medicine, which is a long haul even for a bright eighteen-year-old. Returned men, as they were known, were a different breed. They were determined to *get there.* They were far more dedicated to their work than any other students I met. They had survived the sodding war and were not going to lose this chance. They didn't need explorations with women, they knew that already. Women could wait till later, or so they said.

Not one of them I knew ever spoke of the war. I did ask a friend about the Desert War and he told me I wouldn't have liked it, though it had its moments. He and others were travelling in trucks heading up to the front lines when he saw his friend Peter McIntyre, the official New Zealand war artist, coming towards them in a jeep. My friend lifted a hand, to be answered by Peter: 'Simcock! Don't go up there. They're killing people!' True gallows humour. And never forgotten. Another time when we were all working at exam time I asked another friend how he was feeding himself. Was he getting any exercise? He was doing well, he said. He bought a store of meat pies from Pa Carr's dairy near the campus: one for breakfast, one for lunch, one for dinner. Heated of course. He did heat them. Oh, God yes. As for exercise, he stood up from his chair every four hours or so, walked around it, then sat down for another four hours. I tried to help, handing on to him a mnemonic for the five brachial arches of the dogfish which I thought might come in handy – *Pink Elephants Can't Have Babies.* Unfortunately dogfish didn't crop up, he told me later. Now after so many years of dogfish I remember the mnemonic but see little else except that pink elephants are sterile.

Their proud moment, if they thought of it as such, was VE Day, 8 May 1945. Bells rang and the mayor and councillors stood on the town hall balcony, while the crowds yelled and roared and our returned men stood there looking embarrassed and smiling shyly as they gave unprofessional waves and the crowd roared and waved back. I don't remember any carousing later – good girls didn't do carousing in '45, or not in daylight.

Nor do I remember any emotion at VJ day in September, other than relief. No more of our boys and girls overseas would be killed and now they could return home to become men and women with memories of war.

In my third year I left St Margaret's to share digs with seven home science girls in a high-ceilinged, once gracious and spacious house in Castle Street. The owners had rented it to home science students for years, thereby showing their good sense. Home science girls had high standards of domestic hygiene. They could cook too. Not only had they learned it at their mother's knee, they were now completely competent. I was not. Part of Mum's 'useless as a piece of fixed furniture' routine meant I couldn't be trusted with an oven or let loose in what she always called My Kitchen. In Dunedin I bumbled around with a sausage or two, or a chop, and hoped for the best. None of the others complained to my face, which is the only part where criticism matters.

On other days we ate well.

Slang dates sooner than the jargon of science or art, but at that time I was quite happy to be called a 'chook' and our home to be known as the Chookery.

One of the occupants was my poetry-loving friend Jan, but she was now busy doing well in home science exams. She also had another full-time interest. Jan had met Bill at school dances and had seen no reason to end their friendship. They went to watch rugby together, they went to flicks together, they went to dances, balls, any event which surfaced during the year. They were married the moment Bill qualified as a fully paid-up Doctor of Medicine and lived happily ever after.

There were several such push-me-pull-you relationships around. The female half of one couple used to stand every Saturday evening at St Margaret's gazing affectionately at herself in front of an enormous mirror asking herself, 'Do I look all right for Desmond?'

They had met at primary school and it seemed a little late to be worrying now. They were more than 'going-out' together these pairs, they were glued together from infancy, and all those I know achieved good marriages.

Another friend at Castle Street was Jetta Trotter, who had

arrived in Dunedin a year before me to take a degree in home science. Tall, with long wavy blonde hair and a figure Miss Gishard would have applauded, she became an immediate success. Reading a copy of the students' *Craccum* when I arrived I saw on the social page *All Knox has the Jetta Bug.* Wow.

Another girl doing a degree in home science was pleasant except for occasional moments when she would explode into screaming rage at one or all then storm off to her single room in sobbing incoherence. The next morning at breakfast she would arrive all smiles, 'I'm so sorry I was naughty last night. I had a temper tantrum.'

A weird business to remember for over sixty years, but vivid.

Those working for degrees rather than diplomas were allocated single rooms, which was a help. I was not good at 'swotting' with others, let alone sleeping. Another benefit was that for the first time you could greet a boyfriend and shut the door. Later I came across the American term 'heavy petting'. Not an attractive phrase, but descriptive.

Contraception was a problem. The Pill was far away, and condoms were not available in Four Square stores (the precursor of supermarkets). Nor were they on display at chemists. Young men had to engage in some fancy footwork to avoid the young females behind the counter when they were trying to catch the eye of the male pharmacist. Diaphragms for females had to be measured by doctors, some of whom according to rumours denied them to unmarried girls.

Sexual morality was also confusing. David gave me a solemn talk on the matter. There were fast girls, he said, girls known as 'hot stuff' or 'players'. Men liked them, hell yes, who wouldn't? Then again most men wouldn't want to marry them.

'Why on earth not?'

'Well, they're sort of oh, I don't know, sort of . . .'

'You mean "soiled"?' I snarled.

'Of course not, smart arse. You know what I mean . . .'

I did, with rage.

Girls, be they soiled or sweet as the heather, the bonny, blooming heather, were dependent on their boyfriends for contraception. Pregnancy was the risk of 'going all the way' and both men and women were terrified of slips.

One day my 'current boyfriend' asked me if I'd go and see a mate of his who'd copped it. Had to marry the girl.

'And so he jolly well . . .'

'Yeah, yeah. So you'll come?'

We arrived at a tiny flat with our doughnuts and drank tea with the poor bloke who'd copped it and his helplessly shy young wife, both of them embarrassed and shamefaced. No one wants to be copped.

We were introduced to a baby lying on a rug with pink rabbits. It stared at me and I stared back, smiling vigorously to indicate delight. It seemed to me the infant lying there waving minuscule arms was as out of place as a petunia on the moon. We left our small gift and the father clattered down the bare wooden stairs to let us out. 'My dad's been pretty decent,' he muttered to no one, 'but her mum . . . Cher-rist.'

'It takes two to tango,' said my boyfriend, flinging a comradely arm around his wounded mate.

I was back in Hawke's Bay when my exam marks arrived. I now had a Bachelor of Science degree, with decent marks too. A bachelor of science in the science of life. In my last year I had an A for zoology, an A for botany, and a B plus for geology and chemistry. 'Dad, I've got it,' I yelled, waving the beautiful bit of paper.

'How many thousand times have I told you not to say "got"? "I *have* a bachelor of science." Let me have a look.' There was a pause. 'Pity about the B pluses.'

Prof Marples had suggested before I left that I should work for a master of science. 'You have an enquiring mind, which is always useful,' he said. 'Marine research at Portobello across the harbour perhaps, since you're enamoured of invertebrates and microscopes.'

I didn't explain the pact with my father but remained grateful to him forever.

Glorious.

CHAPTER 13

During the war university students were manpowered into useful jobs during their holidays. Men who had a freezing works in their vicinity were considered lucky; the work was hard and the hours long, but the wages were good. David and I were even more fortunate, having Wattie's canning factory near 609 Robert Street.

Legend had it that when Mr Wattie was launching his enterprise he walked from door to door around Hastings selling cannery shares to raise the money he needed. It was also said that those who bought a few made a packet, as did Mr Wattie. By the time I pedalled around to work there his business was booming to the extent that he paid farmers in the area to grow paddocks of peas for his factory. Mr Wattie, or one of his cohorts, said to the farmers, 'Plant now', and the farmers did. Later, at the exact moment of ripeness, different men arrived to organise the picking. The local newspaper carried notices as to which farmer's paddock was ready for picking next day. The pickers – schoolboys on holidays, the manpowered, the casuals and the professionals – descended like locusts in a different land. All fronted up with their full kerosene tins to be checked by supervisors who gave them a vigorous shake to settle the peas. Sometimes one was handed back with one word, 'More!' The pickers retalitated by giving an empty tin a vicious kick so as to hold fewer peas. Despite this cat-and-mouse routine the fact remained that the going rate was ten pennies a tin and a good picker could earn up to a pound a day.

What Mr Wattie needed now to expand his world was a machine with brains, and he acquired one. The Pea Viner bought mechanisation to Hastings and pea pickers were no more. When the peas were declared ripe the paddocks were cut to ground level and their peas, plants, weeds, thistles and dirt were picked up by trucks, taken to the Pea Viner, and emptied onto a concrete pad where the thinking machine sorted out its wares. This was a miracle at the time and still seems so to me. The workers on the Viner had eight-hour shifts, the machine operated twenty-four hours a day, and men, including David, rotated the jobs required, the worst of which was shovelling the ullage onto an enormous pile, which after a few days in the blazing sun ponged to high heaven. However, Mr Wattie also paid well for such jobs and Viner jobs were in demand.

Women could never hope to earn as much as men and my friend Pam Cashmore, sister of John, and I had a job so easy it was as known as a 'Sweetie'. When we appeared each holidays another of Mr Wattie's supervisors, an amiable large one with no hair, would greet us: 'Back for your Sweetie, are you girls?' Our particular Sweetie was sorting for 'blows'. Blows, in the canning industry, are tins of fruit or vegetables which must never meet the eye of the buyer, the grocer, or worse, the public. A 'blow' is a filled tin whose upper lid has bulged upwards, which means fermentation inside.

Our routine was simple. Each morning we walked along the upper floor of the cannery searching for blows along the long lengths of shelves stacked with tins. We seldom saw any. When one did appear down Pam's or my end, we would yell 'Blow!' in a 'Thar she blows!' sort of roar. We'd stop for congratulations and dump the pariah can into a special box nearby where it waited for disposal as soon as possible.

Having cleared this large batch we then went to an even simpler task, which was sitting beside a hole in the floor guarded with rails, presumably so we would not fall through it. Our job here was to keep the moving chain stocked with full tins before they suddenly disappeared out of sight to the lower floor. This had seemed so simple that at first we bought green Penguin crime paperbacks for reading in turns. We were soon disillusioned – a giant rumble from below followed by a vast clanging roar and all our full tins disappeared and we were scrambling to refill the empty and still moving chain. We became cunning with our stacks after a while but at first we must have looked like Charlie Chaplin in *Modern Times*.

When we were getting low on tins we'd shout, 'Another box, Ceddy. Quick!' Ceddy was half our size and looked about ten but he was a male and thus able to fling forty-pound boxes filled with cans about, whereas we were females and if we even attempted to lift them (which we didn't), something inside us would collapse or snap lower down with sinister results, and Mr Wattie didn't want that.

The best day was Friday, when we queued in long lines at the office to be handed our pay envelopes. On the desk sat a framed piece of advice from higher authority:

Work eight hours a day and don't worry
and in time you'll be the Boss
and work twenty-four hours a day and have all the worry.

My envelope was thin but recipients of Sweeties must expect that. What I did object to most bitterly was that by the time I had reached the shed at home (the one where I received my first kiss from Bruce Cummings) my first wage packet had disappeared. The envelope had gone down the hole in the world. I biked back, searched the grass verges endlessly, then biked home again. Then foolishly told Mum.

She was doing something technical at the stove and turned to me with pained grief. 'You're not safe you know, simply not safe.'

For the first time I disagreed, but didn't say so. I'd got a bachelor of science, hadn't I. 'Got it', what was more, not 'had it'.

I had better luck one year when Wendy found a job for me at an orchard within biking distance. Wendy had worked there before and been promoted to arrange prize peaches into flat trays. I was given a trial but failed. You had to have a light touch the owner's wife told me, otherwise the peaches would be bruised. She and Wendy had this gift but I obviously hadn't. I was heavy handed so I was shown the shed door and began apple picking, where heaviness didn't matter. Apple picking and I were made for each other, and I have never lost a pay packet since. The sun shone, the birds sang, I was a quick picker and I liked my mates who were all regulars. When it rained, which was seldom, we made apple boxes in another shed. There was more talk there, and at smokos, where we listened to the yarns of those who'd been picking forever. One man, a veteran from the 1914–18 war, was convinced that any man who survived the Kaiser's War could do no wrong. He would tell us of lapses ranging from petty pinching, to assault and battery and worse, then he would pause with sad surprise and shake his head. 'You wouldn't believe it. He was a returned man, too!'

*

I applied for a job teaching science at Samuel Marsden Collegiate School for Girls in Wellington and was accepted. My beautiful BSc seemed to offer nothing else. I knew nothing about teaching from the teacher's point of view other than the fact that they always seemed busy and sometimes harassed, but I was determined to get out of the Bay – and Wellington was the capital city, was it not?

In the meantime I accepted Jetta's invitation to stay with her family in Hawera, then a small town in Taranaki – smaller even than Hastings. It was not till much later I discovered that Ronald Hugh Morrieson lived there all his life, a writer whose dry comment to another writer became true. He feared he would be 'another of those poor buggers who get discovered when they're dead'. The smaller the community, the less tolerant, the more morally right, the more *sure*. Morrieson was by no means puritanical, and neither were his books. They were published in Australia during his lifetime and eventually in New Zealand, but not until after he had died.

The Trotter family consisted of three daughters, one son and two loving parents. Their father came home for lunch occasionally, and afterwards played a highly competitive game of ping-pong with one or other of his children before he went back to his office. A process which astonished me. Mrs Trotter did not compete, she was a reader of the nose-in-a-book variety. Every afternoon she retired upstairs to lie and read for an hour or so, which seemed both idyllic and wise. She gave me a copy of Katherine Mansfield stories which were a true discovery. I had never heard of her existence at Woodford or anywhere else.

Another discovery was to find how the whole family would take part cheerfully in any of the others' games and enterprises. Judith, the youngest, was organising a dolls' wedding in the garden. Her advice to us as to how we should dress was the same as Mr Collins's to Elizabeth Bennett when she was about to have the honour of meeting Lady Catherine de Bourgh. We were to wear whatever garment we possessed which was superior to the rest. Mrs Trotter stood elegant and serene. Jetta, the officiating parson, stood waiting in black with two tea towels pinned together about her neck. The rest of us milled around the bride Bluebell and groom Mickey Mouse in expectant good will, then Jetta intoned, 'No smoking in the holy precincts,' and Mr Trotter, with rueful apology, stubbed out his cigarette on a nearby rock and the ceremony began.

My visit to Hawera varied. We climbed through the damp podocarp forest of what was then called Mount Egmont, we visited a dairy factory and were given samples, went to the flicks *en masse*, where Jetta had a good look round before the lights went out and said with interest, 'There's a new man down there. Look Bub, third row up on the right.'

A word about nicknames. We New Zealanders like them and use them freely. They are part of what we like to think of as our easy-going, friendly ethos. Nevertheless, when we meet a fat director called Bones, or a six-foot grandmother called Bub, there is reason to snigger. And I have known worse. One grandmother I know replies happily to 'Tuppence'; another remains calm when called 'Bullet' by her husband and friends. As a baby, she had no hair for years. 'Bub' came from David's lisping version of Baby, and it stuck. I am, as it were, attached to it. I am relaxed if it is used by friends I have known forever but feel slightly shy – a sensation otherwise not felt for more than sixty years – when it is tried by new friends.

When an old friend of his died, Charles Lamb said sadly, 'Now there is no one left to call me Charlie.' Exactly.

Our friends enjoyed visiting us also. Our parents were generous, welcoming and pleased to hear their news. The only thing the young men were denied by my father was requests for ginger ale in his still rare whisky. But as David said, that was fair enough.

My 'current boyfriend' came to stay and went, his reception having been polite but not ecstatic. Other friends joined us at Waimarama. One of David's mates became noted as the only person who could get our mother 'out of the sink'. None of us could be trusted to wash up properly, you see. Nor could she be coaxed to take on a simpler task such as drying up or putting dishes away, or most impossible, leaving us to it and reading the paper. By guile and subtle teasing John Cashmore achieved this miracle.

Occasionally Mum disagreed with them. One of them called Sally told her Villa d'Este hair salon should be pronounced 'Villa d'Estay'. Mum wasn't to be fooled. 'It hasn't an accent, Sally,' she said firmly, 'it's d'Este.' Sally explained, 'It's Italian you see, Mrs

Wright, not French.' Mum laughed kindly, 'Not in Hastings it isn't.' Sally, however, had her day. She unintentionally left behind the largest straw hat her hostess had ever seen, which she then had to post to Oamaru.

Mum was irritated also when one of my early-wedded friends rang to tell her that the blowflies had blown her stored blankets and what should she do? The young wife added that she knew Mrs Wright would be the one to ask. Mum failed her. 'She should have folded the blankets away with plenty of camphor balls,' she told me. 'It's too late. There's nothing I can do now.'

Her young friends (other than me) continued to come to her for advice, as Valerie and Esther and Dulcie had done years ago. Sometimes she failed them but not often, unless it was something 'shady'.

Jill from Napier, now living in Hastings with her husband and three small children, couldn't understand something about the local scandal. A lawyer in Hastings had been accused of indecency – something to do with the extraordinary length of something. The accused had placed a ruler against his client's crotch to demonstrate the unlikely length of the something of which she spoke. Had the client not perhaps exaggerated?

'But Aunty Jessie,' said Jill, 'what had the ruler got to do with anything?'

Mrs Doctor Wright replied, 'If there's anyone in the whole of Hastings who wouldn't know what the ruler had to do with anything, Jill, it isn't me.'

Friends, including Sally and her hat, came to stay with us as guests at one or other of the rash of weddings which took place in the Bay at this time. Returned men returned, some of them took over the family farm, and several were in want of wives. This they achieved with comparative ease. The wise men picked with discernment, choosing the youngest and prettiest available and preferably those who had grown up on farms; young women who knew when the rams were put out and the importance of so doing, when milking cows went dry, and which old ewes looked like dog-tucker. It was also useful if they could knock up a good batch of scones big enough to satisfy a large shearing gang at smoko.

Weddings, be they large or small, were a growth industry in the Bay.

They were also hard work. Marquees were hired, certainly, but the groom and his friends would put the thing up themselves. No one thought of hiring florists to garnish either the church or the marquee. The mother of the bride simply marshalled her friends. It paid, or rather was a help, to have a dear friend who was wonderful with flowers, who could be appointed O.C. Flowers. She would then marshal *her* friends, also ace flower-doers. Early on the morning of the wedding day O.C.F. and her team would drive miles into the country to collect promised flowers cut by more friends, then drive back to deck the appropriate church from top to bottom, from bottom to top. No one in the Bay had ever heard of floral arrangements but sometimes the best friends could be 'worn to a frazzle' by the time the bride walked up the aisle.

'Worn to a frazzle' could also attack the bride's mother, and sometimes even the bride had a touch. All the father had to do was order the grog, make sure the garden was at its best, if his wife hadn't done so already, and pay for everything in sight.

Food was catered, thank God. And the Farmers' were known to be completely reliable.

There was also the question of what to wear. Many years later I read of Janet Frame's longing for a permanently pleated skirt. The most sought-after garment at Hawke's Bay weddings in the forties were navy blue edge-to-edge coats. You were safe for weddings in every kind of weather: not too hot, not too cold. Serviceable but deadly dull.

Another asset for female wedding-goers was the arrival of Mr Noonan and his fabric shop. Before then they would have bought materials in Hastings or bussed or driven through to Blythe's in Napier. 'They have a better range,' as Miss Grant the dressmaker told her clients.

But now there was Mr Noonan who sold nothing other than fabrics, which gave him a definite edge. And beautiful they were those fabrics, a joy to behold. And the proprietor was discreet. 'The XY wedding is it Mrs Wright?' he would ask Mum as she perched on the long-legged chair thoughtfully provided as he flung fabric after fabric across the counter for her inspection. If she said, 'That's the one, thank you,' Mr Noonan sometimes shook his head and saved the day. 'Well no, Mrs Wright. I think not. I happen to know that Mrs Z has acquired the two-tone.' Mum would then drop the two-tone like a hot brick, but Mr Noonan was at hand. 'May I suggest perhaps the French navy silk with the ultramarine ripple?'

The day of materials had gone. Fabrics, like the Pea Viner, had hit Hastings.

I was happy in the Bay, how could I not be, with friends and weddings to attend and a 'secure job' waiting in Wellington? But one night as I closed *Brave New World*, and turned out the light still thinking about the tough life Epsilon Minuses had, I realised I must now concentrate on my job in Wellington. It was a good thing, I knew that, definitely a good thing to be getting out of the Bay. Three years in Dunedin had opened my dreamy eyes. Too many people in Hastings knew what was best, not only for themselves, but for people who thought and behaved differently. Why should men – and women, which was worse – sit around the clocktower and smoke cigarettes? Why should Maori farmers let their farms go to rack and ruin with thistles and gorse and God knows what? Why did those boys and girls hang around street corners on Friday evening in that unattractive way?

But why the flaming hell shouldn't they? It would be better surely than groping around in vast drainpipes provided by Dunedin city fathers.

How did they *know*, these deciders, not only how *they* should behave in their home town but everyone else? Had a finger pointed from on high? No. Then why didn't they shut up?

A returned man (recently married to one of my friends) told me a story. He had worked at a local bank before the war. One day the manager called him into his office. 'Ah yes, Jones,' he said, 'can you tell me if Smith has any Maori blood? He's dark you know.'

'No, Sir, he hasn't. I happen to know Smith has some Spanish blood.'

'Ah good, excellent. I have no feelings on the matter of course, but it is the bank's rule. No Maori. Thank you, Jones.'

'Not at all, Sir.'

We all sang with pride the marching song of the 28th (Maori) Battalion.

Maori Battalion march to victory
Maori Battalion staunch and true
Maori Battalion march to glory
Take the honour of the people with you

We will march, march, march to the enemy
And we'll fight right to the end.
For God! For King! And for Country!
AU-E! Ake, ake, kia kaha e!

Maori had made splendid troops. We all knew that too.

We also knew the rules of propriety. A man with any haircut other than 'short back and sides' would be reprimanded by his seniors, be that at schools (bad example) or in offices, banks, or behind counters (alarm customers). Dyed hair on women was considered suspect. And what if the roots showed? This was considered as risky as a drooping petticoat. Even a glimpse of one showing could result in a friendly (but nauseating) whisper, 'Snowing down south', which would send the culprit scuttling off to rectify it. There was another well-known repellent comment. Overly tall men or women could be greeted with an upward stare and a merry 'Cold up there?'

Small town *ad nauseam*.

My father told me that a New Zealand woman called Ngaio Marsh was writing 'tec yarns' as he called them. Published at Home of course, and receiving good reviews over there. The *Times Literary Supplement* said she was in the 'front rank of crime writers', would you believe? Even more amazing, several of her books were set in New Zealand. I read them and loved them, especially *Colour Scheme*. What a brilliant idea for a plot. Villain changes pegs which indicate safe path through boiling mud pools. Victim suffers horrible fate. Local colour indeed.

I also felt that Miss Marsh, like many female crime writers, loved her detective, in her case Roderick Alleyn. She deals with this problem by giving him a wife both intelligent and a good painter, as was the author herself.

There is an engaging book called *Snobbery with Violence* by Colin Watson which was published in 1971. He acknowledges that his title comes from Alan Bennett's *Forty Years On* and proceeds to give many examples of rampant snobbery in crime fiction in the early half of the twentieth century. Roderick Alleyn, Chief Inspector, CID, has an assistant, Inspector Fox; Brer Fox as he is called by his superior, a man who would give his life for his master. His interest (other than his job) is learning French, which he finds difficult, and the reader is invited to lift the upper lip at his attempts. Imagine such a thicko as Fox attempting to speak the French language!

But then I am sensitive about French-speaking ability and Ngaio Marsh's books are a minor glimpse of snobbery compared with those of Dorothy Sayers and others.

I have forgotten the name of the author or the title of my favourite 'snobbery with violence' story. A loss which I regret; I would like to read it again. Here is the plot: Squire of village has asked local cad to tennis party. Why on earth would he have done so? Why would squire attempt to ingratiate himself with cad? Obvious. Cad must be blackmailing squire. And so he is.

I had now read two New Zealand writers, Katherine Mansfield and Ngaio Marsh. I knew nothing of Denis Glover or the Caxton Press, which he began in 1935 with Charles Brasch, A.R.D. Fairburn, R.A.K. Mason, Bob Lowry, Frank Sargeson, et al. I wonder whether I should have known much more about New Zealand writing and writers if I had studied English in Dunedin in the forties? Don't know.

The best description I know of a New Zealander's reaction of both pride and astonishment when first reading about New Zealanders by a New Zealander came much later. I found it in March 1978 in the magazine *Islands*, a New Zealand quarterly of Arts and Letters, edited by Robin Dudding. Vol. 6 no. 3 was devoted by its editor to a *Celebration for Frank Sargeson at 75*. The article which enchanted me was by R.A. Copland and is called 'First Reading: Only Meeting'. It is written as a pastiche of Frank Sargeson in 'cobber' mode. Copland is in England lying in a bunk in a military hospital in 1944:

So I was feeling pretty much of a loner and a long way from home and Mum; and that was on top of being crook. Then I got hold of a paperback called Penguin New Writing edited by a joker named Lehmann. Well I reckon I'll never forget hitting the first pages of this story by this bloke Frank Sargeson.

I tell you I sat up in my bunk as if I'd just witnessed the collision between planets.

My generation of Kiwis knew two quite separate worlds. There was a reading planet and a real-life planet. On the first you have villages and copses, footmen and squires, Baker Street, the Punjab, yard-arms and keel-hauling. The only book I'd read that wasn't on that planet was called In Pirate Waters by a joker called Garnet, I think that was his name. Never heard of it since I was about ten. But I remember how funny it was to read about this real place called Christchurch, and it had streets called Cashel Street and all that. It felt very queer, like having an auntie in the First Fifteen.

And Copland goes on, each sentence as witty and as true as ever.

CHAPTER 14

The first thing I noticed about the Wellington province was that their rivers were different. The rivers I knew, like the Tukituki, had wide beds, but were not filled with water from bank to bank. What little they had flowed over stones, seldom sand, and they were liable to dry up in our long hot summers, so much so that they may be left with little but rivulets across the parched bed.

I met my first Wellington river just before we came to a small village called Tawa, not far from Wellington City. The road turned past an enormous macrocarpa tree which had been clipped into what looked like a huge green coffin standing on its head, cut back presumably to make visibility better at the sharp corner on which it stood. From then on I could see the river, dark, deep and swift-flowing for miles, its water level with the green paddocks beside it.

'That's an English river, isn't it?' I said, thinking of Miss Avery's 'Lady of Shalott' and her 'river winding clearly'.

'What?' said Dad, who was driving me and my luggage to Marsden. Mum, as usual had said her farewell at 609 Roberts Street.

'The river. Look. It's English.'

'Good God, woman, I'm driving.'

True. Just a thought.

Dad had no problem finding Marsden. It was in the suburb of Karori, which was not far from the centre of Wellington, and near the house where his parents had lived after they had left New Plymouth.

Nor was it difficult to find the staff residence, Innes House, which stood within the grounds of the school. Dad unloaded my luggage, kissed me, wished me good luck and departed at speed.

I saw his point. There was no one in sight. Clutching my suitcase I marched up the steps to my home.

Most of the staff lived in and the establishment was run strictly in order of how long its inhabitants had spent at Marsden, with a nod towards seniority of years. There were, I gathered later, two or three pleasant rooms with *sun*. Others were said to be quite spacious and one even had a pleasant view. None of these astonishments was ever seen by me. Privacy was sacrosanct and doors were kept shut to all except old and trusted friends.

The majority of the staff at Innes House did seem surprisingly old though I realise this thought comes through the mists of years. They were also decidedly set in their ways, which involved avoiding newcomers as far as possible and having a dislike of nonsense in all its forms.

The only three who were near my age were Eileen Bone (geography), Val (physical education) and a delightful English woman called Joyce (history), who was taller than I and one of those endearing people who are happy to make fools of themselves to entertain others. She was a precursor of Joyce Grenfell and just as witty. Her flutey English voice and her stretching and unstretching of endlessly long limbs, prancing around her tiny bedroom, had the three of us begging for more.

Now girls and boys, let us be tall, tall trees, arms up, up, stretching high, higher. Gewd, gewd and once more. Gewd. Now let's all be fairies. Dancing in their fairy rings, let us follow them. Quick, quick. Gewd, gewd, around and around. And we all fall down.

There is something gloriously ham when British men and women with the right voices invite their infants to fall flat on their faces.

Val was about twenty-one and a natural blonde. She leapt about the school glowing with health and easy on the eye. The girls all adored her but I remember thinking that working in an all girls school seemed rather a waste of Val's obvious attributes. She was also as much fun as she looked.

As was our other friend, Eileen Bone, who had been teaching at Marsden for several years. After we had known each other for some time, I discovered she was not only an excellent teacher, but that in earlier days Boney too had been given to staring at herself in mirrors attempting to convince the image that its owner existed. This was astounding to us both, the fact that there was another person in the world who had once been afraid of not existing. Boney, like me, told the image in the mirror firmly that she lived with her nice kind mother and father and brother, the only difference being that Boney did it in Nelson, not in Hastings, and her brother was Richard, not David.

Dear Eileen died before Jeremy told me about 'existential angst' and its various symptoms. I should have liked her to know. It's always good to have a name put to one's oddities or conditions, even if they no longer exist.

There was little chat at the house during the queue for the geyser-equipped bathroom, a queue decked with dressing gowns of plaids, florals, and camel, and sponge bags creaking in chilly hands. The first assistant had first go, though she was usually unseen by the time I arrived. After her came English, maths, French and so on down the line. Physical education and science sometimes tossed for second to last.

In my small, dark and chilly room I felt at first like some benighted hermit in a Lord's grotto, but I became very fond of it. I had brought with me my yellow elliptical radio from my pay cheque as a demonstrator and with my first as a teacher I bought a single-bar heater, which was also excellent in all ways until power cuts were enforced. Every morning I listened to the early morning announcer Morrie Power on 2ZB. Morrie was a cheerful man, or appeared to be so, and I was glad of his friendly presence and the music he played. He began my day at Innes House. Until he intoned at 8.30, 'Ladies and Gentlemen. On behalf of my brother, Vital Electric, please turn off your radio and heaters.' I thought this very witty and so did Val.

It was a surprise to discover that I was the only teacher of science. I had expected a senior figure, competent, available and ready to guide and advise when required but who never interfered. Not so. I found that at the age of twenty I was head of science. Science, in Samuel Marsden Colegiate School for Girls, was me.

As well as teaching forms three to seven I had, like all residential staff, extracurricular responsibilities. These were a mixed bag and revolved mainly around the boarders. House duties with the boarders, dining room duties with the boarders, prep supervisions with the boarders and church attendance with the boarders. The Anglican church in Karori was just across the road from the school so there was none of the marching up and down the hills which attended church duty for the staff at Woodford. Nevertheless it was still a duty, and not the last.

Full-day Sunday supervision with the boarders included ballroom dancing with the seniors in the hall after tea, where the members of the staff were expected to dance with girls who asked them to do so. *One two three, one two three*, once again. I regret to say I found this tedious. Then finally, lights out for the boarders. Yippee! – but softly. The staff house held perils of its own.

One of the responsibilities which was mine alone was the restocking of the science cupboard at the back of the laboratory where I taught. It took me some time before I found where to obtain chemical supplies. Having discovered that, how much should I order? A helpful young man at Kempthorne and Prosser taught me a lot. 'Wellington Girls High usually order about six ounces of copper sulphate at a time. You don't want much of it lying around and Chile is not going to run out of the stuff in a hurry.'

Chile, girls, is virtually a mountain of copper.

Teaching is yakka, a word which means 'hard work' in Aboriginal. I had wondered if this were so from the evidence at Woodford and the immediacy with which our teachers returned marked homework. But that was in the war when some of the staff there were virtually marooned. I was in Wellington, 'the capital city of New Zealand'. I could clang about in trams and see life and fit my marking into my free periods, which were reasonably generous. Which I did for a few weeks, but my marking piled up as I spent nights planning my lessons. Then of course there was the actual taking of the lessons. Did they understand what I was talking about, these green-uniformed girls? Were they interested? If not, why not? Teachers earn every penny they are paid. Less talk, you dumb bums, about the holidays they get.

Many of the Marsden girls I met were bright-eyed and seemed to be more interested in learning than most of us had been at Woodford. Also, many of them wanted to learn the wonders of biology. The chemistry needed for the curriculum was within my range, which had been handed on from Miss Priddle rather than from Professor WON in Dunedin.

The names of the girls I learned first were always of two kinds. The quick-minded, who sat at the back and whose whole face listened, and the others who didn't give a damn, who belonged to the 'Why doesn't she shut up?' school of inattention.

There are many types and conditions of women I admire but

headmistresses of girls' schools, particularly boarding schools, come high on the list.

The headmistress at Marsden never stopped working. Miss Hopper (NHRN) had come from England to take up the position not long before I arrived. She found tension, and more, from one or two senior members of the staff.

I had expected to find the atmosphere in the staffroom to be more relaxed than that at Innes House; after all, here the seniors were not guarding their own comforts. This room was spacious and warm, the cooks produced not only tea and coffee but homemade biscuits, enjoyed by us all except another Miss Wright who did not live in, was wraith-like in black, gave me the spooks and arrived every morning with several pottles containing varying aspects of her diet, which she ate in corners with a silver spoon. The French teacher called us Wrights Ancient and Modern.

The seating was important in the staffroom and Val and I learned the placement quickly. The most embarrassing and unhappy times in the room were at staff meetings. Miss Hopper sat at the head of the table, the first assistant on her right hand and the rest in order of seniority, or what Val and I assumed their positions to indicate.

The first meeting we attended dealt with various problems, the most important it seemed being that of detentions. Not from the boarders of course, nor from girls who lived nearby, but as we all knew, many girls came from as far away as Upper Hutt and detentions issued to these girls would mean they missed their train. Joyce and I looked earnest, Eileen nodded wisely and Val said the same problem happened with teams' practice. If they have to catch trains, she meant.

The senior members of the staff gave Val one of those looks reserved for senior staff to less experienced staff. A glance 'more in sorrow than in anger'.

'We were talking about detentions,' murmured Maths.

Val went as pink as a ripe watermelon and spoke no more.

The same topics turned up, time after time: detentions, parent evenings, the problems of the damage the girls did to the Singer sewing machines during Clothing. And the boiler. Always the boiler.

Each and every one of them was discussed *ad nauseam*, as were others, and each and every time Miss Hooper was flattened by her opponents. It was an extraordinary exhibition. Val and I discussed it afterwards. We were sorry for the headmistress but only she could deal with the situation. She must grapple it to her soul with hoops of steel. Buckle up something. Summon up blood. Deal with it. After all, she was the boss. How easy to say. There are bosses and bosses. Bosses who can boss and bosses who can't – and know it. Their life is hard, very hard.

It was obvious after a month or so that I would have very little time to read, no more in fact than I had had in Dunedin, the difference being that then I had had no hope of reading through the fiction and poetry stacks of the public library if I was to get my letters. I went there only to swot before exams, resolutely walking past anything of interest until I arrived at the poultry section.

Once again I realised reading for pleasure was going to be a treat. Having survived Mum's edict of no reading in the daytime, I had come slap against little reading till the holidays. No wonder Dimsie and Marigold had longed for their hols. The books I would read later had joined the books I would write some day. They would come later when I had plenty of time. Inspired from on high, my inspiration would come down in shafts.

I looked around the capital city in search of people who enjoyed reading beyond most things, who admired the writings of some men and women so much that the knowledge of having one of their books waiting at home could keep them happy all day long. Or less unhappy. I was hoping to talk about books, find writers and poets I didn't yet know. I needed the days when Jan and I used to chant poems at each other, but she was now teaching home science at Woodford saving up for marriage and presumably had as little reading time as I had. I did join a poetry society and was pleased to hear that efforts would be made for us to hear some New Zealand poetry. No such rare beast appeared any time I rattled down to town in the tram. However, I did hear a man called Anton Vogt, who I discovered was a Norwegian, but the fact that he lived here was a good start. I liked him and his reading. One I remember:

Oh, Sister Catherine,
Send me a husband.
Tall, Sister Catherine,
Rich, Sister Catherine,
Soon, Sister Catherine.

I also remember that the poetry society had a tendency to meet in cold places.

I was sad that both Nana and Grandfather Wright had died before I came to Wellington. I had liked both of them and I felt it careless that both of them had demised before I arrived.

Nana Wright had continued to have a sweet tooth since the day David and I were interrupted stealing her chocolates. She also had remained small and round and friendly when we had visited her as children. I don't remember much about the house except that the telephone sat under an unusual padded doll. It started off like an ordinary one then blossomed out at the waist, so much so that it hid the instrument completely. I never understood whether it was to hide the telephone, and if so why, or whether it was just a merry joke. It was a hard question for a small child to frame in words and I never did.

Grandfather and I had always been good friends ('Barbara's the reader'). I also liked Aunt Margaret who was an excellent tennis player and a mean hand at the art of juggling. Not many kids at St Luke's had a juggling aunt. When Grandfather retired from his practice in New Plymouth the family moved to Karori to be near their daughter, Angela, and her husband and family of four girls. Margaret, having been engaged three times, decided matrimony was not what she had in mind. Later she and her partner of many years ran the Blue Cross Boarding Kennels down the other end of Karori.

Another presence I was aware of was Katherine Mansfield who had lived here after her family had moved from Thorndon. She too would have lifted her eyes 'unto the hills', like the psalmist and the rest of us, to Wright's (no relation) Hill on one side and Johnston's on the other. Had perhaps scrambled up through the native bush of the latter to see the view from the top. Well brought-up middle-class young women may have declined but Kathleen Beauchamp had always been a rebel.

I knew she had left Karori and New Zealand in 1908, which was long before Nana and Grandfather Wright had arrived, so they would never have caught a glimpse of each other. Not within a bull's roar (David). Nevertheless Nana Jackson's dislike for my romancing had never done me any harm. I liked to think of them breathing the same fresh air, treading the same pavements in the same winds. Nana Wright and Katherine Mansfield both had strong words about Wellington winds.

I asked if anyone at Innes House knew the whereabouts of the house in which Mr and Mrs Beauchamp and their family had lived so I could have gazed at it with reverence, but no one did. One Saturday I went to the Turnbull Library in town and asked to see some of Katherine Mansfield's original manuscripts. The assistant behind the desk asked me if I wanted to see them for research and seemed disappointed at my reply. However, she gave me some and I sat at one of the tables to have a good read, but found Mansfield's handwriting to be completely inexplicable. I gazed reverently at this undeciphered Rosetta Stone for a while then, feeling stupid, delivered the manuscripts back to the desk and walked along Lambton Quay to The French Maid café, which sold real coffee. I had not met such a thing in Hawke's Bay. My parents never drank coffee. The only thing called coffee in our house came in a bottle labelled Camp Coffee with a picture of a man in khaki surrounded by tents, which was used by Mum when making coffee icing. Real coffee was one of the few sophistications I met in the capital.

Val's boyfriend was now working in Auckland. Mine, Stephen (NHRN), had left university unexpectedly and was mustering in the South Island high country. I found that phrase deeply romantic and still do. Years later I read in one of Janet Frame's novels a character say, 'I should like to have lived in a house whose tall windows face the mountains.' Me too. Or so I thought.

However, my enthusiasm for Stephen had faded and I wrote to tell him. Having done so, I then missed his letters, his tall tales from the hills. Also his words of affection and praise had been welcome in the staff house, even though I realised that life with Stephen would not be a good idea for either of us. He, after reeling from the shock of his rejection, made a quick recovery, married a nice girl and took up farming. Though not in the high country.

Before this he had introduced me to his cousin who lived nearby in Lower Hutt. When Stephen was no longer on the scene, Paul (NHRN) swam into the gap like a cruising paramecium. He was an interesting man with a sense of humour who had recently recovered from tuberculosis and was not working yet. This gave him plenty of time for play. He also had a comfortable car with plenty of room in the back seat. Halfway through a session he murmured passionately, 'Barbara, Barbara, oh my Barbara', then, 'I always make the point of remembering the name.'

Sophistication again, I thought. Only to be found in cities.

There were other pleasures. One was the discovery that I could teach. That some bright faces in front of me were listening. Not all of them, no teacher could achieve that, but a good proportion of young eyes would snap, heads would lift. They wanted *more.* Biology teaching had moments of pure glee, such as the business of mimicry, or more accurately, mimesis. For example, when a butterfly mimics a poisonous leaf, it is tempting to think that it has made itself look like one to avoid disaster from a hungry wasp. Not so. Biology is more cunning than this. The word mimesis means the 'close external resemblance of an animal to another that is distasteful or harmful to predators of the first'. Some moths look like other moths for the same reason, as do butterflies. Who's kidding whom in the Lepidoptera?

Or consider the seahorse, *Hippocampus* (nice name), whom I first met at Portobello, across the bay from Dunedin. Everyone, especially every child, should see it as it wraps the end of itself around a vertical growing seaweed and its changing-coloured eyes stare back at you. The male also carries the eggs, but we all know that.

Other good things were friendships with Eileen, Joyce, and Val, who was the one who introduced me to tramping. I had enjoyed field days in Dunedin but now Val was in charge. She was an experienced member of the Wellington Tramping Club and had access to their huts. Many of the routes, she explained to me gently, might be a bit much for a beginner but the easier ones she planned for the two of us through the North Island beech forest, with the leaves sparkling in the sun and the small creeks babbling (there is no other word), sent my sense of freedom soaring into euphoria, especially when Stephen was no longer a feature in life's rich tapestry.

One of the things I learned is the strong feeling that getting into the bush (which is different from 'going bush') is precious, something which is ours and must remain free for all.

No one in the whole world, I thought smugly, has joys like this

My ancestor Adam Jackson ('Yeddie'). Born at Howpathy Scotland in 1763, he was known as the 'Hunter King' of Liddesdale.

My mother's father, Fred Jackson, at Mangatahi (near Hastings) with my brother David. My grandfather moved onto the land in 1906 and broke it in.

My parents with my brother David in 1924.

My mother and me.

Colin.

David and me.

With David (in the pedal-car) and Colin (pram) at our King Street, Hastings house, about 1929.

David and Colin and my first friend called Jill; my feet can be seen on the left.

With David.

With Colin and David.

With Colin and David at the Waimarama bach we rented every summer.

David, me, Colin.

The Queenswood school play, *Cabbages and Kings*. Mary McIntyre (middle) and I draw swords, while Tiny Groome and Barbara Herrick (the princess, obscured) look on.

David on his motorbike.

My mother, on the right, and her friend Laura outside the new Hastings clocktower.

My parents, about 1950.

Graduating with my friends Pamela Sinclair (left) and Jetta Trotter (middle) in 1947. Note my flat shoes.

On Te Mata Peak with my friends Wendy (left) and Jane (right).

I married Neil Anderson at St Matthew's, Hastings in 1951.

A newspaper photo of Jeremy and Piers welcoming their father's ship, *Taranaki*, to New Plymouth in 1961.

A posed photograph with Neil and our sons Jeremy and Piers. At the last minute we realised my mother wouldn't approve of Jeremy having bare feet, so he tucked them into my skirt.

Our house in Castor Bay, about 1955.

Jeremy and Piers at tea with their cousins Diana and Lizzie at their grandparents' in Hastings, about 1963.

Me with Piers and Neil with Jeremy and Piers at cousin Diana's wedding.

Painting our house in Beauchamp Street, Karori; Jeremy in the blue shirt, Piers in the white.

We walked the Milford track with my friend Janet Drake and her son Philip (foreground).

They didn't think we'd go! Anne McLean and I boarding the RNZAF Hercules, 1980.

I travelled often with Neil while he was Chief of Defence Staff. Here I am on a ferry in Japan, with Japanese students practising their English.

Rear Admiral Oki demonstrating origami.

'Dropping the Pilot', a Nevile Lodge cartoon presented to Neil on his retirement in 1983.

Four publicity and news photos:
Top: for *I think we should go into the jungle* (Charles Jameson, 1989).
Above: for *I think we should go into the jungle* (Don Roy, *Dominion*, 1989).
Opposite above: for *Portrait of the Artist's Wife* (1992).
Opposite below: for *The Peacocks* (Helena Hughes, 1996).

Neil holding Zoë, 1980.

A family photo, taken by Piers. From the left: his wife Sally, Neil, Jeremy, and me among grandchildren Lucy, Harry, Zoë and Sam. Jeremy's wife Heather and their baby son Joe were in Melbourne.

Heather with Joe and Zoë in the Galapagos Islands, a trip they had planned with Jeremy before he became ill.

At our Waikanae bach with Joe and Zoë.

Late summer at our Waikanae bach, March 2008.

A 1999 publicity photo (Kevin Stent, *Sunday Star-Times*).

within an hour or less from their capital city. *Floreat bush.* I loved everything about it: the camaraderie, the friends made, the songs (the words of which would have lifted the hair of every puritan across the land), the comforting, or not so comforting hut, the icy streams for washing and the long drops if you were lucky. Not many sophisticates in sight, though they could be found occasionally.

I also joined Val's ski club which was equally good but more physical. We had to carry our skis up to our club hut which was some distance up Mount Ruapehu. No skill is involved in putting one foot after another but you also have to ski and the sooner the better. There are naturals who strap on skis for the first time and are seen disappearing in a schuss down the mountain, but these are few. I did learn and came to love the icy drafts of air and the mountains high above disappearing and reappearing, from blue, to grey, to white-out. Mountains tend to make you feel small.

Some of the best skiers I met were returned men, who having made it home planned to get to the mountains at every moment possible. Some of them asked me to their parties where I was known as 'the tall one who knows the words of the songs'.

But perhaps the best pleasures were the other three 'less experienced staff', Joyce and Val and Boney. We were lucky. We possessed several useful attributes; we were young and cheerful and friendly.

Some of the 'experienced' staff members thawed towards us with time. One we enjoyed was the French mistress who told us she had been teaching for over thirty years. We looked at her in stunned silence until Joyce asked her why. 'I mean couldn't you have changed to another job?'

'Nonsense,' she said. 'I enjoy defeating ignorance.'

More silence. She also told us that when she was studying the language in Paris their professor told them one morning to write a letter of condolence to a man whose wife had died.

'In French?' asked one of us.

'Of course, but I explained to le professeur that I had received a pile of letters from New Zealand that morning and was far too happy to attempt such a thing.'

'And what did he say?'

'He replied that he fully understood and I was to write a letter of congratulations instead.'

'To the same man?'

'Of course. The French are a wonderful race.'

It was the same French teacher who saved me from worse things. On a long weekend near the end of the second term, Eileen, Val and Joyce had left Innes House in various directions. I had planned to catch a bus with the ski club people the next morning. I had had a cold all week and thought the mountain air would cure it, but by Friday evening I was feeling very odd indeed. The French teacher insisted on taking my temperature. It was high.

'Ring the ski people at once,' she said. 'I'll take you down to the Hawke's Bay bus. That's the only place you're going.'

I did and she did and I fell off the Newmans bus into the arms of my parents. Dad at once diagnosed pneumonia, which was an ugly word in 609. Doctors came and went. Mum insisted on what she called 'proper doctors', which meant any doctor in the vicinity who was not her husband, which was odd as she knew how good he was.

In either case I was ill for weeks on end. So ill that despite antibiotics the situation was a close-run thing. A phrase which Dad told me later he had borrowed from the Duke of Wellington about the Battle of Waterloo.

The end of all this was that the two proper doctors decided that I should not go back to Marsden for the last term. I was enraged. Who would find a science teacher for a third term? Of course I must go back and the sooner the better. I then had a relapse. Pneumonia won. Letters were written and I resigned.

Letters also came from my friends. Eileen told me Fiona (NHRN) had told her that Miss Wright was 'the best we ever had for animals and that'. A bright girl, Fiona, who later wrote her PhD on the lives and ways of cave wetas *in situ*, which involved years of her crouching in dark, damp caves to watch her prey as they went about their business.

Good on y', Fiona.

CHAPTER 15

It was high time I found another job. This was my thinking, not my parents', who were happy to have me in the house as a faintly incompetent unpaid companion. I did the shopping, shoved a vacuum cleaner about (it is difficult to make errors with those), set the table, cleared it and remembered where everything was stored. I went on little errands and was 'pleasant at all times' like a true Girl Guide, which I had never been. Companions, I had read, were not expected to do heavy work, besides which I was recuperating; had been for weeks. I accompanied Mum on her goings out and her comings in. I made tea for her to pour. I handed around homemade cakes to her friends. Best of all, I was a buffer. Both Mum and Dad liked me and I liked both of them. My father continued to go to bed at 8.30pm each night to read in his monastic little bedroom and I played Mah Jong with my mother to sharpen up her game for the club, though I did insist on plenty of time to read later. Fortunately it was summer so there was no question of my stoking the fire.

I scanned the *Tribune* daily for jobs but, as I expected, no one wanted a spare science teacher at this time of year. I pedalled down to the library each morning for a wider range of jobs, preferably somewhere else, though I was beginning to think of overseas, which involved saving money from rent.

On the way home I called into the store with my freshly laundered white cotton bag to pick up Mrs Wright's daily order (half a barracouta loaf). Jessie, the donor of broken biscuits, and her parents had gone but the chews – peppermint frogs, chocolate fish, soft and hard jubes, sherbets and lollipops – still lay in their glass-covered case and the new people also had the habit of disappearing 'out the back'. They too were careful, they too sprang to the front when the ding dong alarm beneath the cork mat rang its warning. Kids were light fingered, and not only kids. 'Mackerel Charlie,' said the owner through his moustache, 'the stories I could tell.' A quick agreement with their problems and on I pedalled round the corner to Cornwall Park Avenue, where the plane trees were in full leaf and the flasher had flashed it a hundred years ago.

Mum had news to tell as we sipped our tomato soup (and never slurped it, goodness me no). She was a diligent reader of the *Tribune*'s Deaths column when she ceased her chores for a moment to drink a quick cup of tea. She also had a quick glance at the Births with its smaller column alongside. And what had she seen this morning? Patsy Morrow must have had hers early, she wasn't due for a week or so.

The rash of weddings after the war had continued, and in the fullness of time the enthusiasm and fertility of the participants had produced brand new babies, to be followed by a notice in the Births.

'You must go and see Patsy,' said Mum. 'I hope the poor child hasn't inherited his father's nose!'

Patsy was not a particular friend but yes, I had been to her wedding. So off I set on my BSA to see her and her offspring at Sister Fahey's Nursing Home where business was booming and the shiny linoleum squeaked when you walked in. With me I took a pink rattle and one of my posies. I was good at posies – had been since childhood when I had won prizes for my prowess year after year at the annual Hawke's Bay Agricultural and Pastoral Show. *Posies (Under Twelve)* were my forte. I had kept a fresh one on Mum's dressing table for years.

Patsy was sitting up in a pink bedjacket so pristine, so bright, it must have been knitted for the occasion. Which could not be said of the new mother who was looking decidedly 'tashed', if not bewildered.

'She had a bad time,' whispered her mother, accepting the pink rattle and posie with thanks.

'Oh dear.'

'She'll be right as rain soon and Doug'll be coming in from the farm as soon as they've finished the docking. Won't he, dear?'

'Yes.'

The new grandmother continued to keep things going. 'And how are you, Barbara? Quite better now? You had a nasty time didn't you?'

'Um, er, a bit, yes. What I need now is a job.'

'Funny you should say that. I was reading the *Tribune* this morning to check out our birth notice and sort of slid onto Positions Vacant, heaven knows why, and I remembered thinking that would be just right for you. At Napier Hospital it was, in the laboratory there. You've got your letters for that sort of thing, haven't you?'

I thanked her and left with haste. 'Don't forget to see Sarah in the nursery,' murmured Patsy.

'No, no, of course.'

No nurse seemed available to show me which was Sarah from several well-swaddled newborn babies. I stood for a few minutes out of politeness. Just as I turned to leave one minuscule forefinger touched its tiny nose. I hadn't known they could do that. I watched, wondering if it was trying to tell me something. That it had – or had not – one like Doug's perhaps.

I bounded up the steps from the back shed, through the washhouse and the Pearson's sandsoap ladies, past the downstairs lavatory and the space next door where I had tried to grow silkworms given to me, I can't remember by whom, but the gift smacked of Mum's young, adoring friend Esther Niblock. Whoever the donor, it had been a disastrous enterprise; perhaps the unfortunate worms disliked the variety of mulberry leaves I stole for them from Cornwall Park. In any case they died, leaving an unpleasant smell which lingered there forever.

'Mum,' I yelled in the kitchen, 'where's the *Tribune*?'

'Don't shout. I'm in the drawing room.'

I applied for the job even though it was in the Bay. And got it. The BSc had saved me again.

I was interviewed by the pathologist, Dr Somerville, who asked me if I would be taking the diploma. I had never heard of such a thing but immediately said yes. Dr Somerville then showed me around the laboratory, where three people were bending over microscopes. I would have been happy to attempt a diploma in almost anything as long as I could be the fourth. Dr Somerville then showed me the biochemistry lab next door and we parted on terms of mutual respect. Or so I hoped.

The Napier Hospital on Bluff Hill was where my parents met in the twenties, and was also one of the places where the '31 earthquake did enormous damage. The new nurses' home, built only in the previous year, had been reduced to rubble, killing eight nurses who had been sleeping there after night duty.

The hospital laboratory was unusual in form. It had obviously not been built for this purpose and was below the level of the rest of the hospital: the wards, the operating theatres, the offices, the laundries, the shelters, everything. To me this gave it a somewhat similar atmosphere to Miss Priddle's crypt-like laboratory across at Woodford House's Chapel of St Francis of Assisi.

Having come down the laboratory steps the visitors had a choice. If they were looking for the pathologist's assistant they would turn left to find Bill, assistant in post-mortems, tidy-upper of morgues and maker of slides of the specimens for Dr Somerville to examine later. A dear man Bill, interesting in many subjects but silent about his job.

He had been badly wounded in the desert war and shipped home among hundreds of others. It took a long time for his wounds to heal, for him to 'buck up', as he called his process of getting well again. He was that rare thing, a returned man who wanted to talk about the war. There were lots of things Bill didn't understand about it. He told me he had seen an infantry man scrape the remains of his best friend off the side of his tank, crawl inside and roll on towards the front.

'If some bloke was squatting down with his tin of bully beef and copped one, why did he become a bloody hero? All that "glorious dead" stuff. Crap, if you'll excuse my French, Barbara.'

If the visitor turned right, the next employee to be found was Alfred, who was in charge of the autoclave, an enormous, roaring, hissing, steaming beast which only Alfred loved. His wife worked in the hospital laundry and arrived to meet him at four-thirty each day so they could walk home together, not exactly hand in hand but amicably enough. I visualised them at home in peace, all steaming, snorting, sterilising machines stilled, all dirty washing cleansed. There was something vaguely biblical about the image, marred only by Alfred's enormous walrus moustache which came halfway down his mug at smoko. He liked three spoons of sugar. 'At home,' he told us when we handed him his unsugared tea plus teaspoon, 'at home the wife stirs it for me.'

In the laboratories and Dr Somerville's room the visitor would find natural light for the first time below stairs. These three rooms looked down over Bluff Hill, sloping down to the Heretaunga Plains. Various kinds of gum trees grew there, beside a track on which people appeared occasionally, going upwards, downwards, sometimes stopping to yarn.

Along to the right on Bluff Hill were the shelters: open airy units considered therapeutic for tuberculosis patients, some of whom remained there for years. We technicians went across to collect blood samples from the patients, all of whom seemed glad to see us. Some were oddly cheerful, including a young woman with tuberculosis of the spine who told us she was coming up to her tenth year.

Laboratory work in those days was one of the interesting jobs available for people who liked finding out things. Thinking machines were fewer then. Specimens of various types came down from the wards, we made slides from them, stained them with appropriate stains, dried them and examined them under the microscope, planted swabs of them onto agar or other plates and put them in the incubator to be examined next morning. Sometimes I wanted the bus to go faster to find out if a plate had grown the unusual bacteria I hoped for.

We had scarcely touched on bacteria in zoology at Dunedin, and bacteriology was a whole new world which I found more interesting than haematology and biochemistry. The latter was Mr Rankin's field. Alone in the large room next door he remained hard working, amiable, and austere. It was he who gave me my first lesson in professional ethics, when I told him about my rare, exciting diagnosis.

He looked at me gently, eyed me down.

'But there might be a cure,' I tried.

'There might be, Barbara. There might be. But not at the moment.'

The most senior woman in bacteriology was Ann Avon (NHRN), excellent at her work, pleasant to be with and crisp with makers of errors.

She was also a heavy smoker. So heavy that a cigarette hung from the side of her mouth most of the time she was working and continuously in the tea room, with the result that a permanent nicotine stain lay above the left side of her upper lip, a mark which didn't disturb her in the slightest, nor anyone else.

About the only time she would stub out a cigarette in the lab was when Bill arrived with an egg and two glass cups to ask her to separate white from yellow, albumin being the best adherent available then to make his slices of specimens stick to the slide. Apparently men didn't separate eggs and Ann was an expert. I was rather envious at not being asked but never having separated one I assumed this was another arcane skill.

Other staff members were Amy and Audrey. Amy, half my size, was also a technician and Audrey doubled in brass, being both typist and receptionist. Her reaction to outpatients when they arrived for various tests was to toss her black hair in the direction of a nearby bench without missing a ping.

Occasionally a young man or two would appear to train for their diplomas. Collecting bloods was their forte and they seemed happy doing that, but in time they all drifted away.

We were a heterogeneous collection and happy being so. One of the things we enjoyed together was Mr Rankin's collection of *Times Cryptic Crosswords*. People who don't enjoy the cryptic ones tend to say that anyone can do them when they get used to the mind of the man or woman who sets them. Not so. In my experience all you need are five or more people to solve the same puzzle, all of whose minds operate differently. In our pokey little tea room Mr Rankin and Ann and Bill were lateral thinkers before the term had been invented. Their solvings seemed as impossible to the rest of us as cracking Swahili, but when they explained them – why, any fool could get it. The speedy typist always achieved the anagrams, I came in with the quotations and Amy smiled happily.

The second year I was there, Ann sat and passed the Diploma in Proficiency in Hospital Laboratory Practice, which now has a much grander name. She went down to Dunedin to be examined by professors of the medical school in both written and oral examinations and came back glowing with pleasure, as well she might. She, and those who followed her while I was there, never had a lesson, a lecture, or a glimpse as to what we might be asked. We did have one book about the subject but it was so impossible to read, much less understand, that I am unable to remember its name.

At the end of my third year I went down to Dunedin in Ann's tracks. I stayed with the mother of a good friend, Pam Sinclair, a fellow demonstrator and enthusiast about all things zoological. She had gained her PhD on the life cycle of some obscure echinoderm (spiny-skinned organism) that lived in the Taieri Flat near Dunedin. Pam was now a junior lecturer at an Australian university.

Her mother made me welcome, but all my friends, including David, had gone. I walked along Castle Street past the Chookery but there seemed little point in knocking on the door to say, 'I lived here four years ago.' 'So what?' is better avoided.

Few things remain about the exams. The practical was all right – a question about laboratory identification of tuberculosis, which was a breeze – and Professor Mercer told me I did a better oral examination than a written one. A comment which I didn't know was good or bad.

I passed my Certificate of Proficiency in Hospital Practice and came back to a cake in the tearoom and pleased handshakes from Dr Somerville and Mr Rankin. Also Dad offered me a sherry that night and Mum made a pavlova.

'In good weather or bad, commuters have it rough,' announced a heading in *Life* magazine at this time. It wasn't like that for me. After a brisk walk (or anxious run) to the bus stop I enjoyed the drive to Napier. I couldn't read like those with iron stomachs but the orchards which then lined the small village of Clive were worth watching in every season, from stark lopped branches to acres of blossom, to ripe fruit trees, and round again. After Clive came the sea, its breakers crashing against the stony beach then sucking the water back down the steep incline. None of these dramas could be seen so well from cars. Buses get better views.

'Port Out, Starboard Home', I learned from my father, is the origin of the word 'posh'. Experienced travellers from Britain to India learned to travel in port cabins from Britain and in starboard ones going home, because those cabins were cooler. Something to do with trade winds. Those who were in the know travelled posh. Dad and I enjoyed swapping snatches of useless and sometimes inaccurate information, an art learned from his father.

I therefore traveled posh on the bus, not for the cooling breeze but for better views. Starboard seat going out, port coming home, especially when the sea was at its wildest.

Faces became familiar on the journey and one interested me. I peered and peered again at the blonde hair of a young woman in front of me. It reminded me of Colin's, though thicker, but what interested me more was that the girl's hair was obviously not dyed. What a bit of luck for a Hawke's Bay girl. A true blonde with no risk of 'roots'. I told her so when I sat beside her. She laughed and told me her name was Shirley. We discovered that we lived round the corner, within shooting distance more or less, from both Mr Wattie's canning factory and each other. Also that our mothers were both on the committee of the Plunket Society. We told each other it was a small world and we must learn to drive sometime, though I didn't bother to tell her of the debacle at Ashley Clinton.

Usually a licensed member of one's family showed the unlearned how to stop and start, and having done that, go backwards and forwards. Neither Dad nor Mum though would play. However, Mum said yes I could borrow her car occasionally if and when I could drive.

I biked across town to Bailey Motors and made Mr Bailey a proposition. Presumably, I said, all the men who worked for him could drive and I needed to drive and I wished to pay one of them to teach me. Mr Bailey, like Prof Marples years before, said he could see no reason why not, adding as long as the hero who would take me on did so in his lunch time. He left his clean and tidy office and came back with a young man who was happy with my terms. His name was Tom Crow and when did I want to start?

'Next Saturday?'

'Done. See you here at twelve noon.'

Mum said I had to learn sometime and did Tom Crow know what he was letting himself in for? After that I drove Tom around the town, backing and parking and starting and remembering to look in the back mirror. We then finished each session by shouting each other to a double licker at Mr Rush Munro's Ice Cream Parlour on the outskirts of town. Before long I presented myself before Mr Herbie Green, a man of power in Hastings, as he was the only person who could give you your driving licence, or refuse to do so. Herbie gave me the nod and my horizons widened. I was now able to take my friend Jan, and others at Woodford House staff house, tramping in the Kaimanawas.

I spent occasional Sunday suppers at Hodge House, which was a new addition to Woodford House. Named after Miss Hodge –

the original precursor of the school – it was designed for the less academic pupils. 'We hope that here . . . many girls will learn to be good homemakers,' announced Lucy Hogg. The end product being considered desirable for matrimony. Also Hodge House was a haven for staff and friends on Sunday evenings.

At this time the true blonde, Shirley, asked me to play tennis despite the fact that she was good at it. Her brother Neil was home for the first time since, at the age of seventeen, he had left for training with the navy. The tennis ended; Mrs Anderson's tea had been delicious; I began thanking everyone in sight when it was time to leave. Neil asked me if he could give me a ride home on his motorbike. I declined with more thanks. I was going to see friends in Havelock and Mum's car was outside. He said the car could stay there and he could take me to Havelock on his bike. I laughed merrily.

'How would I get back?'

'Give me a time and I'll come and get you.'

I looked at him as I had frequently during the Fitzroy Avenue tennis party. This time with particular interest. Tall, blue eyes, slight smile.

'Yes, please.'

'Let's go.'

I became well acquainted with Neil and his motorbike. He traded his old BSA for a new Matchless Springer; a much smoother ride for me, he told me, when he picked me up at the laboratory lunch hour. I missed cryptic crossword sessions to cling tight as we hurtled around the tight corners of Bluff Hill to arrive with sandwiches on the stones between the thudding waves and Marine Parade.

We packed a lot into those hours, day after day and week after week, as he used up the end of his war leave.

I introduced him to my parents, and discovered Dad had brought him into the world. Well, well. We explored favourite places he hadn't seen for five years: the Tukituki River and its deep swimming holes among the shallows where Neil and his friend Terry Goldfinch, both aged twelve, sailed down the river for days in the canoe they had made together; Waimarama and its beach and the Herring Pond we had known forever; the Te Awanga lagoon where he fished for eels in a small dinghy in the twilight, caught one and was so alarmed at the enormous thing threshing about in the dark he threw it out and rowed home.

He borrowed his father's car. One evening in the back seat he asked me if I would marry him. I said I would like to very much and kissed him yet again.

Next morning Mum was making pastry on the marble slab she used for the process and at the same time looking out the window at the blue poppy from Kathmandu and wondering yet again why it would never flower.

I told her my news. She dropped the rolling pin and swung around in floury horror. 'You're what?' she gasped.

'I am going to marry Neil Anderson.'

'You're mad!'

I don't know why she reacted like this. I'm sure that in her mind she was not being vicious or unkind (let alone idiotic). I knew she loved me, warts and all. She had liked what she had seen of Neil, and surely she must have given up by now her vision of the Hawke's Bay farmer of Scottish lineage with a suitably generous number of acres. I was, after all, twenty-three.

It was just that she knew best. Another reason, perhaps, was she had slipped into the pleasure of having a companionable daughter at home. I liked her friends, they liked me, I was cheerful and I could make her laugh.

Each day when I came from the lab and we were munching our way through another well-cooked meal Mum would say, 'Tell us the funnies, Bub', and I would do so. I became a good teller both of drama and mirth: the blow up of Alfred's rage at the recalcitrant autoclave; the loss of an important blood plate, temporarily, not funny; how Bill had given me the honour of separating yolk from white (Ann was sick) and, even better, he had asked me if I would read the sun hours on the roof while he was on holiday and would tell me how tomorrow. My parents' interest in this venture was as good as an audience waiting for the *Crime Does Not Pay* serial at the Cosy. How we shot up in the lift to the flat roof of the main building. How Bill showed me how it worked. Each day I must put out a new sheet of paper which registered the hours of sun per day. When the sun shone it burned a track around the paper as it moved on its celestial way. No sun, no burned track. Occasional sun, occasional burn marks. I thought this was very clever as did Mum. She also liked Bill's comment, 'If it's impossible to read on which side of the marker the burn is, give it to the sun side. We've got to beat Nelson's sun record somehow.'

Members of my audience varied in their preferences. Mum was appalled when I relayed Bill's story that occasionally the off-duty ambulance men turned their siren on if they were running late for lunch. Couldn't do it often of course. It would get a bit obvious.

Whereas Dad was more interested in the crosswords, especially those with particularly subtle clues.

Q. Jones takes the plunge.

A. Inigo.

'Neat. Very neat.'

Young New Zealand men who wanted to make a career in the navy, and whose parents could afford the expenses involved, had previously always joined the Royal Navy. Another thing which made Neil suspect to Mum was that he was in the Royal New Zealand Navy. She, like me, had not known that such a thing existed. This was not as ignorant as it seems. King George VI had created the Royal New Zealand Navy as a separate entity as late as 1941, as a mark of respect to all New Zealand sailors.

Mum knew the Royal Navy was a fine and noble institution. Occasionally a young New Zealand woman's photograph would feature in the bridal page of the *Free Lance* or the *Auckland Weekly*, under captions such as 'Naval Bride' or 'Over the Seas'. I had been to one of these weddings as a child. All that dressing up for the men as well as the ladies was bliss to an awestruck child in white gloves like those of the White Rabbit.

There was a certain sense of a coup in the air surrounding a girl from the Bay who was invited into matrimony by a Royal Naval Officer. Some mothers were proud their daughters would live in a revered and ancient place which their parents still called Home. Also, such officers were unlikely to be impecunious.

Neil, courage high and heart aglow, had joined the Royal New Zealand Navy in 1944 and left immediately for training in the Royal Navy.

By this time his leave was over and he joined his first New Zealand ship, HMNZS *Rotoiti*, which was soon to sail. From

Auckland he wrote a formal letter asking my father for my hand in marriage, which I thought quaint but pleasant. Dad replied in the affirmative and told me that he liked Neil and we would have bread and butter but not much jam. He also, rather endearingly, became over all Yo Heave Ho, and drained the Hastings library of all things nautical, beginning with a reread of *The Diary of Samuel Pepys*. He wanted to check his exact position under Charles the Second.

Mum said all she wanted was for me to be comfortable.

I thought this kind and said so.

Jill from Napier gave me advice. 'You must have something concrete – well, not exactly concrete – before he goes. Try a ring.'

I took leave from the laboratory and chuff-chuffed up to Auckland on the main trunk line. Neil met me and we chose the ring; he then put it on with suitable ceremony, or what ceremony can be achieved when putting on a ring inside a jeweller's shop, but yes, Jill was right.

HMNZS *Rotoiti* sailed at 1100 next morning for a year in Korean waters. Neil was due to go on to England from Korea five months later to do a specialist course in navigation. The navy's plan was for him to go straight from Korea to Portsmouth, but Neil had other plans. After strong arguments on both sides, his prevailed. He would fly back to Hawke's Bay at the end of April, marry me on the fifth of May, and we would sail for England ten days later in the New Zealand Shipping Company ship RMS *Rangitoto*.

Seven months was a long time but a year in a war zone was longer. I realised that as I saw the dazed faces of young mothers with wailing children clinging to their fathers' bell bottoms as the ship prepared to leave. Things seemed oddly formal as I stood about with miserable strangers, though I noticed that the women and children looked much more miserable than their men.

Someone had given me a book when we were engaged called *The Grey Mistress*, written by a wealthy South African woman who, when her mink was lost, wrote to Daddy for another. She had married a man in the Royal Navy and stressed the importance of sailors' wives wearing brave faces on these occasions. Buck up, stiffen the sinews, etc. Looking around the crowded wharf I knew

I would have to stop being hopeless, absolutely hopeless, or worse, simply not safe.

Neil introduced me to various wives. We smiled at each other and left it at that. Periodically a voice from the ship roared an order and uniformed men leapt to obey. The one I liked best was 'Six hands to inboard bread'. The bread was inboarded before it had a chance to notice what had happened to it.

The final roar was 'All Aboard'. Neil kissed me, turned to go and came back. 'Only seven months,' he said over the hug. Feeling faintly sick I agreed, 'Only seven.' Then watched his back disappearing up the gangway.

Neil's previous captain was watching the ship leave and introduced himself. 'You're going to marry Lieutenant Anderson I understand, Miss Wright.'

'Yes.'

He nodded. 'He will go far in the service.'

'Oh, um, ah. Thank you.'

'Not at all. Good luck to you both. Goodbye.'

CHAPTER 16

Mum, having realised that 'this Wedding' – as she spoke of our coming nuptials in deep tones – would undoubtedly take place, began dealing with the situation in her usual competent way. It was, after all, her task, and Mr Noonan was already murmuring about the Wright wedding as he flung fabrics about on tables. My job at the laboratory continued, as did hers on the home front. One of her first jobs was to order the marquee for the front lawn of 609. 'Your father is so hopeless,' she explained, 'and they get booked up.' I murmured that he hadn't had much practice at ordering marquees and she replied, 'Thank God for that.'

She calmed down though and became happier as things hotted up, so much so that she began taking afternoon rests, not on her own properly made bed, goodness me no, but lying down in the sunporch, brain ticking, pad and pencil to hand. My father found her there one day on his return from the surgery and mentioned his problem. He really must have his hernia dealt with soon. Mum told me her answer over our Mah Jong fix that night.

'I said, "For goodness sake let me get this wedding over first."'

'And what did he say?'

'He agreed – Pung! Hurray. Mah Jong.'

St Matthew's church was booked and the Reverend Mr Button said he would be pleased to officiate on 5 May. I chose the hymns and went to see the organist, who was brisk. 'There is no need to fuss, Miss Wright, just name the hymns. Though I did decline one I was asked for last week. I felt it unsuitable.'

'Which one was it?'

'"Abide with me / Fast falls the eventide." I simply declined.'

Fabric was bought and fittings began in the house of my friend Miss Grant, in the presence of her Egyptian cigarette stand and her husband opening the door as usual.

'I wish it was all over,' I said one day. Miss Grant removed her mouthful of pins and stabbed them with vigour into the padded pinholder on her bust. 'It will be over soon, Barbara. And you'll make a lovely couple.'

Another problem solved.

I had shown Miss Grant my copy of the photograph Neil had had taken for his parents. The photographer of choice in Hastings was Mr Lovell-Smith in Heretaunga Street opposite Mr Redgrave's garden shop. Neil, who was wearing the cap and rig of a fully paid up lieutenant of the Royal New Zealand Navy, was surprised when an agitated woman rushed up to him saying, 'I'll only be a moment, Officer, just a second.' Neil smiled and assured her that her Morris would be safe for a minute or two. It was a good photograph and served us well, though I agreed with Mrs Anderson we could have done without the cap.

Time was ticking by and Mum continued to have everything under control. The bridesmaid's dresses for Shirley, Jane Wood and Pam were coming along nicely. Pam, with whom I shared the Sweeties at Watties canneries, was about to share the ship with us and required a few anti-sickness pills. Noel Wilson, a chemist and one of the Sunday tennis four my father played with, one of those who Mum described as 'four bald old buffers bounding around with bare knees', told Pam not to bother if she'd never been sick on the ferry. 'Barbara Wright had them by the bucketful. Ask her if you're desperate.'

Letters arrived from Neil in blue airmail envelopes and Mum left them waiting for me on the hall table beneath the painting of Colin's 'funny Jesus', Saint Sebastian.

There were also cables and telegrams. I miss telegrams; they were dramatic things, whizzing through the air with a whiff of *King's Messenger*, another serial, which like the rest of 3A, I listened to on the radio every Tuesday.

Some of my telegrams to HMNZS *Rotoiti* were more pragmatic.

'What size sheets are you getting?' asked Mum with a dangerous gleam in her eye.

'Double, I've ordered them from Westermans.'

'How do you know Neil will like them?'

'I guessed.'

'You must send a cable.'

I did. Why fuss?

There was one problem which was beyond Mum. The very thought of it was beyond her, it made her feel . . . No. She knew it was a mother's duty but . . . Honestly. The thought of it made her feel ill. She consulted her friend Peggy who lived on a nearby farm. Could she, would she, take on this dire mission? Peggy was also a friend of mine. She asked me whether I knew, well, did I know the facts of life?

I said yes I did thank you, and added that I had since I was eight at Waimarama and even the details hadn't put me off. Also I had learned zoology for three years. Every living animal does it, give or take one or two. 'There are diagrams,' I said.

'Diagrams?' squeaked Peggy.

I hugged her, told her not to worry. All would be well.

She told me it was just that she had never liked it much though of course the children were worth anything. Fortunately Henry had never been very keen and . . . How about a cup of tea? Oh yes, and had she told me she was organising a recipe book with the name of their farm stamped on the front and a contribution from all the women guests? Did I think that was a good idea?

I hugged her again. She was very huggable, Peggy.

All was ready and in its place except the bridegroom. Neil's progress from HMNZS *Rotoiti* to Hastings was complicated. He said goodbye to the ship and all who sailed in her at Sasebo, Japan, where they were enjoying R&R. Then he went by train and car to the Commonwealth Air Terminal at Iwakuni, where he was granted an official hitch on an RAAF plane heading for Australia via Manila and Darwin. Sydney was achieved the next day and he caught a flying boat to Auckland, then an NAC plane to Gisborne. The plane was late. Undeterred, Mr Anderson, who had flown up from Napier to meet him, persuaded the airport people to speed both of them to the airport fence and the waiting railcar *en route* to Napier. And thus to Hastings.

The day before the Day a cable of good wishes from HMNZS *Rotoiti* was sent to 609 by the Hastings Post Office. Mum answered the telephone and took down the message from a female voice. Having finished, the voice said, 'And we're all hoping for a fine day tomorrow, Mrs Wright.' Which was kind, but ignored by the gods.

The great day dawned pouring with rain, so much that the reception was transferred to St Matthew's parish hall where

Wendy and I had stood during the St Matthew's parish concert and recited our total flop by Rupert Brooke.

Now my brother David stood resplendent at the door ushering guests into the parish hall which had been decked with a bounty of flowers destined originally for the marquee and rearranged by the exhausted C.O. Flowers and her helpers. David took his spiel from the hustlers at the sideshows of the Hawke's Bay Agricultural and Pastoral Show. 'Hurry, hurry, hurry,' he roared. 'You'll see nothing on the outside.'

Photographs had been taken at 609, not in the squelch outside as planned, but indoors. Mum declined Mr Lovell-Smith's suggestion for a shot of the bride flanked by both parents. I was to have a photograph taken first with my mother dressed entirely in grey with an astonishing hat resembling a grey flamingo about to take off from its nest, long neck arching one side, long legs sticking out the other.

My father wore a grey waistcoat but looked more cheerful.

I remember little of the ceremony except that naval uniforms are flattering and that I was presented afterwards with both my marriage certificate and passport by the Reverend Mr Button.

The reception, over which Mum had worked herself into a continuous frazzle, was a glorious scrum, a true-blue heads-down Hawke's Bay scrum. And by no means a Hawke's Bay picnic. Jammed together, men met women and women met men and both shrieked with joy. Gaiety was the message of the day, added by the presence of eight officers from a Canadian cruiser berthed in Wellington.

Mr Brown, another of Dad's tennis four, who doubled as the mayor of Hastings, had heard of the ship's visit to the Bay. Might it not be a good idea to invite some officers to Hastings for the weekend? Enough to form a guard of honour with their swords, that sort of thing?

Drunk with goodwill and with his newfound love of all things naval Dad agreed with enthusiasm. By this time Mum was beyond worrying about catering and also welcomed the idea. She had always been good at flirting, and, like Jetta, who was now in London, took a healthy interest in new men. And the Canadians, especially the French Canadians, responded happily to new women. I heard one murmur to Pam Cashmore, 'I shall always remember Hastings by your beautiful –' (moment to check) '– blue eyes.'

All the staff from the laboratory were there except Alfred, who told me they didn't do that sort of thing. Mr Rankin told me I would be missed for the cryptic quotations. Dr Somerville gave me a kiss, which was a surprise, as did Bill, which was not.

Yes, it was a good party. Nevertheless I changed into Miss Grant's 'going away' coat and skirt as soon as it was decent. I felt we were wasting time, and wanted to say hullo to Neil.

Mum flung herself into my arms, her hair immaculate, her eyes wet.

Jill from Napier told me later that one of the more Rabelaisian of my father's colleagues had lifted a glass after the confetti had settled and proposed a toast: 'Here's to a beautiful consummation.'

He need not have worried.

Neil's parents drove us to that disappointingly unsophisticated city, Wellington, where we boarded RMS *Rangitoto* and sailed overseas. As usual we stopped at their favourite picnic place to eat sandwiches and drink tea from the thermos. It was considered foolish to stop at tea shops when one could make better sandwiches oneself. There were no cafés *en route* and going into a pub for lunch was unheard of.

Neil and I returned to the back seat feeling well fed and happy. I put out my left hand to his and snatched it back. It had gone, my beautiful engagement ring had disappeared, gone the way of all. I felt physically sick for hours. The moment we were alone in Wellington I flung myself at him. He responded with enthusiasm. 'No, no, you don't understand. I've lost my ring. It's disappeared.'

He looked at me calmly. 'So it's disappeared. Don't worry, it's insured. We'll buy another one when we arrive. Worse things have happened at sea. Come here.'

Such sense. Such beautiful sense. Such acceptance of lapses.

Later I found a second-hand one in Brighton where Prinny pranced among his discarded cravats and my parents heard Colin had died.

*

The long and bitter dispute between the shipowners and the watersiders was at its height when we boarded RMS *Rangitoto*.

Depending on their beliefs, people spoke either of the Strike or the Lockout. All our farming friends thought the wharfies were holding the country to ransom, as did my father. But Mum was so engrossed in getting 'this Wedding' over and done with she put the situation to one side with Dad's hernia. She would make up her mind about it later. I was as bad. All I wanted was to get onto the boat with Neil immediately and go overseas with him.

The armed forces had been moved in to work the wharves but obviously there were no handlers for luggage. We carried our luggage and took turns to roll a sealed tin containing the second layer of our wedding cake. Once on board Neil revealed his cure for seasickness, which was to drag me onto the deck in any kind of weather and pound around in the bracing air. This, plus the new anti-toss pill, worked. Sea voyages with a new and friendly husband are to be recommended.

Overseas is a word loaded with emphasis for Antipodeans. It is where we go when we leave home. We never go abroad, whereas to the British that is any place in the world where they happen to be, from Paris to Cotopaxi, from the Yukon River to Papua New Guinea.

Those who sailed the seas to 'make new lives' in other countries looked forward to the day when they went Home to have another look. Not to stay there, necessarily, but to see where they came from, to 'find their roots' again in ancient places. In Britain the whole place seemed old. It reeked of age, from castles to slums, to picturesque thatched cottages around the common, complete with duck pond and upending ducks.

My parents probably belonged to the last generation of New Zealanders who treated Britain with such reverence, like children who looked upwards to benign but distant parents.

Our cruise on a luxury liner ended in June when RMS *Rangitoto* berthed in Southampton. There we were met by Aunt Lillias and her husband Captain Egbert St Bede Kirkley, neither of whom I had seen since I was eight. One glance and I was glad our cake had been stowed in the Not Wanted on Voyage section of the hold. Two nutters trundling a tin cake in their direction would not have been a good arrival.

Aunt Lillias (now reduced to Lillias by request) had done her best for David and me when Colin died and Egbert had always been friendly, but when I saw her tweed coat and skirt and suitable hat with its suitable small feather I knew she had not changed. She had always been scared of difference; now she had a wider range of horrors to avoid, a more subtle refinement in clothes, behaviour and ideals. Firmer views on wrong religions, wrong political parties and stupid, stupid voters.

Before the war she and Egbert had gone abroad every year. One had to be careful of course, the French had always been odd, but even then some places had been filling up with trippers. The only other comment I ever heard about her pre-war holidays was that one drank a lot of coffee abroad and you couldn't get a good cup of tea for love nor money.

Egbert had been too old to return to the 3rd Carabiniers during the war but Lillias went back to nursing, and became matron of a small local hospital. Like Mum, Aunt Lillias was a proper nurse. Her photograph in uniform showed a strong eye, her nursing medal worn proud and high and a starched white veil perched on her once Titian hair.

She had also learned fine distinctions expected of an ex-army officer's wife within shooting distance of Sandhurst. She would run her finger over invitations to endless sherry parties, and occasionally a 'Drinks 6.00–7.30'. Usually the pasteboards were engraved and she could relax. If the message was merely printed she would sigh 'I wasn't sure about her but he seems all right. I suppose we should go. What do you think, Egbert?' Egbert would look up and reply, 'I'm sure you're right, dear.' She would pick up an invitation as it plopped onto the front doormat and inspect it with interest. 'I see Lady Wetherspoon is having her sherry party late this year, Egbert.' To which Egbert, still behind the *Times*, would murmur, 'Ah.' And their routine would drift on, gentle as falling snow.

Lillias had never returned to New Zealand since she left and obviously the bonds which tied had snapped. 'You people out there have no idea what it was like here during the war. Not an idea in the world.' To which I agreed. They had earned their smooth routine, part of which involved their Rover. The poor thing had been up on bricks during the war and now they obviously felt it only decent to give it an occasional run, and, time permitting, a good run.

The towns of Bagshot and Camberley follow each other on the London road. The road sign which indicated then when Bagshot was about to appear read *Bagshot welcomes careful drivers.* Nothing as soppy as that for Camberley. The driver knew who was in charge when the next town's sign appeared. *Camberley and Frimley District. No accidents please.* We should be grateful for the 'please'.

Matrimony remained satisfactory and here was a brave new world to explore. Here was a country I thought I knew about from books and more books, from parents and grandparents and teachers. Here was the land of opportunity that our best brains had been emigrating to throughout the years and had seldom come back. The instinct to bend the knee had faded for our generation. For our forebears it had been instinctive. Even after a long gruelling war we knew this was the place to be: better, bigger, older. But not forever.

Like thousands of other overseas visitors my first visit was to London. Neil was eager to show me everything: Buckingham Palace, churches which contained the histories of centuries, Trafalgar Square with Lord Nelson up high above the Landseer lions and voracious pigeons below. All these I recognised and had expected. Unexpected pleasures were recognising advertisements I knew from *Punch*, when Dad was still 'getting it for the surgery'. I had grown up with them, right back to my 'What's funny about this one, Daddy?' 'Let me see, ah yes. This one is funny because . . .' The advertisements I liked best were for Guinness, blown up to giant size on sky high hoardings. Guinness was undoubtedly good for you. Two cheerful large-beaked birds said so. 'See what Toucans can do.' Wrightie had started me on advertisements and London was good at them. Bigger, better, wittier.

I knew about the parks too. The 'lungs of London' were not forgotten, nor the bright red double-decker buses. Mum must have bought a Dinky Toy version of one for Colin – he was still at the 'brrm brrm' stage – but it was too late and the bus lay hidden away in the chest of drawers on the upstairs landing.

Red buses sent us to Kensington, that haven for museums. The first one for me was the Natural Sciences to inspect the stuffed dodo, the last remaining one in the world, or perhaps the one who didn't get away. Neil was more impressed by the giant Foucault's pendulum hanging in the ceiling.

Next we bought a 1936 Baby Austin which served us well when looking for somewhere to live, close to HMS *Dryad*, the Navigation School. Once again we were lucky and found a place in Wickham, an attractive village near Portsmouth. I knew about the man after whom the village was named. Somewhere in his treasure hoard of useless information Dad knew that William of Wickham's motto was 'Manners Maketh Man', a sentiment of which my father also approved. He also knew that William became Bishop of Winchester, founded Winchester College and bequeathed the school his motto.

We rented the upper storeys of Lower Wickham Lodge, which was owned by a major in the marines and his wife. Their parents, Major and Mrs Duncan (NTRN), owned and lived in the lower storey. These two storeys had once been united and used as the living quarters of the staff of the big house, Wickham Lodge. At some stage a high brick wall had divided the two buildings. Our side was Georgian, plain as a large house could be, the other side Early Victorian, more elaborate and embellished with window sills and a portico above the front door.

We never saw the people next door, try though I might with twitchings of curtains. You can't find out much about semi-detached neighbours with a high wall dividing you. Nor did we know their names. All we ever saw was an occasional glimpse of the top of the red Royal Mail delivery van appearing twice a day.

Major and Mrs Duncan's small lawn at the back was divided from ours but not with much effect. We could see them in their cane chairs beyond the privet hedge and presumably they could see us flopping about on our patch and me sneezing when the privet was in flower. Below us both was a large lawn which must have once been a tennis court, though not, presumably, for the staff. It was our responsibility to keep this area cut with an antique hand lawnmower. The court seemed noticeably larger when Neil was at sea, and I was in charge of the brute.

An unexpected joy for us both was a handsome kowhai. This specimen was espaliered, which we had never seen at home, against a white Georgian wall. It must have been very old; the top layer lay not far from our bedroom window.

The Duncans were fond of our tree but had no idea what it was.

We told them with pride. 'It is a native New Zealand tree. A kowhai.'

They told us we should see it in the spring when it was covered with beautiful yellow flowers. We said we would look forward to seeing that.

Major Duncan also told us Wickham Lodge, both Upper and Lower, had once belonged to a captain in the Royal Navy. Around the eighties, nineties, somewhere like that. He must have bought the kowhai home with him. 'Sensible to have planted it on the south side,' said the Major.

Mrs Duncan said she liked the idea that both their tenants and their pretty tree came from the same place, and didn't Henry agree? Major Duncan, like Egbert, courteous at all times, agreed.

I had hoped that Sir Joseph Banks might have brought it home as a seedling as one of the botanical treasures he collected during his journey to the Pacific with Captain James Cook in 1770. I imagined Banks potting up our kowhai, tending it. A good word, tending. I realised a two-hundred-year-old kowhai was unlikely but, as I have said, romancing doesn't do any harm.

Neil preferred the RN captain for the role of tending and potting. Like all sailors, James Cook was his hero, and one is either a Cook man or a Banks man. Botanists laud Banks for his achievements in discovering so many new species of plants and the precious collections he left to the British Museum, whereas navigators, explorers and geographers vote for Cook. To them Banks is a wealthy amateur scientist who made Cook's life more difficult than it already was with the demands he made on the son of an agricultural labourer who had joined the Royal Navy and had happened to have a reputation for scientific skills.

J.C. Beaglehole sums up the situation in his book *The Life of Captain James Cook* when he mentions their dissension over landing in Dusky Bay in the South Island. Banks wanted to go in there for a botanical exploration and maintained a permanent grievance that Cook would not. What was a day or two's fair wind against the interests of science, thought Banks. The captain had reason enough and knew a great deal more about winds than Banks did. Also he was responsible for his ship and his company.

Major and Mrs Duncan, like Lillias and Egbert, lived in contented retirement and clockwork routine, though the Duncans had no car, or none we ever heard of. Twice a week at 10am exactly they set off arm in arm down the gentle slope to Wickham Square, where stately Georgian houses ringed the space. In front of them were village shops. There were two ironmongers, who carried on a vendetta as to which had stolen the other's customers, and a pub on the corner which I never entered until I marched in to buy a small bottle of ale for putting in Aunt Lillias's Christmas pudding. On the other side were a chemist, two grocers (more rivalry), a doctor, a stationery shop and, most wooed and cherished of all, a butcher. Rationing was still in force, and according to Mrs Duncan, the meat ration was now more minuscule than ever.

Having collected and paid for their pittance of mince from Mr Brown, the butcher, Major Duncan and his wife headed up the road to Lower Wickham Lodge. Several miles beyond was the handsome city of Winchester.

Their hot lunch finished, they had 'our little nap' then off they set once more, arm in arm, each with the assistance of a stick, both sporting a silver ferrule and hers further adorned with a fine leather tassel. I watched them with interest from our wide windows. Sticks in the Bay were for the halt and the blind; here they seemed to have different functions, more evidence of their owners' ease, useful to lift for pointing, to swing along with panache. They demonstrated that their owners had time, lots and lots of time. Mum and her friends would never admit to having time, let alone enough of it to go for a walk for pleasure. If asked how they were some would reply, with a slight indrawing of breath and sagging of shoulders, 'Busy, very busy.' Busy is not how you're feeling about the world, it is what you are doing. Major and Mrs Duncan had also survived the long horrors of the war, of years of rationing and blackouts and bombing, and they had come through to enjoy their gentle days together.

They were an interesting and unexpected pair. The Major was English to the back of his straight backbone. He had met his wife when his regiment was stationed in Egypt after the Kaiser's War.

He was then in his thirties, she seventeen and as beautiful as the dawn. I know this because when we became friends she told me everything, including the fact she had good cheekbones. 'They are essential for looks to last,' she said, patting hers affectionately. 'For the face to hang on.'

She told me what a shock life in England had been, the chilly reception from Henry's parents, the loss of the warmth of her large and adoring family and friends. 'The first, the very first meal I had with Them –' (her in-laws were always Them) '– there was vermicelli custard. Pasta worms in custard for pudding. Think! Think! The shock.'

She was an excellent cook and told me how to make the best spaghetti bolognese in the world. 'Don't worry about the mess in the kitchen, Barbara. You can always tell *una cucina inglese*, an English kitchen. They have no soul, *inglesi* women.'

In the same way, a French housemaid can always tell whether an unmade bed has been used for love or for money. 'Love,' Mrs Duncan said firmly, 'is messy is it not Barbara? No mess, *no love*.'

'Oh, yes. Ah, yes.'

She was frank also about how she had coped with the endless queues of wartime. 'I just elbowed myself to the front saying "Scusi, scusi" and they are like sheep, *inglesi*, they move away, well mostly. But Henry couldn't look. He always left me to get everything, went outside. Him a brave soldier with an MC in the trenches. Imagine!'

Mrs Duncan and Mum could have been friends despite their differences. Both had lived their lives as beautiful women, were generous, strong minded, good cooks and good at laughter, though I don't think the after-effects of passion on laundry would have cropped up.

CHAPTER 17

From the time we arrived in Lower Wickham Lodge I had been learning how to cook. Peggy's recipe book contained the favourites of experts but many of them were designed for hungry farmers in a land of plenty. I learned useful things such as to how to achieve crackling on a leg of pork (you must give it a blast of high temperature at the end) and that a quart of cream should not be overwhipped. Each morning I selected one suitable recipe to be shorn down to a *one pea and one bean* meal within the bounds of rationing. I found imagination is useful in cooking, also that if you can read you can cook. It is not an arcane mystery, all it takes is dedication and time, and I had plenty of both.

Also John Lehmann had begun to publish Elizabeth David's forthright – in fact crisp – cook books for gastronomes with their heads screwed on. It pleased me years later to find her publisher was the same man who published *Penguin New Writing*, where R.A. Copland found Frank Sargeson's stories in a British military hospital during the war.

One asset in breaking the code of cooking, and in fact anything, was having Neil around. Of course I could cook, I was wonderful, I could do anything, though he wasn't quite so sure about my driving. 'You don't need to pull out the choke when you're going up hills. In fact don't. Otherwise you're coming along nicely . . . Christ!'

I refused to be daunted. I had to drive to Fareham, not for its charm but to see two New Zealand friends, one married to a Royal Navy man and one to a schoolie in the New Zealand Navy. Both became good friends, especially Jackie. We got off to a good start the first time we arrived at their rented house. The sight of unending length emerging from the Austin's low squatness made her laugh. Like Mum and Mrs Duncan, much made Jackie laugh, she was also good at it. She also taught me many things: everything I know about the gentle art of coping, which is useful for naval wives; also dressmaking, and how to shop sensibly. She was older than me and her memories of the Depression were sharp. Her good sense and wit flowed in all directions. 'Me? Cook a dinner on Sunday?

Certainly not. If Stanny gets pangs on Sunday Stanny knows what to do about it.'

How wise, how carefully followed.

She was also a compulsive reader and we agreed that local libraries were a sad disappointment. They didn't even have Katherine Mansfield. And the Jane Austens were worn out. Well, of course they would be, but you don't expect that, not in good libraries like home. Winchester was good but there you had to get used to sombre buildings and po-faced librarians. However, Winchester was the place where Jane Austen had died and thus a pilgrimage must be made to gaze at her plaque in the Cathedral cloisters. Jackie read all six of her novels once a year and we had heated discussions as to which was the best. She was shocked at the irreverence of the English reader in general, having read somewhere that an unnamed book came back to an unnamed library with a kipper between pages 186 and 187. Presumably both reader and kipper had passed on at the same moment, or so she hoped.

Why I don't know but I moved on from fiction to biography in Fareham and became knowledgeable about male English writers. Many had similarities. They began with distant parents, kindly nannies and night lights, and progressed through nurseries and on to prep schools, where they were bullied, and public schools, where many had their first homosexual experiences. Then universities (preferably Oxford or Cambridge), where lives blossomed and wits and intellects met others of the same calibre, where muddied oafs and flannelled fools were rejected and debagging was frowned upon.

What I should have been doing was to see if I could write something myself, instead of sending long letters home to feed Mum's famished letterbox. She told me frequently she lived for it, panted for letters, they were her whole life. As I enjoyed writing letters and she enjoyed receiving them the twice-a-week routine continued.

When we arrived home in the Bay I asked for them to check an address but she had thrown them out. Like the woman in W.H. Auden's poem 'The Shilling Life' who was adored by the greatest figure of his day, who 'could whistle; would sit still . . . answered some / of his long marvellous letters but kept none'. My letters were not marvellous but I would like to see them now, to see how I tried to describe the places as I walked for miles around Wickham, soaking in the greenness of the fields and the beauty of the deciduous trees: oaks, elms, chestnuts, walnut, sycamore, beech. I knew them all of course, not only from botany but also from the early ones imported to New Zealand by homesick pioneers, but these were different, hundreds of years of difference. I also knew them from Illingworth's drawings in *Punch* as backgrounds for country cricket matches, which Wendy and I also knew in Cornwall Park.

Deciduous trees are no more beautiful than our indigenous ones but they carry the benefits of change. I had watched the difference from the Napier bus, seen the changing of the seasons in the Clive orchards, but it is better to watch this recurring miracle on your feet. Not only the trees demanded attention but also the beauty of the cut hedges and stone walls and picturesque villages. All were new, except as scenes on calendars. Once I admired a thatched cottage to a woman standing at its door.

'Huh,' she said. 'You tell the owner that. Wet like a duck in the winter it is.'

It was not until two or three years later that I longed for an untidy landscape, an empty road stretching for twenty miles without a car in sight. Space, emptiness, and especially space, take a while to pine for. In the same way we sailed through our first English winter. It was later, our second or third, before the snow lost its wonder. You never see slush on Christmas cards, and snow chains became essential and 'greasy Joan doth keel the pot . . . and coughing drowns the parson's saw'. But you know the rest.

One pleasure never failed. I was surprised and pleased to find the number of beautiful men in Her Majesty's Navy. They were probably no more beautiful than in the Bay, but *en bloc* and in uniform they were impressive. Certainly they were better dressed – it is hard to go wrong in a dark navy uniform. They were also attentive hosts, either in ships or shore establishments, and seemed to enjoy talking to women. As one aware of Hawke's Bay picnics I found this both pleasant and flattering. I loved each and every one.

Another matter of interest was that some of their wives were not beautiful to match. Some of them were, I'm sorry to use the word, *plain*, and I don't think dark uniform would have helped.

It never did much for the WRNS and that hat was a disaster. To make things worse, some of the above wives were also lacking in politeness, let alone charm. J.M. Barrie had a word for the latter: 'Charm is a sort of bloom on a woman'. And if you have it you don't need anything else. A *jolie laide* can charm the birds from the trees but a touch of amiability is required.

I discussed all this with Mrs Duncan. Her theory was that some *inglese* men would marry a woman with good connections and money no matter if they looked like a camel, though she was generous enough to say she had never seen one spit. Marrying for money in the Bay was unheard of, though I knew it happened from novels. How could such beautiful men do such a dire thing?

Another moment of patriotism shone when Neil was playing in the HMS *Dryad* rugby team against Aldershot. I watched with well-wrapped-up and camel-coated wives. A trench-coated man said to a nearby linesman, 'Excellent lock over there.'

'Yes,' said the linesman. 'New Zealander.'

'Ah, yes. Rugger and sheep.'

'Three sheep per person,' I said, 'but we're trying to catch up.'

The coats melted away.

There were other differences. If you were renting your house in New Zealand and a doctor and a naval man both wanted it, the likely winner would be the doctor. Nothing wrong with the naval officer but the doctor would be a 100% payer. As of course would the naval officer but . . . but the doctor must *never* slip. His reputation must not fail, cannot for a second. In England it would be the other way round. Why?

One week Neil and I were in a pub with New Zealand friends (it was safe if escorted by men and I took every opportunity to do so). The cheerful barmaid, hearing our accents, asked where we came from. Our friend sat upright on her stool and patted her hair. 'I,' she said, 'am married to a New Zealand doctor.'

'Oh yes.' And you dear?' she asked Neil.

'I'm in the New Zealand Navy.'

The barmaid beamed, 'Now isn't that lovely, dear. I didn't know they had one.'

'They certainly do.'

'I'm sure they do, and a lovely one too, I bet.'

*

Neil had been appointed to HMS *Vanguard*, and there was a hiatus of three weeks before the ship was due to return to Portsmouth. The Admiralty followed their usual routine for 'gash personnel' and sent him on another course, a three-week Joint Anti-Submarine course in Londonderry, Northern Ireland. And yes, I could go too if we paid my expenses. We sailed overnight to Belfast and on to Derry where we were booked into the Moville Hotel, which had seen better days, and gave me the impression it missed them. Though not us. Hotels were a novelty and we enjoyed unexpected treats. The only thing which gave me pause was the look of the bed, which was large and lumpy and dressed in shiny orange satin. 'Tashed'. Or worse. I made Neil get in first to see if anything had died down there. Assurance given, all was plain sailing.

After breakfast Neil went off to learn about submarines, leaving me to run upstairs, flop onto the orange bed and get on with *Tess of the D'Urbervilles*. I prefer to read on the horizontal, an atavistic preference which I like to think, in my more pompous moments, comes from reading only in bed during my formative years. All went well until I leapt upright each morning to greet the diminutive housemaid who appeared at varying times. With goodwill on each side we tried to communicate but could get little further than friendly smiles and gestures. This was a surprise to me. After all we were both speaking English, were we not? But with her brogue and my accent we never got much further than 'Good morning, Rosaleen', 'Good morning, Barbara'. After which I set off to explore my second island overseas. There was much to see; everything was so old with histories and battles old and far away. None of which I knew anything about except for the Great Famine in the 1840s and Gladstone's failed attempt at Home Rule in 1893. We didn't do Ireland at school and I knew little about its people except that most of them were Catholic and had the gift of the gab. I was also aware of the conflicts between Protestants and Catholics in Northern Ireland, but I didn't know till later that in the 1950s half a million left Ireland, nearly half of them for Britain.

On my way back to the hotel after my first exploration I stopped with mouth-hanging astonishment. High above me a red brick wall, which had been naked yesterday, now proclaimed in large black letters, 'Fuck the Pope.' I had never seen 'fuck' written before. It was swearing *in excelsis*, something to be heard behind the bike sheds by a tough kid confronted by a flatty, when all the air had gone to the top of his tube. And here it was in huge letters for all to see. And how had he or she risked getting it up there? They must have meant it, have had the courage of their convictions.

Things were different in Ireland.

Next day I set off with the guidebook like a fully paid-up tripper to complete the circuit of Derry's ancient walled city by walking along the top of their walls. The day was fine, the locals friendly and their instructions interesting. 'The river dear? Just around the next corner and she'll be waiting for you.'

We crossed the border to visit Buncrana where we overate on large Irish steaks with sourdough bread and loved every minute of it. On the morning after our return a waiter appeared in the dining room with news that I had a visitor in the foyer. Surprised and pleased, I left my soggy cereal and went to meet the stranger, a seven-foot-high officer of the Royal Ulster Constabulary. An impressive sight in a dark olive greatcoat, made more so by a large revolver in the black holster on his belt, he handed me a letter I had posted to 609 Roberts Street.

'How do you do, Madam. This letter was found nearby. We had to open it so we could return to the writer.'

'But I remember posting it.'

'I think not, Madam,' said the officer. He saluted smartly and departed.

The last paragraph of the letter read, 'We go to Buncrana tomorrow and hope to return laden with contraband.'

Neil joined HMS *Vanguard* and I met loneliness for the first time. It was a time of disillusionment; I had always thought I was self-sufficient, not in practical ways, but happy on my own if there was the proverbial good book to hand. A thinking radish, that was me, never bored if I were present, let alone lonely.

It was also disappointing to find that time alone does not produce inspiration. I wrote bad poems but I had done that for years. Being lonely as a cloud didn't seem to make them any better. However, life in Hampshire remained interesting. So many differences in large and small things, from the different dialects of English, to the numbers of newspapers available, ranging from the *News of the World* to the stately *Times*, when at home then it was a case of one size fits all, and none on Sunday. Their small town libraries were worse than ours, their museums sublime, their food less and their winters colder. People seemed less friendly but if the shell cracks the English are the best friends in the world. Or as good as us, and we have a few duds.

I had been introduced to one nearby ('You're a New Zealander, you must meet Pauline'). If you want to or not. I did and on a drear Sunday I trailed up the road and rang the bell in search of humanity.

Pauline answered. 'Yes?' she said.

Vacuum. Total vacuum.

'I wondered if I could come and see you for a little while,' I stammered. But the door was not flung wide. I looked at her moustache of icing sugar (sponge, dry, bought, I bet) on her upper lip. Pauline was taking part in that sacred custom, tea, with her English stockbroker husband and I had trespassed.

'I'm sorry,' she said, the icing sugar lifting in little puffs as she spoke, 'but we're busy at the moment.'

Beware of New Zealanders who anglicise.

I wrote to 609 Roberts Street that night with the news that I was pregnant. Mum wrote back immediately. Yes, it was time I had my babies. She added the welcome news that my father would pay for a New Zealand Karitane nurse for the first two weeks of the infant's life, as I was a long way from home and she supposed Neil would be away in 'that wretched boat': the wretched boat being Her Majesty's Ship *Vanguard*, the pride and glory of the Royal Navy.

Sheila and Jackie rallied to the cause and Jackie increased her dressmaking lessons. My triumph was a bright red maternity jacket and a navy blue skirt. The fashion in maternity circles in '52 was to have the jacket large enough to cover a slim (yes, slim) skirt. The secret for achieving this was to have a large U-shaped scoop in the skirt for expansion in the affected area. The breakthrough did not last. Think what would happen if the jacket lifted.

I avoided such hazards but my skirt and I had some dicey moments when assisted down companionways by courteous men standing below, ready to offer a steadying hand. I came from a generation of little girls who blushed when little boys cried 'Poppy show' at a glimpse of bloomers and later thanked young men for whispering if one's petticoats showed so we could scuttle away to correct this, thus avoiding sartorial shame. Navy blue bloomers and wayward petticoats were nothing to the revelations my Ubergap could reveal.

It was said that pregnancy had come out of the closet in the fifties. The condition was after all, a fact of life. It was not, however, yet something of which one could be visibly proud. Queens and Princesses still 'cancelled their engagements' and employers such as in department stores expected their employees to retire before they looked unseemly. And you never saw bloated air hostesses enquiring 'Tea? or Coffee?' when this was still a glamorous career.

HMS *Vanguard* was now operating out of Invergordon and Neil suggested a break from Lower Wickham Lodge might be a good idea. He made a booking in the type of boarding house now extinct, places run by firm landladies with strict rules to be obeyed by both casuals and permanents, or take the consequences.

Several other wives were staying in Invergordon and once again we were surrounded by interesting and beautiful men whose sole aim seemed to be make sure we were all happy while on board. We were. It was on board *Vanguard* that I first breathed my affection for wardrooms. On Sunday evenings guests were invited to what was called 'an informal supper', after which a film was shown. I have always enjoyed Sunday evenings since Jackie's advice and these evenings had all the ingredients. Good company, good food not prepared by me (and certainly not by our hosts), and a good film. The duty of the attending staff seemed to be somehow both friendly and invisible.

It was in Invergordon also that I met my first whiff of female protocol. The wives were standing on the jetty waiting for the coxswain to arrive with the picket boat to take us out to the ship when I heard an earnest female voice say, 'Who is the senior wife?' Did she mean the oldest? Surely not. Neil explained later. The most senior officer gets into the boat last and gets out first. He hadn't thought this would or could happen with wives but he supposed it could.

'It did.'

'She's an admiral's daughter. She must have learned such things early.'

Back in Hampshire Stan Hermans showed his valour by escorting two heavily pregnant women, Jackie and me, to the Fareham cinema. The sewing machine was red hot.

Lillias did her bit. She kept in touch, gave Egbert and the Rover a run down to Wickham occasionally, but stopped asking me up to Camberley until 'afterwards'. Once we went to Portsmouth but that was not a success. 'This place is full of pregnant women.'

Sheila Lane, whose husband was also at sea, said she would be happy to stay with me for the last fortnight and drive us to the nursing home in nearby Shawford when required. As we cruised along through chilly Hampshire lanes in February she said casually, 'I suppose you feel like a new girl at school?'

'Yes.'

A sensation which increased when I waddled into the delivery room and saw the small garments warming in front of a gas fire exactly like the one in the dining room in 609. The nursing home was small and the staff kind. I suppose this gesture was to lift the heart of the incipient mother with joy. My reaction was different: pure alarm.

The doctor arrived and in the fullness of time Jeremy Neil Romaine Anderson arrived complete with a mass of black hair. Sheila sent telegrams to his father and grandparents and all was well. She also arrived to collect us both after we had been there for a week, the usual 'lying in' time in Hampshire in '53.

We stopped in Bishops Waltham (nice name) for me to pick up Jeremy's all-important ration book. I came back with it and glanced at him asleep in his carrycot. There was no one else responsible for this helpless scrap of humanity. I knew that, how could I not, but I found the situation alarming. *Me.* All I hoped was for him to stay asleep until we reached the safety of Nancy, the Karitane Nurse, waiting in Lower Wickham Lodge.

As I climbed into the car Sheila said, 'Is he still breathing?'

'Of course.'

'How do you know?'

Nancy the Karitane nurse was at the door to meet us. Noble,

wonderful, marvellous Nancy. She taught me everything about the wide world and joys of motherhood, starting gently by bringing Jeremy to me three times a night to be fed. She told me things as elementary as deburping. He was the best-behaved baby she had ever met, she said as she held his hand in hers and waltzed him around the kitchen. She knew the country I knew, a place of cows and sun and wide acres. One day she came up the stairs with the milkman's bottle in her hand saying, 'That rain's put the butterfat up.' I hugged her. We sang our favourite cowboy songs together between bouts of Perry Como, and the three of us went for brisk walks in plastic raincoats and cold mists. Nancy gave me all the confidence and love in the world, and pride in Neil's and my achievement. It was a sad day when she left. She was aware of it, leaving a message for Jeremy.

'Chin up, Jeremy. I am just a phone call away.' She was the best present Mum and Dad ever gave me.

Neil sent loving messages by cable from Gibraltar. He arrived home six weeks later, with the largest teddy bear available on the Rock, to a warm welcome from us both. He immediately became a rarity among English fathers we knew: what would now be called a hands-on father.

In June '53 Nancy appeared again to take care of Jeremy while I attended the Coronation Review in the Solent, when the newly crowned Queen Elizabeth II took the salute from ships representing her various navies and others, HMNZS *Black Prince* being our representative. It was a wonderful day, combining spectacle, drama and changing scenes as the Royal Yacht steamed along between the rows of ships, each one firing a 21-gun salute as she passed. There was the sense of being lucky to be there, amazement at the organisation involved and thanks for a beautiful day. Neil was about to leave *Vanguard* and I met his relief, a pleasant young RN Lieutenant with his equally charming wife and his witty mother. We were all up on the bridge, delightful, couldn't be better. Champagne as well. Excellent. And then the son began. 'I suggest you go down the companionway backwards, Mummy. It's safer.

'Well done, Mummy.'

'Quite comfortable, Mummy?'

Mummy assured him she was happy as a lark and looked it, and the Royal Review rolled on.

Jeremy also had his moment on board *Vanguard*. He was baptised in the ship's chapel by the Anglican padre whose long fingers flicked water onto the child's face from the upturned ship's bell which was acting as the font, a traditional baptism available only to the members of the ship's company and their offspring.

After the ceremony our guests, the padre, and some of Neil's shipmates moved on to the wardroom to wet the baby's head.

Jeremy was not present. Having opened calm eyes as the water trickled down his face he slept again. The admiral's flag lieutenant, William Stavely, offered his bunk near the wardroom and Jeremy slept beside an ancient, beat-up teddy bear. His owner became an Admiral of the Fleet. History didn't relate more of the bear.

Aunt Lillias and a now frail Egbert made their last run down to say goodbye and Mrs Duncan cried hot tears at the loss of her renting baby. All farewells made, we sailed for home. We divided our time between the swimming pool and the crèche, where Jeremy had an elaborately iced cake for his first birthday and won a prize (as an All Black) in the children's fancy dress.

The three of us hung over the rail as the ship swung around the entrance into Wellington and we watched the painted wooden houses flung against the steep hills above the harbour. These were our Hills of Home, the hills returned men saw first, the ones viewed with alarm by early immigrants. And not so early. 'You don't mean the houses are *all* wood?' asked a nervous voice beside us. We looked at her kindly.

Next morning I looked out from the hotel window at the galvanised iron sheltering the pedestrians beneath from rain and wind below. How practical. How sensible. How wise.

Neil was appointed to the survey ship HMNZS *Lachlan*. I suppose I must have asked my parents if Jeremy and I could live at 609 Roberts Street for a year or so but I have no memory of doing so.

Mum and Dad were delighted to see us but neither of them were enthusiastic about babies. Why should they be? We all take our pleasures differently, as Dad and others say. He himself was tolerant towards his grandchild and the newspaper was always a good means of retreat. Fortunately Jeremy was past the mewling and puking stage. Before long he was helping Mum to make her bed and wheeled an ottoman around her bedroom to cries of, 'Ticalator truck. Push, Nana.'

Then I broke my new news to her.

It was like a rerun of the scene when I told her I was going to marry Neil, though the set had changed. This time Mum was sitting up in bed finishing her pre-sleep routine as advocated by Louisa at the Elizabeth Arden counter. She had already removed the filth of daytime with cleansing lotions applied with swabs of damp cotton wool, and was now applying the nourishing cream best suited to the calibre of her skin. This process took some time and care, not a quick slap around the cheeks, but a careful upwards sweep with the backs of both hands, beginning at the neck. This was essential, according to Louisa. It was that dragging motion *downwards* that led to those dreaded wrinkles, though not for Mum and other users of Elizabeth Arden Orange Cream for overnight.

Routine finished, Mum put on her night hairnet, a heavy-duty variety, not the spider thin one she wore in daytime to keep her hair immaculate.

'Mum,' I said, 'I'm pregnant.'

'You're not!'

'I am!'

'You're mad! Stark raving mad.'

'I don't see why. And anyway I am.'

As before, when faced with ridiculous behaviour on my part, Mum calmed down and resumed our amiable relationship. Mah Jong began again, country friends reappeared on their way home to be greeted by Jeremy, a social animal from birth, calling, 'Come in, Peggy. Have a brangy.'

Friends were kind to the grass widow. One or two told me how guilty they felt not 'having me round', or 'out' if they lived in the country. Being told you make people feel guilty is one of the more dispiriting and infuriating comments people can make, but as usual my snarl was gentle.

Mum and Dad continued to be calm and Mrs Anderson, a woman with a friendly view on life and a devotion for babies, helped in all ways.

Life drifted on until a month before the baby was due. Jeremy and I had had a long session at Cornwall Park playground, and like all dictators he was reluctant to leave his empire and expressed his displeasure. I pacified him with a small licker from the kiosk and we headed home. By the gate where David hid his shoes before school it became obvious all was not well. Mum took one look at me and turned into Nurse Jackson. The ambulance arrived and I departed to the maternity wing at the hospital, leaving Mum and Dad and Mrs and Mr Anderson with an active and enthusiastic sixteen-month-old child. I lay in complete bed rest, reading all day except during visitors' hours which were equally pleasant. I worried about Jeremy until I found that he was delighted to see me but trotted off with whoever was in charge with every appearance of happiness. As for Mum, she bore up well apart from a few comments to the effect that I needn't think she would be available for this sort of thing ever again. Neil told me she was probably having the time of her life, but as his appearances were few and far between I felt his evidence was shaky. 'In peacetime surveyors' wives are the most left-behind of all naval wives,' he said airily.

Bella Landels, one of Hastings' beauties and wits, sometimes came with Mum to see me. She had been the joy of the Knitting and Sewing Society (renamed by my father the 'Sitting and Knowing') who had made comforts for our boys overseas during the war. I had loved going to Mrs Landels's house as a child. She had a picture of Napoleon looking grim with one hand in his coat, and at the end of her section her daughter Barbara had painted hollyhocks on the back fence, which seemed handsome beyond words. Bella also made presents for all her friends at Christmas and shocked me when I heard her say to Mum, 'Jessie Wright. If Jesus has another birthday I'm not going to his party.' She also said as they were leaving me one afternoon, 'Jessie Wright, they're not getting us in here again, that's one safe thing.'

Michael Piers Romaine Anderson's birth, according to the captain of the *Lachlan*, was one of the best arranged births he had ever known. The ship was surveying in Hawke Bay and Neil was able to get ashore to see me both during the afternoon when labour began and next morning to greet a brand new beautiful son, after which he sailed off with the *Lachlan*.

Christmas came and went. My father lifted his glass to Mum and me with Jeremy's latest greeting. 'Happy Heemus,' he said, and that was more or less that.

Neil's next posting was to HMNZS *Philomel* in Devonport as Queen's Harbour Master. Now we were home again we planned, like all New Zealanders, to own our own house. With this in mind we had bought a new car in England to sell when we arrived home. At that time the rough equation to buy a house went something like this: Three years of buyer's salary = price of house. Twenty-five Peter Terrace, our newish two-bedroom house perched on the last section of the street in Castor Bay, North Shore, cost £3000. Neil's salary was £1000 per annum. Perfect match.

Despite the match Neil was not able to get leave for the big move and the convoy set off from the Bay to Auckland. Mr and Mrs Anderson took off with Jeremy to be followed by Dad, Piers and me. The excursion remains a blur but we all arrived eventually, and Neil was there to greet us.

Twenty-five Peter Terrace was compact (as in tiny), sitting on stilts out over the valley and possessing a view of the sea and Rangitoto Island. The developer, as usual, had removed what topsoil remained, so my dream of a cottage garden faltered, but continued. The main problem for gardening on rotten rock is the lack of water. Castor Bay's water supply consisted only of rain water, which ran into tanks. This of course depends on the vagaries of nature and size of the tanks. We had four tanks. It had never occurred to us that this was not a great deal but it became obvious, especially when visiting friends would look down onto our four open galvanised iron tanks below and say something like, 'Cripes, they're getting low.'

We would have been in the direst of straits had it not been for Des, our neighbour across the road. He was a builder, had built the house he and Gay now lived in, and was the man who became the salt for our parched earth. He and Gay had acres of water hidden away in a big concrete tank beneath their patio. Nevertheless he made Neil a proposition. If Neil passed his heavy-duty driver's licence, Des would lend him his large work truck and a tank he happened to have at home. Neil could then drive to the Takapuna council hydrant, fill the tank, pay for it, return to Peter Terrace, and back down the steep rough slope until the truck was level with our nearly empty tanks. He would then toot the horn and Des would amble over, leap down the rough slope and pick up the piece of guttering he lent us on these occasions. He would then adjust the guttering for the water to run into our tanks. Operation completed, not a bucket wasted, and finished with a beer or two with Des and Gay on our front verandah.

When heavy rain falls Neil and I still nod at each other. 'Tank rain,' we say. Heavy rain is the best in the world when needed, but like others of nature's repertoire of opposites (rain/dry, sun/snow, flood/drought) can also be the worst.

Words have been written about the practicality of New Zealand men who achieve wonders with a length of number-eight wire and a tweak here and there. Thanks Des.

The boys and I enjoyed each other's company and we became used to climbing up the road from the beach. Our friends with cars knew where we were. As one of them said, 'It's good dropping in here. You're always home in the winter.'

The meetings and greetings with other naval wives and their husbands at HMNZS *Philomel*, Devonport, were limited for me. Buses and babysitters were thin on the ground in Castor Bay. One evening I do remember. A Scot on loan from the Royal Navy confided in me after a Vat 69 or two, that his problem was a certain New Zealand naval wife. 'She bosomed me against the coat-racks,' he said, 'and wailed, "Why are ye so cold to me?"' That was worth a few buses, and better still, Jock gave us a lift home that night.

In 1957 Neil was posted to Wellington. We sold the house, packed up, hugged Des and Gay and departed to rent a house in Eastbourne. Neil caught the bus with other commuters for the early morning scenic ride around the harbour to the capital. He had two offices there, one in the navy office and one in the army, I can't remember why.

Our cottage in Eastbourne was nearer the sea and there was no hill to climb. The boys and I lived on the beach all summer with other idle housewives. There is a lot to be said for doing the ironing in your bathing suit before, as Mum said, 'getting the meal on.'

'Summer time and the livin' is easy', or so we found at Eastbourne. Jeremy went to kindergarten and volunteered to mind the kindy bunny during the holidays. Piers and I spent a lot of time singing 'Day-o, Day-o' with Harry Belafonte. 'Come, Mr Tally Man, tally me banana' on the wind-up gramophone.

Mum and Dad came to see us, with acres of food, and were startled by the tartan carpet at the local hotel but otherwise happy.

The only time we felt the need of a motor was when we were bidden, with a few thousand other lucky citizens, to a garden party at Government House in honour of the Queen Mother. This required careful timing with babysitter, bus and meeting Neil (in full fig) at the corner of Stout Street at fifteen double O – not a moment later. I left plenty of time, but Wellington is windy and her corners are not kind to large-brimmed straw hats. I was a mess, so much so that Neil hailed a taxi, which was against his grain.

The Queen Mother, however, was in fine form, and looked as though she was enjoying every moment. Watching the faces on the other side of the aisle as she passed I could see smiles deepen into gormless gasps, then as she passed I felt my face muscles do the same. As the bus swept homewards, me with my mangled hat on my lap, we saw a large painted hoarding above the Ngauranga Freezing Works – 'Haere mai, haere mai te Queenie.'

CHAPTER 18

We returned to Britain three years after we had left, with RMS *Rangitoto* berthing at Southampton and spring bursting out once more. The only difference being the presence of two small boys jumping up and down with excitement, the absence of Lillias and Egbert, and no roll-along cake tin buried deep in the hold.

Dear gentle Egbert had died a few months before our arrival and Lillias's letter with the Queen's image in the right-hand corner had informed us, understandably, that she had no wish to go charging all over the country meeting people.

Like Neil, I was getting used to arrivals and departures. You were posted, you went, you arrived, and after a given time you were off again. Things were not so simple with dependants but now I felt I was becoming the Antipodean equivalent of an Old China Hand. We knew furnished rental places were easy to find in Hampshire, where naval men and their families were continually on the move. Clutching bag, hammock and a few treasures from home, off they were again, round and round the mulberry bush of the Admiralty's postings, some of which were good, some average and some stinkers.

This time Neil was to attend the Advanced Navigation Course at HMS *Dryad* and we were able to rent a small piece of what had once been a large Victorian manor near Swanmore, on the beautiful Hampshire Downs near Winchester.

Our manor had once been one of those large piles surrounded by parklands. Regrettably it was not still graced by grazing deer, nor were we guarded by endless stone walls topped with barbed wire to deter felons, or my favourite, my best of all, stone pineapples, those symbols of hospitality which topped high gates.

All such accoutrements of the wealthy pleased what Egbert used to call 'tootlers', by which he meant 'trippers in motors'. Many of the tootlers would stare with reverence at such piles as ours saying, 'So sad, so sad to see these beautiful old places being cut up', their inference being that in the good old days of mantraps and floggings they, the tootlers, would have been made welcome beyond the lodge gates.

Not in a stag's roar.

Another illusion tootlers had, or have, is that all such piles are beautiful. Not so, particularly those designed for baronial late Victorians like ours. However, we loved our bit of the pile. It had been divided into eighteen small homes, twelve of which were in the manor and six, including ours, in the stables nearby, which added a rustic and pleasing air to the establishment, which consisted of a large courtyard with the original coach house on the left and the houses around the other three sides. The stables of my equestrian days had been little more than wooden sheds with a few bridles hanging on the wall. All the romance and none of the ineptitude.

The other houses around the yard had been involved with the *gear and tackle and trim* plus maintenance and welfare of the horses who slept nearby.

Our two-storeyed houses had two or three bedrooms and were in beautiful surroundings. We felt particularly glad our diminutive sitting room looked onto the original peony walk. How could we not be proud? Thankfully it was out of sight of the coal bin round the corner which fed the Rayburn, the poor man's version of an Aga, and where I gave my weekly order to Mr Gander, a nice man and ambassador from the local grocer, who, although rationing had stopped, would begin each time, 'Let's start on the rations shall we Mrs Anderson?'

One day he mentioned his children. I asked him were they boys or girls? He replied he had one of each. I said that was nice. Mr Gander removed his pencil from his order book and sighed. 'Yes,' he said, 'it's nice to have all that sort of thing over and done if you see what I mean. Rations then, Mrs Anderson?'

There were some unexpected moments at Swanmore. Joan, an American who had married an RN officer and was mother of two boys the right age, told me that if I was lucky Mrs Croxley, the boss of the Mothers' Union, might ask me to join. Mrs Croxley did. In theory the only requirements to be a member were to be a churchgoer, a good mother, and united, but there was a noticeable division in the seating. Mrs Croxley sat behind the table in the church hall, with an offsider to take the notes. On her right side sat the non-village women, who lived in large houses some distance from the village among beautiful trees and absent children, and who said 'palay' when they meant 'polo' and 'haise' when they meant 'house'. Also they said 'specks' when they meant 'glasses', but that was easier to understand. They all adored the Union, as did the village members who sat on Mrs Croxley's left side, and who lived in the village with their children and had no beautiful trees.

Defeated by unknown placement I hovered middle back and hoped for the best.

I also loved the Union but in a milder way. Especially singing Blake's 'Jerusalem', which I had not met for some time. Who could resist it?

And did those feet in ancient time
Walk upon England's mountain green?

You bet. Though I was aware I was not the only member of the Union who failed to hit the high notes.

Other pleasures were occasional trips in a charabanc which took me back to Nimon's buses, though twice as large. The best trip I remember was to the embroidery section of the Victoria and Albert Museum, where a series of experts discussed the finer points of *Historical Designs for Embroidery: Linen and Cross Stitch* by Louisa F. Pesel, who happened to have been a good friend of Mrs Munro who lived nearby. For a pound donation to the Anglican church each week, the seekers after truth gathered at her house to learn. She was running out of pupils, she said, and made me welcome. She also told me that she didn't think she could have survived the war without Louisa's canvas work and the joy of long-legged cross stitch, and how glad she was to have taught both boys and girls in the village school and how several men who had joined the navy in the war had written to tell her the same thing. 'I wished Louisa would have known.'

I didn't tell her that after Virginia Woolf had drowned herself, her sister had found her bag of wool threads unbearably moving. There didn't seem any point, just something you remember while putting in the soothing thread and pulling it up again.

There were other feudal aspects of Swanmore which I had not met in Wickham and which I found interesting. The local Squire and his wife lived near our ex-stately pile. His children had long passed beyond the teaching of their governess and the school room remained empty. Mr and Mrs Squire, out of the goodness and charity of their hearts, had enabled Mrs Moore (NHRN), who lived nearby, to continue to teach a few local children the rudiments of reading, writing and arithmetic in the otherwise empty school room. Mrs Moore ran, in fact, a dame school, again one of those things I had met in books and was glad to see appear in real life.

Joan told me Mrs Moore had a vacancy and her son Michael loved every moment there and what about Jeremy? The school room was nearby, the fees minuscule and the local school miles away. 'What about Jeremy?' I asked Neil. 'They do that sort of thing here,' he murmured, knocking out his pipe.

There were other extra-curricular activities in Mrs Moore's school. When the cook was making the plum pudding weeks before Christmas, all those who were in the house, including Mr and Mrs Squire, Mrs Moore, the cook, all the indoor staff and finally the dame school pupils, were called to have a stir and drop in a threepenny piece. They also assisted in decorating the Christmas tree and gave an end of year concert for their benefactors. The ceremony was both real and archaic.

Neil was now posted to HMS *Saintes*, which at this time was in the Mediterranean. One cannot be lonely with small children around and I became enamoured of the Rayburn. We could come home cold and miserable at four o'clock on a winter afternoon to be greeted by warmth; welcome, true warmth.

We became enthusiastic fans of television, which was new to us. Before Jeremy went to school we lined up for *Listen with Mother.* In the drear dark November we were there, me in the middle and a boy either side. First came the music, and then our friend, our friend who could be relied upon, who would never let us down, come wind come weather, began.

'Good morning,' came the wide vowelled male voice, 'this is *Listen with Mother.* Are you sitting comfortably?' (in four syllables).

Jeremy and Piers wriggled their Antipodean behinds deeper on the sofa. 'Yers,' they said. It was a wise and beautiful moment. And this was only the beginning. Our favourite song was sung in a firm baritone:

There was a man lived in the moon, lived in the moon, lived in the moon,
There was a man lived in the moon, and his name was Aiken Drum.
And his breeches made of haggis bags, haggis bags, haggis bags.
And his breeches made of haggis bags, and his name was Aiken Drum.

'Do it again! Do it again!' they squealed. No fans were ever more ardent.

Later HMS *Saintes* (named after one of Nelson's victories in the Caribbean) and her crew were fighting the Cod War off Iceland in wet weather gear and duffel coats. At the same time, Piers had his tonsils removed at the naval hospital at Haslar, Gosport, with an unending view of a cemetery containing the graves of hundreds of sailors who had died of 'the fever' many years before. My instinct was to pick up the child and run, but he was now busy swapping comics with the boy in the next bed. Next morning, when I went to pick up the patient, he was sitting up with purple rings under his eyes and eating a boiled egg, asking what had *The Flowerpot Men* done today on the telly and where was Jeremy?

The *Saintes* was what is called a happy ship, and it rubbed off; all the wives were kind to us, especially Iona and another called Susan who suggested we should join her, her children, her mother and her brother who were hiring a refurbished train on a siding at Wool, Dorset. Not only was it fun for everyone, the people themselves were. The only good thing about her father's death, said Susan, was that her mother need get only one copy of the *Times*. Previously they had had to have one each for the cryptic crossword and the competition was intense.

We were near Bovington Downs and watched the tanks at work and also what looked like play, including one which laid down its own bridge, drove over it, picked it up again and shot onwards.

Glorious.

Saintes wives were bracing as well as kind. Iona said of course I could drive to Plymouth on the forthcoming Bank Holiday weekend to see our men before they sailed. Of course I could. And I did, and was probably the only woman who got onto the Exeter bypass in a Bank Holiday rush and could not get off and went round and round and round, bellowing with the boys their favourite verse, 'And he played upon a ladel, a ladel, a ladel, and he played upon a ladel and his name was Aiken Drum', until even the boys rebelled and I found the Plymouth exit with joy.

HMS *Saintes* sailed from Plymouth and Aunt Lillias came to see us at Swanmore, bearing gifts and leaving me a bottle of Dubonnet, a 'tonic wine' which I had not met before. However, she told me it was a pick-me-up which I found to be true. She also bought the boys duffel coats, complete with toggles and hoods and tartan linings, all of which met with high approval from both. She even risked taking Piers to matins once when he was staying with her and Lady Spence shook hands with him and approved of his toggles. The visit came to a sad end, however. His host found him crying underneath the dining room table wanting to go home to Jeremy. 'Not you. Jeremy.' Being a sensible woman like her sister, she climbed into the Rover and drove him home.

Lillias was always kind to me in a rather daunting way. Once she rang me with news which she obviously thought would be of great excitement for me. Lady Weatherspoon (the hostess who one year had her sherry party late) had invited me too to a similar knees-up. My heart sank. Joan would take the boys for a night, but driving there and back, to stand around with Camberley 'no accidents please'! I began making excuses.

'Nonsense,' boomed Lillias. 'I've told her you'd be delighted.'

So there I was doing my best at a sherry party with unknowns. Fortunately, a good-looking man came over to talk to me. He was pleasant and his moustache reminded me of my father's. Conversation picked up.

However, on the way home Lillias hissed, 'Why did you stay talking to Colonel Ballantyne all night?' as the Rover purred its way back to Watchetts Close, Camberley.

'He was talking to me,' I said mildly. 'I didn't know anyone else. I thought he was very kind.'

'You were making an exhibition of yourself,' said my aunt.

This was so ridiculous that I snorted with laughter, as the Rover swept into the motorhouse.

There was another treat she insisted on taking me to. Egbert had had a ticket (if that is the term) to the Royal Enclosure at Royal Ascot and I could now take it. This sounded exciting – Royal Family in open coach, horses thundering around which I had last seen on the racecourse of the Hawke's Bay Jockey Club – where Pop and other Hastings doctors and staff from the damaged Royston Hospital had set up a makeshift dressing station and hospital for the wounded from the 1931 earthquake. I don't remember seeing the Royal Family which seems ineffective on my part. The horses thundered as always but apparently Lillias never bet which was a relief.

She had told me to bring the thermos and a bacon and egg pie and at the right moment we 'retired' to the Rover. However, this became rather a disappointment for Lillias. Apparently I had given her a slice without a whole egg. I begged her to allow me to correct this error and things picked up.

Another memory which remains is that many of the men were better dressed than the women and many were more handsome.

Strange her reactions during these odd treats, but she did love the boys.

There was bad news, I told Neil when he arrived home. Prudence, one of the pupils at Mrs Moore's school, the bright-eyed daughter of Captain and Mrs Philimore, who, as far as I could work it out, was second-in-command in the district after the Squire and Mrs Squire, had decided she didn't like Jeremy and wouldn't have him to play any more. Jeremy wasn't concerned about the boycott but he had half finished off a beaut tunnel in the hay barn and he wanted to finish it and Prudence ponged anyway.

Neil kissed my concerned nose. 'Darling heart. Balls to Miss Philimore! Wonderful news, we'll be gone in a fortnight. I've been promoted. We'll be off to Buckinghamshire for the Joint Services staff college.'

I also learned that Neil would be the first captain of HMNZS *Taranaki*, the new New Zealand frigate which was being completed at the Isle of Wight. He would stand by the ship with some of the other officers and I and the boys would go back to New Zealand.

The new frigate was to be launched by Lady Freyberg and we were invited to dine with Lord and Lady at Windsor Castle before we left. And dine we did. There were no other guests, or if there were they have disappeared into oblivion. The evening was not a merry one. Lord Freyberg was old and not well, and his wife (Barbara) did her duty, but not with the élan and enthusiasm she had shown when he was Governor General of New Zealand. I was glad to hear her still call her husband 'My General'. Another thing I was glad to notice was that Lord Freyberg did not dig his fingernails into the back of his neck. One of his aides-de-camp at home told me it was a sure sign of boredom. He was digging out bits of shrapnel still embedded there.

We were shown the Windsor Castle dungeons and saw names carved hundreds of years ago by prisoners as they lay mouldering in freezing cells. We left at ten.

The Joint Services staff college had also been a stately park. In this case handsome terraces looked far down the valley to water meadows and a slow running stream, the Chess. Beyond, there was a grove of chestnuts which surrounded Bois Mill. There we lived, and once again we were not alone. The owners, Colonel and Mrs Someone, lived in the house proper and had obviously fallen onto good times when the staff college appeared. The course lasted six months and there was a steady turnover of tenants. They appeared pleasant people who maintained that stately British attribute of keeping themselves to themselves.

We were again living in beautiful surroundings by the babbling (there is no other word once again) of the Chess. Next to us was an Indian Colonel, a Sikh, Jaswan Singh, and his wife, and nearby was a Royal Navy Commander, Tony Tyers, and his wife Megan, whose little house looked like some sort of antique lodge built on the bridge over the stream.

The only time Mrs Someone entered our slice of a cottage was when I cracked the porcelain hand basin in the lavatory. She stared at the damage for some time and turned to me in pain. 'How on earth did you manage to do that?'

'I dropped a shampoo bottle into it and the whole thing exploded.'

She sighed, lifted a flaccid hand. 'I have never known a shampoo bottle to explode, but tenants achieve the most astounding things. Especially colonials.'

The tenants were more relaxed, but then it was not their basin. Jaswan Singh spoke perfect English and enjoyed conversation but his wife was shy beyond happiness, and spoke only in smiles. Jaswan told me about his religion, how important it was to him, how essential it was to be up at five each morning for his prayers. From that we drifted on to the turban. Yes, it did take some time to get the turban correct, but only at the beginning. One can become expert in all things, said Jaswan.

Practically all I could do in greeting his beautiful wife was to exchange good mornings at the clothesline when she was pegging her husband's vast white trousers on one line and me my less interesting garments further along. The boys and I were interested to see how Jaswan's trousers operated. 'Six foot at the top, then tapering away. Good in the wind, eh, Mum.'

Megan and I were both book drunks; we swapped them from the Chesham library and chewed them over. Tony was also a dear, and her fighting weight. He told me that Anthony means 'the runt of the litter', news which I passed on to my father. Tony also endeared himself to me when answering Neil's query as to his new car: 'The Rover? Warm and comfortable. That's all you need.'

The children went to school at Chenies, a small village near another handsome house, again surrounded by a large park. The teachers were good but for Jeremy and Piers the highlight of the day was the cooked lunch for every child, a system recently instigated. 'They have Bird's custard Mum. Not like yours with mucky old eggs.'

I was lying in bed with flu while Neil and the young were watching the television when I heard a roar: 'Quick! Quick! It's a New Zealander!'

I stumbled down the steep little stairs and flopped on the sofa to watch the Rome Olympics. Neither of us had heard of Peter Snell or Murray Halberg.

Now it was the 800 metres. 'Look, look for the black shirt dumb bum. Look!' roared Neil. Hysteria took over as our man pounded on to win. '*And a record*.' It was too much, too good, too wonderful. What a man! I began heading back to bed.

'No, no. There's the other one,' they yelled, and so there was, longer and longer till Murray Halberg passed the line, collapsed flat on his back and rolled over while we sat speechless with awe and pride. And another record.

'Now you can go,' said Neil.

Megan and Tony held a mulled wine party for friends from the Joint Services Staff College, including one of the wives who had broken her jaw while dancing Scottish reels at the college and who brought her own straws. It was a happy party and a relief from packing.

We spent our last overseas Christmas in Shropshire with friends who had known Neil ever since he arrived at the naval college at seventeen to train in His Majesty's Royal New Zealand Navy. David Barratt joined the same day but although he was in the Royal Navy the powers that be didn't go further than the alphabet, so Anderson was next to Barratt. They were in adjacent bunks, same class, same part of the ship, etc. David asked Neil home to Shropshire during their first leave and they were in the same ships for four years.

During the war Major Barratt had been in charge of the local Home Guard but Mrs Barratt was the only person who could start the Home Guard's Bren gun carrier. When the siren rang she leapt out of bed, put on her blue dressing gown, then, having started the beast and backed it out of the barn, debussed and went back to bed while the Home Guard carried on with their duties. Not unnaturally, she had an abiding love of *Dad's Army* on the television, which she handed on to us.

Not only had Major and Mrs Barratt made Neil welcome in 1945, they had continued to do so with this band of Andersons. We had heard the news that Major Barratt had died just before we set sail for home. Since then Mrs Barratt had moved from the nearby county to Ludlow, one of the loveliest towns in Shropshire, the home of *A Shropshire Lad* and A.E. Housman.

Come all to church, good people;
Good people, come and pray.

Though I am not sure Housman did. His grave is not in the usual graveyard.

The second Jill I met and loved also before we climbed on board RMS *Rangitata* with her two small boys *en route* to New Zealand. Jill's husband was the engineering officer of HMNZS *Taranaki* and was also 'standing by' the building on the Isle of Wight. As he said, it was a good idea to get it right, as the ship was the first naval ship the shipbuilders had made with bunks for all, not just for officers.

None of this hammocks and 'show a leg' business for God's Own Country.

Jill and I won the fancy dress hands down. It was a walkover, so obvious, so sweet. I was the neck end of the giraffe and Jill the legs. All we required was acres of yellow paper daubed with black splotches and we had the makings of a complete dancing, prancing giraffe out of one five-foot grass widow plus one six-foot one. The applause was long, and I pranced higher until I realised all was not well at the rear end. We had forgotten to install some mechanism for Jill to breathe and soon she was lying flat on her back panting for air. Flinging off my head I began respirating, as Mum had practised on me when she was in the Red Cross. Irritated by this, Jill was now sitting up and we began prancing around, minus giraffe head and in very little else, to even more applause.

If you have to be a grass widow it is wise to do so on a ship with plenty of friendly men around. One of them told me he had never seen two women talk cheerfully to each other for twelve thousand nautical miles. Another was a physicist, a race for whom I have always had great respect. He and I spent a lot of time leaning over the ship's rail (at last) while he pointed out reflections which he said have different names and functions, such as crinkles, wrinkles and whinkles. Can that be true? Anyway it led to amiability.

Mum and Dad had sold 609 Roberts Street and bought another while we were away. I was enraged but not surprised that all my books had been disposed of (except my text books, which Dad thought might be useful). Mum and Mrs Anderson found us somewhere to rent, which, according to both, had been filthy, absolutely filthy, cobwebs stuck to the walls, imagine.

The obvious thing was to get a job teaching. Hastings High being no longer co-educational, boys remained at the old school and girls now biked in the opposite direction to Lindisfarne. The teaching was as good as ever but Miss Steele had retired long ago.

It was easy to find a part-time job as the science teacher was pregnant, and I was grateful to have it. Life was not much fun and I was glad of the money, though, as always, the endless 'marking' ate up reading time. However, it was in Hastings I found Janet Frame's *The Lagoon and other stories*, which had been published by Caxton Press about fifteen years before. The book jacket reads: 'The stories were immediately recognised as outstanding in their perception of childhood and the child's world.' And what was more, a New Zealand child's. A sentence in one of the stories reads: 'We took baskets with fruit and sandwiches but not tomato as it goes damp, though some like it damp.' I was back on the bench outside standard four swapping with Wendy who liked them like that. I realise a woman from another country could have written with similar insight, but it would not have given me that exact stab of recognition. The weather would be wrong, the sky, the smell of the damp asphalt. The friend.

I pedalled back to the library next morning on my bike, which had survived the sale. No, they had nothing else of hers. Yes, she was good. Quite exciting wasn't it?

Hastings seemed exactly the same, as did my friends, most of whom now had four or more children to rear on their respective ranches. The same ones invited us to stay and others didn't, as the mood took them. Days passed. Depression came and went. One day I discovered my underpants had disappeared from the whirligig clothesline. I rang the police station and a large man with a strong Scottish accent appeared. I tried flippancy: 'Perhaps it was someone who was short of pants?'

'No,' said the officer, 'I'm afraid it's more likely to be a perverted man.'

Which didn't cheer. Ten feet between me marking and a perverted man did not lead to merriment. Nor did the woman in the corner store who told me if her Arthur didn't come home each night she'd die, and one glance at Arthur and I'd run like a rocket didn't help either.

The boys got everything right. They brought home a yellow plastic colander from de Pelichet's store because their teachers had told them not to forget Mothers' Day. To my shame, I burst into tears. Was it the wrong colour? The man said they could swap it. No, no, it was beautiful and now we could bike up to Rush Munro's for a licker! The panacea for all pains.

Another of the pleasures was to be with my parents again. Whether it was the move from a house too big for them, or some other reason, they seemed to have reached a *modus vivendi*, a calmer acceptance that neither of them would ever change. I even heard them laughing together occasionally, even when no visitor was present.

On Wednesdays, when I finished teaching at noon, I pedalled round to lunch with them: soup, kedgeree or macaroni cheese (shades of Mrs Duncan), and a fresh white barracouta loaf brought home by Dad in its same spotless white muslin bag. The boys were at school and Wednesday lunches were fun. It is a strange business waiting for a husband or a father to come home but we were lucky to have parents all around.

One surprise to me was Cecil and Jessie having been early buyers of a television set. It sat serenely in the corner of the dining room waiting to burst into the News at Six. Where would they be without it, sipping their first whisky and gin. It was turned off, of course, while the meal was eaten and the dishes put away before Mum's joy of the week arrived. If only Lucille Ball's *I Love Lucy* had arrived reliably each day like the boys' *Listen with Mother*, life would have been better than ever. Mum sat in a small chair with her feet on a small stool and tears rolling down her cheeks with merriment while Cecil sat smiling as he lit another Craven A.

The boys had 'settled in' once again, to their third school and so far their best. After a few days Jeremy came home with interesting news.

'I heard a boy talking real New Zealand this morning, Mum.'

'Tell me.'

'He said, "Hell man, these new dunnies are demo."'

We were home, beautiful home, and glad to be so for the rest of our fortunate lives.

HMNZS *Taranaki* was due in New Plymouth in October and excitement was booming in Hastings. Dad was coming home after eight months with a brand new 'boat'. There were not many sailor fathers at Windsor Park Primary. I resigned from Girls High with thanks, cleaned the reasonably clean house between the railways and the Aerial Mapping Company, packed up and was ready to set off to Taranaki. Once again in formation were

Neil's family: his parents, Shirley, followed by Gerald, the younger son, and his wife. Tootling behind them came the Wrights and us: my father, having grown up in New Plymouth and, as I said, having become interested in all things nautical; and, for the first and only time for a family arrival or departure, my mother, elegant, smiling, and looking forward to seeing this weird business of a ship coming home, especially when her son-in-law had done it, got it all the way from England. She also enjoyed good parties, like any sensible woman.

The weather was appalling. The rain (tank rain) had not ceased for days and the wind not only blew like a whetted knife but came from every possible direction. Nevertheless, New Plymouth was not going to miss the arrival of their own frigate. From mayor and councillors to squealing children, the drama was not to be missed. But where was the thing? Gradually out of the mist and rain a grey prow appeared. A ragged cry, then solid roars, came from the crowd as she was seen rounding the breakwater and steadying up for the wharf.

Neil was on the wing of the bridge giving orders, the last being 'Stop both engines. Finished with main engines.' A naval officer beside me said, 'Perfect alongside.' He sounded faintly disappointed.

Children, including ours, were soaked, beaming, couldn't keep still. Everyone was laughing, shouting, waving, from pure delight. Solemn-faced sailors trying to hide smiles lined the upper deck.

The gangway was put in place. We were first on board to greet Neil who was both smiling and harassed. The children were now squealing like small pigs. Neil grabbed us all in one conglomerate fierce hug or clench and dumped us with his eyes on the gangway. 'Quick, quick, get behind here,' he said and shoved us behind something looking like a gun.

Escorted by Rear Admiral Phipps, a large man in a tight suit and a brown hat marched up the gangway. 'The Minister,' Neil yelped and leapt towards the gangway. The bosun's call sounded, and Neil, the officer of the watch and other sailors sprang to attention. The brown hat was lifted.

What on earth?

'The Padre?' I tried, and saw a glimpse of an exasperated glance towards the gangway.

'*The Minister.*'

I got it finally. I got it.

'What minister?' said the boys as we peered round our gun.

'The Minister of Defence.'

'Oh.'

The official party moved on.

After some time Neil arrived back. He came back to his gun, smiling at his loved ones. 'Well,' he said, kissing us, 'great to see you. Come on down to the wardroom.'

The wardroom was Coke and potato chips and kindly men.

'Yeah, yeah!'

It was a good party. Excellent. And the men were home.

CHAPTER 19

Up bag and hammock and in November 1961 we were installed again on the North Shore, this time in Calliope Road in the seaside suburb of Devonport, overlooking Auckland. This area is naval ground between the shore establishment of HMNZS *Philomel* and the dockyard below. Many of the houses nearby had been bought for the navy, part of their policy that the hill remain navy property. They were pleasant old villas with expansive views across the harbour, though our view was marred by a whirligig clothes line and a messy compost heap.

The North Shore, and especially Devonport, is a good place to live and once again the boys 'settled', this time at Stanley Bay School. For me there was walking distance to the Devonport library and the joy of being the near the sea again. Just an amble down to Stanley Bay for a swim then back to the ironing in bathing suits before 'getting the meal on'. No writing yet.

HMNZS *Taranaki*, like HMS *Saintes*, turned out to be a happy ship, and so it was with her wives. The ship was away a good deal (that, after all, is where they are meant to be) and we shared our minor problems and major triumphs. How four boys had sailed out to sea at Stanley Bay in a small rubber boat and Jill (giraffe's hind legs) and I had rescued them with skill. How I found Henry James in the library, who would keep me going for months. How a bus had backed into our car outside the greengrocer near the gasworks and the owner, Mr Bone, promised to give evidence for me if required. 'You got enough on your plates, haven't you, girls, without buses banging into you.'

True, and consoling, Mr Bone.

Our allotment from the Royal New Zealand Navy was not overgenerous and we were glad one day when Jill and Norma (Number One's wife) heard of a good second-hand clothes shop in Auckland. This, we decided, might be a good source of ready money. We packed outgrown clothes, dead clothes and not-bad-at-all clothes in ancient pillowcases and set off for the 10am ferry.

'What's the betting Lois will be on board,' said Norma, Lois being a Devonport naval wife known to all. She wore silver spangly eyeshadow and scarlet nail polish (professionally adhered), had glorious legs and, worst of all, had private means, which we considered dirty fighting.

Norma was right. There was Lois, who naturally asked us what on earth we were doing. Norma looked at me. I could get them out of this one. I told her we were going to sell some old clothes. Lois laughed merrily, real Tinker Bell stuff, and settled down with a copy of the *Tatler.*

The *Tatler.*

We did not do well with the second-hand clothes vendor. We retreated for a deflated cup and a bun nearby and headed for the ferry which would get us home before schools came out.

The boys also were disgusted, both with our errand and our failure.

'But I *like* my blue pants.'

'They'll split any moment.'

'They won't.'

'They will.'

'What's for dinner?'

'Sausages.'

'Neat.'

'And I've got two more *Biggles* from the library.'

'Neat. Where are they?'

I envied our children's unlicensed time for reading.

Two years later we were back to Wellington. David was practising in a newly developed suburb appropriately named Newlands. Neil was already back working in Wellington and he and Jenny had found a new house which they thought would be perfect for us. Also, as the real estate man told us, with our amount of money we could wipe the prestige suburbs: Karori, Khandallah, Kelburn – the lot. He had a place in Happy Valley by the tip but that was a bit shaky. All we could do was go far out.

Newlands was not too far out but it was not welcoming. The developer here was even more ruthless in his removal of topsoil than the one in Auckland, and there were remarkably few trees. As we drove in to inspect our prospective estate we passed a house with two or three ancient-looking cars lying about the place. They were in need of attention. I commented on them and the real estate agent sighed and sucked his teeth. 'Yeah,' he said, 'it's a disgrace. They should get the Progressives onto them.' And who were the Progressives? They sounded more alarming than the abandoned old heaps. Progressive for whom? And what?

I discovered the Progressive Association did good work, but still trees refused to grow. Neil and his good friend Stan Hermans dug the front lawn with a Kango Hammer and built a fence either side. The cliff below steepened onto rough country and what I hoped would become a forest of New Zealand natives. Total failure. The forest fizzled to nothing.

Beside the carport was the ever-present whirligig clothesline, which worked like a typhoon in the endless wind.

Nearby was my herb garden. In the sixties cooks had discovered herbs other than mint and parsley. Elizabeth David once again. Also herbs are difficult to kill and have the advantage of clinging to the ground. The boys learned not to park their bikes on Mum's Herbert Garden though they had never asked who Herbert was.

The bikes were new acquisitions from grandparents for riding to Newlands Primary School. Even more exciting was the arrival of the television. Television had been around for several years and David and Jenny's two small girls were conversant with theirs. Also there was the old cry of 'Lots of the kids at school have them, Dad'. The day our black beauty appeared they fell about with joy.

'Was it on special, Dad?'

'Yes.'

'Neat.'

My parents came down for Christmas. The weather was ridiculous for December as Mum said, but thank goodness the fire didn't smoke. And why on earth had I decided to have purple and green for the sofa? As I was beginning to wonder about this myself I was slightly unnerved when she continued by telling me the only person she knew who had had purple and green together (especially *purple*) had been Martha Ken's sister Edna, who took her own life. Poor, tragic Martha's sister and her purple and green sofa.

We had a happy Christmas Day with David and Jenny and their young, Diana and Elizabeth. I enjoyed having the small girls to stay. The boys loved them and the girl cousins were so beautiful people looked at me with awe when I had them all together. Two sons, two enchanting younger girls. 'You don't often see that,' said a smiling woman holding up a *Janet and John* in Whitcombe and Tombs. 'It's usually two boys and then if the third's a girl, that's it.'

Shades of Mr Gander in Swanmore and my grocery orders. Rations first, Mrs Anderson.

There were empty sections in Longcroft Terrace, Newlands, and most of the houses seemed empty too until their occupants came home again from the day's work. They reminded me of the Yellow-eyed Penguins we had seen in the Catlins in the South Island. They too were programmed to dive in, work all day, come home, leap out of the sea/bus, and waddle up to the nest as the day darkened, the busy world hushed and their day's work done.

An exception to this were Angela and Frank, who had an unusual enterprise at home. They had bought the franchise for selling cigarettes from a machine installed in their house. Buyers would put the money in and a packet of fags would fall into their laps.

'But why wouldn't they get them at the store?'

'When they're right here? Not likely.'

The neighbours across the road were also interesting. Every Sunday morning about twelve friends drove up in their cars. They marched in carrying crates of beer, reappeared in the front room, stared over the view available, drank solidly for four or five hours, then departed with no visible sign of increased gaiety, wobbly legs or wanton driving.

It was time for me to join the Yellow-eyed Penguins and find a job. Fortunately there was one available at Queen Margaret College, the Presbyterian girls' school in town who already had one part-time science teacher, and also a full-time head of the department. A situation which drove the maths teacher stark, staring, raving mad when she was making up the timetable, but covered science well.

Every morning at six Jeremy arrived in our bedroom with the wake-up call 'Everybody *art*'. And everybody was 'art', out of the house at seven-thirty with our individual needs for the day, including sandwiches.

Queen Margaret's in the sixties deserves all the accolades I can give it. The staffroom was not only a 'nest of singing birds', as Samuel Johnson called his contemporary poets, but one of the teachers described it as something like a well-conducted nunnery. 'Living in charity within the rule.' Teachers cared for their pupils in ways I had never seen before.

Occasionally the headmistress would ask at morning break for anyone who taught Rose Blue to speak with her for a moment. Without hesitation, cups were abandoned and smiles maintained as the headmistress explained that things were not well at Rose's home and she would be grateful if everyone would remember this. Wise heads nodded, Rose was remembered, help was given where possible.

If I could have spent my time in that staffroom I would be there still, give or take a few changes in circumstances and years. The English teachers took me back to Miss Avery. They loved words and the men and women who could make them dance or weep. Also they let me join in their discussions. Dylan Thomas for example.

'Who?'

'"Whacking thighed and piping hot."'

'Oh.'

'I'll lend him to you if you like. Perhaps you haven't read enough men, Barbara. What about Hemingway? Or Conrad. Start with *Victory*.'

'Thank you. Yes.'

The two other science teachers also knew their onions. They were competent, so much so that they were surprised when I admitted that sometimes I was relieved when my experiments worked (especially the triumph of Hydrolysis of Water). How could it not work? That is the whole point of science. That which can be proved – and is.

At lunch they discussed essential films.

'Ingmar Bergman, magnificent.'

'Who?'

'Swedish. Amazing man.'

'Oh.'

One of the older and smaller teachers thought he should have cut the scene when the woman was violating herself in bed. Had she? Goodness me. Well well. 'It just goes to show,' as Nana Jackson used to say, though not in this context.

They all agreed about the scene in *Zorba the Greek* when the poor old woman was dying and equally poor women sat around like vultures waiting to snatch her possessions. Appalling, quite appalling. And – and this is the real horror – the dying woman knew. How did she know? Because it was the custom of a country where poverty breeds different depths of shame. This was definitely a film to see, a must see, I told Neil that evening. He lowered the *Evening Post*. 'Oh God, not another bloody must.'

Not long afterwards our friend Judith Trotter was taking lessons in Greek before she went to live and work in Athens. *Zorba the Greek* had come into the conversation. 'Surely,' said Judith when talking to her teacher about another alarming part of the film, 'they wouldn't have stoned the young woman to death. I mean, not nowadays.' 'Yes,' said the teacher. 'You're right. They would have waited until she had run from the churchyard. That, of course, is sacrosanct.'

Queen Margaret College was undoubtedly a happy ship, all the staff cheerful and competent. Lynley Dodd, the creator of *Hairy McClary* at a later time, was Art; Sewing looked as though she had stepped out of a bandbox. Husbands and boyfriends did their stuff most beautifully well at the school dances. Almost, you could say, like well-behaved wives when the ship was away.

Think if I had missed *Zorba the Greek* and other treats, including finding the best camping site in New Zealand, which was passed on to me by the senior science teacher. It was there Neil, the boys and I met the prefect Norma (now with husband and six children) who had told me how to deal with the beefsteak tomato on my first meal at boarding school. They too went to Anaura Bay every year, camped in the empty shearers' quarters and made us welcome to all their pleasures.

The beauty, the sheer beauty of pleasant unexpected synchrony. Nothing can beat it. And where does it come from?

Bad things at this happy time were that neither Mrs Anderson nor Mum was in good health. David and I made many short visits to Hastings. David drove with speed and talk. He was worried about Mum. 'No Jackson ever gets past seventy. Not one,' he said firmly.

One of Mum's irritants lately was the arrival of Aunt Lillias, who had come home with all her goods and chattels to the Bay after an absence of thirty years. Some of the chattels were stamped with 'Antique' marks to prove they were. She also bemoaned the fact that there was nowhere to 'Wear my Clothes'. A statement so infuriating and daft that Mum's sense of humour died. She and some of her friends wore earrings made by local potters. Lillias, seeking information as one does in a foreign land, asked Mum about them. 'Why do so many of you people,' she said, thoughtfully stroking her diamonds, 'wear buttons in your ears?'

But the thing which maddened Mum most was Lillias being haughty to her friends, who for thirty years had helped her with her corsets, her hair, her dry-cleaning.

'Who in heaven's name does she think she is?'

'The Little Flower of the Sheep Dip,' I tried.

But little helped.

'Forget her nonsense, she's all right,' I said. 'She can be kind and generous as she was to us.' But Mum could be neither cool nor calm in a ridiculous situation. It seemed sadder when *I Love Lucy* was there to laugh at each Wednesday night and Your Father was finally helping a little.

Colin's death had nothing to do it with it I'm sure. That heartbreak was long ago, when pneumonia was so lethal and before Alexander Fleming (both Scottish and a bacteriologist) discovered the enzyme which became penicillin. Aunt Lillias had been a good nurse. She had done all she could.

I was getting ready for one of our routine run-ups when David rang. Mum was in hospital, we must get there at once.

It was dreadful, the small ward at the Memorial Hospital. Appalling, because Mum would have thought everything was perfect, would have approved of all available. She wore one of her prettiest hospital nightdresses, handmade and embroidered by her friend Miss Burt around the corner. She had always called them 'my hospital nighties' and had them folded side by side for years in case she was called in suddenly; had worn them otherwise occasionally when she stayed at the Midland in Wellington or at the Eastbourne Hotel with the tartan carpet when our little house was not large enough for anyone to stay.

Her hair above her closed eyes was immaculate in her daytime net. But the worst, causing grief which rushed tears to my eyes, was not so much that her mouth was dribbling down one side of her face but that Sister, good, kind, competent Sister, had folded a pristine handkerchief on her cheek to stop the irreverence of dribble.

'Oh thank you, thank you, Sister.'

'Mrs Wright wouldn't have liked it,' said Sister in her veil and hands together because David was a doctor, and Mum had been proud of that.

David was examining the charts at the end of the bed. He was silent for some time then dropped them. 'Hell's fangs! What am I doing? I'm just, just . . . This is my mother. It's *terminal.*'

'*What!*'

'Would you like a word with Dr Ballantyne, Sir?' said Sister.

'He can't do anything now,' said David.

'But what is it? *Tell me.*'

Mum had gone to the letterbox that morning, as she had done every morning, to collect the mail. She had continued to 'live in the letterbox' when we came home and my letters continued to flop in the box each week. Dad saw her collapse at the gate.

The diagnosis was Subarachnoid haemorrhage. Terminal.

My father's first task after my mother's funeral – of which I have no memory at all – was to answer the letters of condolence. 'Grisly,' he said. 'Reminded me of bears.' He made every letter different in some way, he told me, but they all ended similarly. 'My wife and I had forty-two years of perfect happiness together, and no man could ask for more.'

He also told me he was learning to cook and found the hardest part was to get everything done at the same time.

He then decided it was time to retire. David and I agreed. We also agreed that he couldn't live alone and the solution would be for him to stay with each family for six months of the year. David looked at me, and said with his usual crackling honesty, 'The thing is, Bub, Mum was ten years younger. We've backed the wrong horse.'

A remark all his friends would recognise as a true David comment.

*

David's prophecies were correct. Lillias was the next Jackson to die. She became unwell and decided she was displeased with her local doctor. She told me later with pride that she had asked for a second opinion. Unfortunately the courteous GP was not one to deal with Harley Street routines and told her he thought the best solution would be for her to go to another doctor, rose from his chair, and bowed Mrs Kirkley out the door.

The problem was that other doctors in Havelock North appeared to be unable to see her. I wrote the letters for Lillias and received the answers. Lillias wept. I finally found one in Hastings. It was sad and inexplicable.

She died not much later of a heart condition.

Her will must have cost her many hours. Yes, she was generous.

So Pop, as the boys now called him, for years to come upended one black and one tan suitcase twice a year to travel between our households.

Like his own father he had never been possessed of laugh-out-loud merriment, but the young, especially Piers, appreciated his dry wit and ancient jokes, such as Gelett Burgess's 'Purple Cow':

I never saw a purple cow
I never hope to see one;
But I can tell you, anyhow,
I'd rather see than be one.

'Say it again, Pop.' The dearest words for ancient jokers.

In 1967 we were back in Auckland to another rented villa in Calliope Road and the seventh school for the young.

Piers came home on his first day from Auckland Grammar with a query. 'Mum. What's calculus?'

I could think only of Mum's answer to Jill's question long ago about the length of the suspect lawyer's ruler and the importance thereof. 'Piers, I would be the last person in Devonport to know what calculus is.'

'Well, I've got to do it. And Dad's at sea.'

'How about Pop?'

'Won't know.'

'Try him.'

He did, and Pop did, and was glad as well as Piers.

He must have been lonely during the day, my father. I blessed the five-day radio broadcast of international cricket matches and mourned with him when rain stopped play. I became, like him, knowledgeable about the commentators, his favourite being the clipped tones of John Arlott: 'Someone to Someone. He bowls.' Then he became so excited he shoved himself forward in his favourite cane chair in his bedroom, making those small squeaks known to the old and the young.

But the best time for him was when all five of us were gathered together and Neil had given him his first glass of whisky. That was when real life began again. Sometimes for a little joke when Neil was being a bit dilatory with the refill he would hold his empty glass on his grey head and pretend to balance it. A joke appreciated by the young rather than their father who might well have had a bad day in Stout Street or at HMNZS *Philomel*.

Pop also approved of the North Shore, especially as the house we were now in had a full-length verandah which looked across to the city and its shipping. Neil would read him the *Shipping News*. Who's in, who's out. Who was sailing and at what times. And the one who arrived in the middle of the night with an audible rattle of the anchor chain as it waited for a berth. He also enjoyed yarning to the boys, giving his views of life at Auckland Grammar when they arrived home. The school gave far too much homework. Ridiculous. Also of course, it was a tragedy both of them were no longer taking Latin.

'At ½ past One a Small Boy who was up at the masthead called out Land,' wrote Banks in his Journal for 6 October 1769.

The bicentenary of the landing of Captain James Cook in his ship *Endeavour* was of importance to many: Maori and Pakeha, Cook enthusiasts around the world and, more immediately, those living around Young Nicks Head, the name given, as promised, by Cook to any hand on board who first sighted land. The landfall was the coast of Poverty Bay, also named by Cook and near what is now the town of Gisborne.

Official and local arrangements were set in train. Naval ship visits were invited from five countries and a total of eleven ships were to be present. Neil was to be the co-ordinator of all services' participation. He would be there for two months and I would go down for the bicentenary weekend.

Pop and his mates were parked, where I can't remember, and I set off towards Gisborne. Neil had made many friends in the district, all of whom told me how well he had done and how popular he was. One or two wives were surprised, if not astonished. They would never have thought I would look like I did. Shorter perhaps? More cuddly? Obviously a disappointment in some way.

Nevertheless I had a good time at the functions and the fireworks, with my ex-prefect, now Norma, and her family. Also the ball was excellent. I had a dress made by a dressmaker in Devonport which I thought was extremely soignée. And so it remained until I went to the lavatory and discovered the sleeveless top and the all-in-one split trousers zip met at buttocks level. I would never be able to get the whole thing together again if I opened it, even with a little help from my friends, if available. But by this time I was calling for madder music, stronger wine. I slapped on more lipstick and sailed out to find an attractive looking man who would come when I whistled.

Next day the rain fell like tank rain but the show went on. A re-enactment had been arranged of Cook and his men coming ashore at Anaura Bay to get some so-called scurvy-grass, which Cook used as an antiscorbutic. This was followed by a hangi, and friendships made on all sides.

I said goodbye to the Murphys next morning where I admired Peter's huge vase of bulrushes in the hall. 'Stop and get some near the swamp,' he said, giving me directions. 'Got a slasher in your car?'

'Something like it,' I said, amongst farewell waves.

The stillness of the morning by the swamp was intense. I stood listening to it: not a bird, a beast, a breath. Then slowly, one after another, frogs began to croak: that deep, hoarse, indistinguishable sound. Had I heard it before? If not, why not? This noise was true wonder, and I had dissected some of these harmless formalin-stinking honkers, though they were dead before we met. Shame. It was the best half of Captain Cook's bicentennial. He might have heard their forebears when he landed.

Later I found this could not have happened. The only frog around when Cook landed was the indigenous frog who has no croak. Bother.

It was a dark night in Devonport. The clattering clang of a ship anchoring finished. Nothing but dark stillness and the reflections of neon light shivering on the black sea. Neil had been working all night.

'Late,' I said. 'Come on. Monday tomorrow.'

'I've got to finish this.'

'Tonight? What is it?'

'The *Lachlan*'s Inspection Report.'

'Well, I'm off.'

'Nn.'

Hours later his light went on.

'What on earth . . . ?'

'I've got a pain in my chest.'

I sat up. 'How long?'

'Hours.'

'I'll ring *Philomel.* Someone'll be on duty.'

'It's not as bad as that.'

The telephone sat on a table in the hall covered in black-and-white-tile linoleum pretending to be marble. A good effort, laid by a previous renter, but cold on bare feet.

The duty doctor answered. 'How long has he had the pain?'

'About two hours.'

'Probably indigestion. Get him a couple of aspirins and tell him to come and see me first thing in the morning.'

The pain passed away. Neil was up as usual, told me all was well. 'I'll hand the report in first. Get rid of the thing. I'll ring you after I've seen the doctor. Bye, love.'

The washing machine was thundering to command as a uniformed doctor appeared up the drive.

I told him Neil was on his way to see him in his surgery but he was going to deliver something first. He replied he had waited for him in his office and thought the patient might still be in bed. Disappointed by Neil behaving in a loose way without reporting his intentions to a senior officer, the doctor saluted, thanked me, and departed.

I had begun work in a private laboratory in Auckland City and usually I drove the boys over the bridge to school, including one time when the radio bellowed, 'Love is a big shit following me.'

'What!'

'Ship, Mum. Ship.'

One of the features of this laboratory was that the authorities gave you what they called a 'day in lieu' – a system which meant that as well as paying you for urgent work on Saturday or Sunday they gave a whole day free for a few hours' work, weekends being sacred at that time. *Day in lieu.* Do they still exist? A beautiful phrase, something *given*, a dedicated obligation, a pact.

This morning the boys were on the ferry, Pop was still relaxing in his bed, my day was mine in lieu. Yippee.

I was crawling around in the living room, cutting up patches which would eventually become a patchwork quilt, which in its turn would grace the master bedroom.

The front bell rang. Removing pins and swearing gently I went to open it. A younger doctor stood there who asked if he might come in. Of course he could. Please sit down. He took off his cap, put it on the floor, sat down and told me his news. Neil had had an ECG taken after the senior doctor had examined him, which showed he had had a heart attack and he would be in Auckland hospital for at least a month.

It is true, your heart does fall. Plummet even.

I burst into loud bawling tears and told the younger doctor that Neil was only forty-three and fit. Very fit.

Then the bearer of bad news told me I was lucky Neil did not have terminal cancer.

I told the cap lying on the floor I would like to have been given a little more time before being told I was lucky. He picked up his cap and apologised. I did also. He departed.

Pop said Neil would make a splendid recovery and he did. The patchwork quilt also pulled through.

After three months' convalescing and nine back at work, the next posting for Captain Neil Anderson, RNZN, was to attend the Royal College of Defence Studies in London, during which his dependants would be entitled to accompany him.

A whole *year* in London. A flat in Lansdowne Road, Holland

Park, W11, which we took over from another New Zealand officer. The flat was one of a modern block of three flats built to replace a bomb strike, the only one in a street of handsome houses and beautiful gardens within a few yards of Holland Park Tube. Piers, who had been accepted for next year at the newly established Auckland medical school, would be with us for a gap year, a term known to the UK young but not to ours. Ours had OE, the year before getting y'boots on, and getting down to something. Jeremy was established in second-year medicine and in a flat with friends. And I would have a year doing just what I liked.

Pop would spend this year with David and Jenny. After which, he told visitors, 'They will be deprived of my company when the Andersons come home again.' When this heavy irony became too much he quoted Dr Johnson: 'He who is tired of London is tired of life.' So that was all right.

And not only London. Neil bought a second-hand campervan, a Volkswagen, the only car with which I became enamoured. Cars called Popsy or Tootsy give me the creeps but the VDub was a battler, a warrior, ready for anything in any country.

First we explored Devon and Cornwall, travelling to places with names like Roseland in St Just with snowdrops covering its graveyard. Where primroses straight out of *Flower Fairies of Spring* lined lanes so narrow the tops of the trees sometimes met.

This was England as it should be, or rather as it was in the first books I knew. At the same time I heard an Englishman on the BBC discussing the work of an exciting new African poet. Something which surprised him was that the African wrote about snowdrops and primroses. Why did the man not write of his indigenous flora? I could have told him.

We drove up to Scotland for what Neil called a dry run for our big summer expedition abroad. The VDub went with ease in all places and many camping sites, the best of which belonged to the Duke of Argyll, a situation I felt was as it should be.

On our first morning with the Duke I woke to find that Neil was not in his bunk. This was not a surprise to me or Piers. He leaned over from his sleeping bag muttering, 'Typical. Grabs the only dry towel and he's off like a rocket.'

The door swung open with good news. 'The Duke's done us proud. The water's piping hot.'

'What're his towels like?' snarled his son.

The next day we saw the battlefield of Culloden in the rain. One of the saddest places in the world for a Scot, or even half a one. Mum would have wept.

The dry run being successful, we were going to Europe for the RCDS month's leave. Piers, an amiable youth and fond of his father, asked me a serious question on the night before we left.

'Mum. Will I like it being in a campervan for a month? With *Dad*?'

'You'll love it.'

Which he did, considering.

The last time we had left the homeland of my father things had been different for me and more so for Piers. He had left the United Kingdom to the strains of 'Aiken Drum' and his hat of good cream cheese. This time we left New Zealand with the strains of the Beatles singing in our and the whole world's ears. Last year Piers had been part of the Swinging Sixties. The seventies would be even more interesting for him.

This time also we had come by aircraft, with with men's long hair streaming everywhere. Not four weeks on a luxury liner with short back and sides. Neil was not concerned with the length of his sons' hair and I enjoyed those rippling waves. After all, Lord Melbourne senior had been appalled when his son had his hair short – another of Pop's more helpful pieces of information.

Piers was more interested in a job. He enrolled in Manpower, an efficient establishment for casual workers all over London. The hopefuls rang at six-thirty each morning about work available.

'Dad, what's a 2.9 ton truck look like?' he asked.

'A pantechnicon? A big box on wheels. Why?'

'I'm driving one for Biba tomorrow. Picking up outwork in the East End and back to Biba in Kensington.'

'Christ.'

The next day his son was painting the back area of a Gentleman's Club and was almost fired for walking through the ante room to the dining room with a ladder on his shoulder and nearly decapitating a waiter *en route*. Another time he was shown the door when he stopped his truck outside the Army & Navy Stores after seeing a large sign saying 'Wine Tasting'. When asked by a floorwalker where he was going, he replied he was going to the wine tasting. A uniformed official appeared and said he thought not and showed him the door. These escapades of Wild Colonial Boys needed someone of the same age to laugh and understand and laugh again, but these were rare in Lansdowne Road.

'Abroad' saw us drifting through Chartres, the Dordogne, Provence, and the Côte d'Azur, where Piers said my philosophy of 'how disgusting it would be to be rich' took a severe pasting as we watched beautiful people in glorious clothes – albeit brief – lying about on handsome yachts.

Neil had the unfair responsibility of a) driving, b) navigating and c) keeping the VDub going (it occasionally went 'phut' some distance from garages), while I enjoyed the wild flowers and found every place more wonderful than the last. We also did a lot of lying about. The French are good at it, I noticed. Several times I watched old men fish while their wives knitted beneath a nearby tree. Then sudden action from wife, large *pique nique* laid on white cloth and much food eaten. Husband and wife then rolled over and slept. The French, as the French teacher said, are a wonderful race.

On we went to Florence and the Fort Belvedere, where there was a superb Henry Moore exhibition and a camping ground by the Arno. Piers declined a second day in Florence. 'There are some guys over there. And I like *small* galleries.'

I saw his point, but what a wallow we had – Santa Maria Novella and the monastery, the Museum of St Mark and the Fra Angelico museum. And all the way, riding shotgun for us in every gallery, were Rixon and Padbury.

See Venice and Die. And duck the mosquitoes if you can. Piers was the worst wounded. A dark limpid-eyed young woman in the chemist stroked his arm sadly and sighed, '*Ah, puncta insecta*,' which was an appealing phrase and cheered Piers.

We had been advised by a friend not to miss a pensione in the centre of Venice. Leave the van at a camp miles away, that's the trick. We went up by vaporetto and arrived with greetings for our host from our New Zealand friend. 'Ah, Colonello Jones,' followed by beams and laughs and incomprehensible Italian. We agreed with Piers: 'I like Italy.'

Next morning our host produced a cable forwarded from New Zealand. Jeremy had left medical school. Naturally we were anxious to know how he was, and rang him at once. He sounded amiable and calm; he wouldn't arrive for some time.

'Far and few, far and few, / Are the lands where the Jumblies live,' said Edward Lear. Far and many, far and many, would be more accurate for the keen exploring London.

First came Art. I heard Dolores Padbury's gentle voice among the rooms where Rembrandt's self-portraits were and I found the one with green slashes on the painter's coat shoulder. 'So vivid, girls, see?' And so long ago. I can't remember how we all saw the green slashes on the postcard reproduction but I can remember the attempt. After a time I loved the whole of the National Gallery as millions must have done before me. Turn to the left on arrival and there is Cimabue, another winner, and one I had never heard of. This is how favourites should be, available at all times.

Then on I went, further afield and more diverse in my hunting, blessing the New Zealand Defence Department as the days rolled on. Why not the Museum of Children's Toys? The Hayward Gallery across the river? The Chelsea Physics Garden, 'founded in 1673 and situated in the heart of London'?

I had plenty of time, all the time there is (Miss Holland), and I was determined to see as many delights as possible while we were here. The museums were excellent, as were the libraries of dear, dirty old London (Lillias). I made tracks for the British Museum and all its riches, the first being the Reading Room where, if you had the correct ticket, you could sit and write books with your own individual green lamp in the place where Karl Marx wrote *Das Kapital*.

All these places had to be found and the Underground was invaluable. As Neil told me, 'Any fool can work the Tube.' I agreed in theory, but he is a navigator by trade which means you have to learn to know where you're going. You also need a sense of direction. Mine, if it ever existed, left home early and left the door open. My reverence for the Tube is great. The map itself is the work of a genius.

I usually had the luxury of avoiding the rush hour, though this was not always possible. One day I had made a surgical strike to Sainsbury's for food on the way home from a visit to Whitechapel Gallery. Laden with that, plus a wet umbrella, I charged onto a crowded tube (Mind the Gap) and flung myself at a city gentleman with a beautifully rolled umbrella. Somehow I managed to clutch the end of his umbrella rather than mine. He looked startled, presumably because he thought I was attempting an intimate grope at his private parts. His alarm appalled me. I couldn't look at my boots, they had disappeared in the scrum below. Apologies would show I had been doing something for which one should be apologising. There was nothing to do except long for Holland Park. I stood staring at the edge of his left ear as we passed through station after station. At the moment before he left he extracted his umbrella with a brilliant sleight of hand, gave me mine, nodded, ducked for the door, avoided the gap and disappeared.

His station was Queensway. I took an interest in it ever after.

One day I had a commission from Pop:

Your great, great, great, great grandfather, William Romaine, DD MA was Rector of St Andrews of the Wardrobe. (Charles the Second by the way.) It is a funny little old church not far from the Holborn Viaduct. His sermons are still extant. His portrait is in the National Portrait Gallery. So if you are ever brave enough you might look him up. (I have a photo of the portrait here.)

We headed for the gallery. A man behind the desk arranged for William Romaine to be sent up from the stacks. We looked at him and he looked at us, a benign-looking man with his right palm raised. A follower of Whitfield, the Methodist and evangelist, we learned. Also that William was painted by Francis Cote, who also painted Joseph Banks. Another thread with the Antipodeans.

Jeremy arrived in September and, like his brother, fell headlong into the pleasures to be found in London in the seventies for the young and frisky. The music, the noise, the everything. Jeremy, who had an interest in clothes to rival Pop's in his earlier days, fell for flared jeans, wasp-waisted purple jackets, and 'flowing hair'.

He was made for all these and more, and Manpower did what they could to keep them both in meagre but ready money.

We all enjoyed Emperor of Wyoming, a shop with a plain wooden floor and saddles hanging on the walls. It was also, except for the piles of clothes for the young at heart, exactly like Peter Murphy's tack room at his station near the croaking frogs, with bridles, saddles, wooden floor.

> *You ask me why those teardrops fall?*
> *It's that bridle hangin' on the wall.*

The smell, however, was different. Nothing horsey at the Emperor, but an unusual one I didn't recognise. I asked the boys if they knew it. 'Marijuana, Mum, marijuana. There's a lot of it about.'

It was good, another good time for us, the year of '72. We flew back to Wellington in time for Christmas and stayed in the same hotel for one night, looking across at the pedestrians sheltered from the rain by the corrugated iron above them. Next morning was Christmas and Neil and I walked up the hill to the cathedral.

There we met a good friend, an American army officer who told us he and his family had come back to live here, they had all liked it so much. He was now the diocesan secretary. 'Yes,' he said, 'never worked so hard in my goddam life.'

I wondered if Great Grandfather Philip Wright in Copford, Essex, would have agreed.

PART III

CHAPTER 20

Neil's new posting being in Wellington, our house hunting began again. Our main requirement was that it must be on flat ground. Pop would be living with us and hills were not for him.

Houses with flat access do not leap to the eye in Wellington but can be found in Karori, Kelburn and Khandallah, etc – the prestige suburbs as our sons reminded us. Also both of them were now at the Auckland medical school, Jeremy in third year and Piers beginning first, so beds must be available for holidays.

'Three bed, flat access, villa in prestige suburb' – 36 Beauchamp Street read like a real estate agent's dream. The ad did not mention *old* but undoubtedly it was, having been built in 1906 which gave it much of its charm. It had kauri weatherboards and doors, the panelled cupboards in the dining room had handsome carvings – the work of a maiden lady who, said the present owner, had lived there for many years – and the small fireplace in the parlour had a carved mantel with ceramic panels. Best of all, the original water pump in the garden was still in working order. We loved it from the moment we sat on the back steps hugging ourselves, not knowing we would live in it for over twenty years.

The owner then asked if we would do one thing for her.

Of course, anything.

Would we light a fire before we ripped out the fireplace?

Of course, and did she not realise we were not ripper outers?

Besides which, we couldn't afford to rip anything anywhere.

Our new house had several links with my previous days. Samuel Marsden Collegiate School for Girls was not far along the main road, and around another corner had lived my Wright grandparents, where I had learned how to juggle, though not as well as Aunty Margaret.

It was also where Katherine Mansfield and the rest of the Beauchamp children had trailed up the hill in a cart from the city to the more salubrious air of suburban Karori; the place where on arrival they saw a white duck running around with no head, the duck which appeared later on the dinner table.

Our street was called after her banker father although he and his family had never lived there.

Another good thing was that Pop was happily ensconced in his bedroom, glued as ever to the radio whenever there was a five-day game of cricket. His sight was worse and his promises never to smoke unless he was outside, or we were home, became of great importance. Neil smoked a pipe and understood. 'You can't stop the poor old pot,' he said. 'Anyway he couldn't.'

Pop enjoyed meeting our friends but was not always an easy conversationalist.

'Are you interest in politics, Dr Wright?'

'No.'

'Art perhaps?'

'No.'

It was nearly time for his empty glass on the head routine.

He never mentioned that his main interest was books and the men (and occasionally women) who wrote them. The wisdom and beauty and fun to be found in other men's words which he could read now only in talking books.

Always he was pleased to see his grandsons when they came down from Auckland, especially Piers with whom he had long talks about all things including changes of social mores. 'No Piers, in my day a glimpse of a lady's ankle raised one's pulse.'

'Pop!'

'No, no, I assure you.'

Then he would tell the old story of General Smuts, who when asked about the elegance of the ladies' gowns at a grand dinner party replied, 'I can't tell you. None were visible above the table.'

He also took a friendly interest in their girlfriends, treating them with utmost courtesy but lamenting to me the fact that he couldn't see much of them, but what he could see looked very fetching

However, after several false alarms and several lost cigarette butts it became obvious that something must be done. David was now practising as an anaesthetist and living in town and we had many discussions. Our father couldn't see and was not safe even with what he called a little puff. Once I found a job I wouldn't be home all the time, and Jenny was just as busy.

We found the Home for the Blind at Tawa, the village where

I had first found that the rivers flowed higher and quicker in Wellington than in the Bay. The time when Dr Wright was driving me to my first job.

He was sitting on his cane chair and me on his bed with the heavy blankets he preferred when I told him the news. He was appalled. No, not appalled, *saddened* would be better. I felt like the woman in the Russian fable when her husband was about to take his mother to the equivalent of a Russian Old Person's Home on the sledge. He was wrapping a large rug about her, when his wife spoke.

'No,' she said, 'cut that in half. Half will be plenty big enough.'

'Yes,' said their young son, 'that will be for you when I take you there.'

We all went to inspect the home. It was pleasant, the staff very much so, and the superintendent said the food was excellent. We were assured one of the staff would pour his whisky at four-thirty and at five o'clock one would escort him to the dining room.

Pop agreed it was a well-run institution. The highlights of his days, beyond even the five-day cricket, were our visits. I became expert at pouring and sharing his whisky after organising his talking books.

Not many things puzzled him at the home but he discovered one. Why were there so few men about when there were women everywhere? He liked women, always had, but it seemed odd. Neil's comment that men worked themselves into early graves was not repeated to him.

I had begun looking for a job at a laboratory but was soon back to hunting in the Jobs Available columns. In the days soon after the war jobs for women fell into our hands, a situation which did not continue into the seventies. All I could find was one in the Wellington hospital laboratory, in charge of the autoclave, sterilising used plates and making new agar plates. It was a job roughly similar to Alfred's in the Napier Hospital, though I assumed twenty years had improved the mechanics and would have reduced the roaring and hissing of the Wellington's machine. And presumably Alfred had retired with his well-conducted wife years ago.

My friend Vivienne, another of the residents of the Chookery in Dunedin when I was there, was also looking for a job, one congruent with her home science training. No more teaching for Vivy.

I had an idea, an idea which improved with thought. Why did we not go together clutching our certificates of merit to show the authorities in the hope they would let us share the job? I then had an even better idea. Nothing as simple as morning by A and afternoon by B. No one would take us aboard on that; there would be no continuity for them, nor for us. Anderson's Plan was simple and efficient for all. On Monday morning Barbara would present herself in the Laboratory in her ridiculously short white uniform. She would work each day that week (there was no weekend work). In the next week Barbara would appear again and would work all day Monday and Tuesday as before, and – here is the beauty of it – would work until twelve noon on Wednesday, when Vivienne, the smaller one, with the uniform of suitable length, would take over. Then Barbara would disappear for ten days, plus weekend, while Vivienne would take over and so we would continue *ad infinitum*.

We presented our plan to the head of the hospital laboratory, Dorothy Reynolds, who to our relief saw no reason why it would not work. Job sharing was becoming quite frequent said the splendid Dorothy, who was loved by all and later distinguished herself by being married in a long lunch hour. She would speak to the consultant for microbiology, Dr Manning, who would interview us together. We tried to wave our Letters in his face but he declined. When would we be ready to begin work?

'Now?'

'Good.' He rose to his feet in courteous dismissal. 'Thank you.'

I used to watch Dr Manning walking along the corridors in his spotless white coat. He walked reasonably near the walls as we all did, but he differed from others: his right hand touched the walls at regular intervals. Was he aware of this? If so why did he do it? No, it must have been a subconscious touch. For security? Of course not. I wondered whether others would have liked to ask this calm, well-respected man whether he knew he was tapping, tapping, tapping the wall away.

Viv and I worked for several years. Seeing each other but briefly at changeover, we walked Box and Cox into perfect harmony. It worked for us; it worked for Pop, who knew when I would be coming; and it worked for the laboratory. It was not an interesting job but it had its pleasures, such as simplicity and knowing there was only two and a half days' work before another short holiday.

And freedom. I used to head for the National Art Gallery in Buckle Street, which was on the way home, to check on my favourites: Sidney Nolan's *Greek Coast,* several Christopher Perkinses, and Frances Hodgkins. Always there. Always waiting. Then coffee and a sandwich at the café and home.

Glorious.

Things were changing in our country and had been before we arrived home last Christmas. We were away when the Labour Party had been led to victory by Norman Kirk, the prime minister who said, 'We recognise that we have come of age and must stand on our own feet to reject the role of the dependant and at every opportunity to seize the initiative.'

Only thirty years earlier another Labour prime minister, Michael Joseph Savage, expressed different emotions when he declared New Zealand at war. 'We range ourselves without fear beside Britain. Where she goes, we go. Where she stands, we stand.' Emotions shared by my father and virtually every New Zealander.

Even Pop, and presumably many others of his generation, no longer spoke of Home. More and more, as we sipped a glass of whisky at four-thirty in Tawa, he spoke of 'this wonderful little country'. How it had been good to him. Very good. He was even glad he had given up *Punch* before he left the surgery. It had gone off. Since Pont had died, poor man, he died too soon. Pity, but there you were.

More and more he liked to hold my hand, with his left usually, while the right was holding a good talking book or a glass. He also wanted to know more about things he heard on his radio. Who was Germaine Greer? And the Women's Movement. Fined, was she? For saying 'bullshit'. Really. Well, well. Why don't you join?

I had realised the ridiculous situation of women when we came back from England for the first time and I attempted to open an account at Kirkcaldie and Stains. I was denied one. The account was to be in Neil's name and I gave him the required money, which I had earned. Mad. But that was long ago.

'I made the sandwiches with Barbara Hanna at the convention here. When I had just arrived home. Does that help?'

'Not much,' said Pop still stroking my hand.

His health became worse and he could no longer stay at the Home for the Blind. Fortunately we were able to find a bed in Ewart Hospital near where I worked so I could visit on my way home.

The English naval officer I met on the Devonport wharf when the *Rotoiti* was sailing for Korea about twenty-five years before had prophesised well. Neil continued to do well in the service. In 1978 he became a Rear Admiral and Chief of Naval Staff. This pleased him but meant he was much busier. There was more 'Shally humps and Shally hoops' with flags flapping and salutings all about. Also there was now his driver, Heather Casperson, Leading Wren driver, who became a good friend.

And I became a Hostess. I could cook like an expert as all New Zealand women can, but that is different from Entertaining.

I don't remember how the system worked. Nobody told wives of senior rank in any of the various services to give dinner parties for ambassadors and their wives from all over the wide wide world. What we did know was that young men so beautiful they must have come from central casting were available from RNZAF Shelly Bay where they were training as chefs and stewards. Usually I preferred to do the cooking, but willing young men about were always useful. They did anything and I use the word advisedly. I think they thought the whole thing of 'entertaining' was as unusual as I did. They would wait, serve, attend and then leave the kitchen like an advertisement for Ajax.

One evening I remember especially. All was going well and the Ambassador of the Netherlands laughed so hard at one of the comments made by one of our witty friends he flung his head back into a large dish of whipped cream being handed around by Steward Jack Castle. I was on my feet instantly but in a moment Jack had put down the dish, pulled back the ambassador's chair and escorted him to the bathroom for a quick wash and brush up. On return both were as calm as ever and the Consul-General of

South Africa was telling us we must all be putting our money into rands. Fortunately there was more cream available for a quick beat-up.

Another odd business about our high-life evenings was that our house, beautiful and comfortable as it was, had not been built for such occasions. The drawing room or parlour was diminutive, half the size of the dining room next door, which meant the solemn young men proffering pre-dinner drinks on a silver tray had to be athletic as well as attentive.

Also at the beginning there was no other door into the dining room, although eventually we had that altered. When the moment came to dine, the hostess (me) suggested that we should march into the hall and turn left into the dining room, where we were ushered to our seats by other young stalwarts.

This was a comparatively simple procedure. What became more interesting was if one of our guests wished to relieve themselves as the merry evening continued. All they had to do was turn left, march down the hall again, and walk into the kitchen where young men were busy doing dishes. One would wave the guest left where they would be confronted by an ancient Shacklock coal range which must have been installed when the house was built in 1906 and used until the house achieved electricity and it was closed over. We found the coal range and revealed it, liked it and tidied it up. It was a beauty of its kind though not perhaps to every eye. All the searcher for the lavatory now had to do was to avoid the washing machine and tub and head for the door beside the bathroom. Then trek back to the party.

I even kept a little notebook with the names of guests and the menu so the same people would not be meeting the same (a) food and (b) people. There are also some comments. 'Good', 'OK', 'Ghastly', 'Never again'. But they refer to food not guests.

We met some interesting people who 'asked us back' and enlarged my horizons. What was the name of the woman who was nicknamed 'The Den Mother of Manhattan'? The one who said, 'If you owe a bore a meal send it to them.' We never had to in Wellington.

A digression. What is the difference between Lunch and Luncheon? The dictionary, as always, helps. 'Lunch is a light meal in the middle of the day.' Luncheon, on the other hand, is 'a formal lunch'. Authors seem no help on this social problem. William Stanley Moss in his book *Ill Met by Moonlight* (published in 1950) tells the astonishing story of how he and his friend Patrick Leigh Fermor and some Cretan andartes kidnapped the German General Kreipe in Crete during the war, and marched him from one end of Crete to the other where a small boat carried the Englishmen and the German General to Cairo. Reading it lately I found among other things that the writer called every midday meal 'luncheon', be it boiled potatoes, a few onions and nothing else. Hardly a meal for hungry men on the run, but why 'luncheon'? Whereas Philip Roth's *Exit Ghost* (published 2007) is equally particular: 'lunch' always, even to the lengths of meeting someone at a Lunchette for lunch.

My one attempt at lunch/luncheon took place only because all the restaurants were shut, which seems odd nowadays. However, Shelly Bay, like the Windmill in London during the War, never closed.

The occasion was the visit of Admiral Gravely, US Navy, who was doing what he called a Swing Around the Pacific. He introduced himself to me as the Black Admiral, which gave me nice connotations of Muhammad Ali who was going to 'Float like a butterfly, and sting like a bee'.

The admiral was a large, pleasant man and I had a feeling that if he was the first black admiral in the US Navy in the 1970s, he must be pretty good at it.

'It will be an all-men,' Neil told me before the occasion, adding, 'except for you, of course.'

But that's the sort of odds I like. I felt like a cross between Madame Recamier and a geisha girl, and the Black Admiral gave me a smacking kiss goodbye.

And there is always Pop's quotation from Thomas Hood, 'For one of the pleasures of having a rout / is the pleasure of having it over.'

So God bless the Shelly Bay stalwarts. Plus those in the New Zealand Armed Services.

And their wives. Although Anne McLean, one of the good friends I made in Wellington's social whirl of Army, Navy and Air Force wives, was not a New Zealander. Anne had grown up in Argentina, where her Scottish parents had emigrated before she was born. Her husband Denis was seconded from Foreign Affairs and became the Secretary of Defence when Neil was Chief of Defence Staff.

Anne and I had a few useful ploys. If one of us failed to introduce someone to whom they were talking, we followed Ploy 1. Ploy 1 meant that neither of us had the slightest idea who they were, so introduced ourselves, thus avoiding that infuriating comment from the unknown: 'You haven't introduced us, Barbara (or Anne).'

Ploy 2. If a wife insisted on telling you how brilliant her children were, let her rip. Nothing could stop her and it is no use telling her your sons used to be able to stand on their heads.

Ploy 3. Great and excessive enthusiasm for skills and ability of husband in his job was also best met with polite smiles.

Ploy 4. Restraint when a young woman told you she could not think why she and her husband had been invited to Government House. Don't say, 'It's the job, thicko.'

There was a lot of routine pecks and kissing as well as talking. Coming from a non-kissing family I found this unnecessary. I once mentioned to one of the nicest and most sensible men around that I found it silly if not ridiculous.

He smiled his wise smile. 'Ah Barbara, I just regard it as part of the job.'

Ever a man of correct procedure, Pop would have been happy to make sure I would avoid too many gaffes with placements and names and even kisses, but he was now too unwell to help. He was in complete bed rest and cigarettes were never seen. Again his courtesy – and his conviction that he deserved it – helped him. The staff liked him and he all of them, particularly a senior male nurse called George. He was happier when George was on duty, becoming almost chatty and telling me what George had been doing. One afternoon he said, 'It's odd you know, Bub, I have a lot more puff when George is on. And with you and David of course. Where's your hand? Ah, that's right.'

He died later that day, after I left, on a late Saturday afternoon when Neil and I were having drinks with some nearby friends. As I was about to leave him I had asked, 'How do you really feel, Pop?' He kissed my hand again and answered with one of his Latin tags, the one in which gladiators were reputed to have saluted the emperor before entering the ring: 'Morituri te salutamus – We who are about to die salute you.'

George had not been on duty that afternoon.

Pop's funeral I do remember. So few people, so few, I thought, although I doubt he would have cared. He had not needed many friends, and had never bothered God.

Once, trapped at a party with an unknown man, he asked him whether he was going away for Easter. 'No, er, no,' said the vicar, touching his dog collar. 'Easter is a busy time for us.'

'Ah yes,' said Pop, unfussed.

A tolerant gentle man, and tolerance is not necessarily a negative quality. He is remembered with love.

I have mentioned the man in Lyttelton with his tannoy bellowing, 'There's six carriages round the corner, six carriages round the corner, six carriages.' And his subtext of 'Get on y' no hopers, get y' luggage round the flaming corner, there's six effing more carriages like I said.'

The tannoy man and David were right. 'It's your suitcase. It's your business. Push it.'

It took me longer to find that 'drifting and dreaming' was not enough. So much so that I was faintly pleased with myself when I made a pact with my father, for paying me the three years needed for me to get a bachelor of science and no more. Medical school was a lengthy and expensive business and David had years to go. I knew I was lucky to have *got* my letters.

Since then I had made other resolves. The list went like this:

1. To leave the Bay.

2. To go overseas.

3. To marry Neil Anderson, which was not only important but also lucky as it meant I sailed out of the Bay and overseas all in one go.

Now at fifty-three I needed another shove. Nothing, I knew, would make me write books alone, but what I did know was I had been most aware of writing and writers when I was teaching at St Margaret's and Mrs Cochran and the other English teachers encouraged me to discuss English literature with them.

Why then – and here comes the beautiful thought – what if I went to Victoria University as a mature student? I would have to read great writers, and perhaps something might rub off. Also I would write essays, which had always been the highlight of the week at Woodford, and surely I would receive something better than 'watch your commas'.

And what about Art? Tons of it. And essays in that too.

Vivienne was happy to leave our Box and Cox job at the hospital and we resigned.

I enrolled at Victoria University on the appointed day in 1980. There was no sign of Dolly Flower, David's friend, but the process was not without problems for the mature. Why did I not find 'How to Use the Library', which school leavers were attending for the morning. Neverthless, mature students then were *paid* to attend. How astonishing.

Milling about in the quad I met my third friend called Jill, Jill Barton, the owner of a shop in Karori which sold pottery, silk scarves, cards, paintings and prints all made in New Zealand. 'Goodness, Jill,' I said helpfully, 'how on earth are you going to have time to be coming here?' To which she replied she didn't know but she intended to try. Which she did and added to my pleasure in the academic world.

We sat together always in the same place as students tend to do. Intent Asian students were always in the front rows, relaxed New Zealand young sat high at the back. It was one of these whom Jill heard say to her friend as they passed, 'Who're those two colour-coordinated old dolls down there?' It was a sobriquet of which we became proud. Early next year when the flag fluttered and Heather and the car waited at the gate of 36 Beauchamp Street and Neil was about to depart he asked me what I was doing that day.

'Sitting in the sun reading *Lady Chatterley's Lover.*'

He picked up a battered briefcase. 'Ah yes, she was the one who was active on the estate was she not? The academic world must be hell.'

But he was wrong, he was indeed wrong.

CHAPTER 21

Now I was in the fortunate position of being paid to attend university. To read books written by writers who knew how to do it. To read some authors I had never heard of and others with alarm or ecstasy.

Somebody somewhere said good writing can only be learned from good writing. Lies, all lies. Good writers are good writers because they are good writers. Remember Jane Austen slipping her pages of script under a book when a visitor enters the morning room? Or Emily Dickinson keeping her poems hidden, and only five published while she was alive? These women knew they wanted to write more than anything else in the world, and very sensibly, they did. They had a finger on the pulse of words.

I loved sitting in the lecture rooms listening to every word from lecturers good and slightly less so and knowing I would have to read each and every book. And you *had* to read in the daytime.

Glorious.

And there were other pleasures. I was back to writing essays, this time at the kitchen table dissecting what I thought about Captain Ahab in *Moby-Dick*. Or by the same author, that obdurate oddball, the gentle *Bartleby, the Scrivene*r.

Tutorials also were new to me. No such things had existed in science. How could they have; no small groups of students could have gathered much from '*One* here and *One* there'.

In the humanities you could fight for knowledge if you wished to. You could ask questions. Could be encouraged to do so without being considered a skite, that long last lingering shadow of youth. *Skite* is not an endearing word but there was a worse phrase in the Bay. In my youth you would be said to 'have tickets on yourself'.

New Zealanders were said to be self-deprecating but we have become better, especially the young. And wait till you meet Americans.

It was not long before Jill and I met Dorothea Turner – one of the most memorable women I have known. She was the older sister of

John Mulgan who wrote in the beginning of his book *Report of Experience* of his country 'of places and a sound that is the tide coming in the early morning in Manganese Point, or the surf at evening at Whatipu, or a bush river in flood somewhere north of Karamea'.

Both Dorothea and her brother were adventurous from childhood. She told us they were once lost for forty-eight hours in a dinghy in the Hauraki Gulf with nothing to eat but golden syrup, cooked rice and presumably water. And were perfectly happy when found.

We met her not long after we had enrolled, when we were hoping to obtain what Dorothea called our 'warrants of fitness', some sort of certificate entitling us to continue doing what we have done all our lives, read books.

Dorothea had already written two books and been a literary and music critic for years. When a music critic asked whether her brother was musical she replied, no, her brother was 'not interested in music – he was very much a listener of words'.

Why didn't I think of that?

Now at the age of seventy Dorothea was working to complete her thesis for a PhD in, as I understood, the stylistic variations of Herodotus. The ENGL LIT work we told her about she continued to devour as a side dish. In the ten years she was there Professor Dearden of the classics department described her as an 'icon at Victoria'. And both of them knew what the word meant.

Dorothea would learn how to work a computer before the days of Senior Net, but occasionally would have to give it a kick, which meant taking it under one arm and marching around the department until she could find someone who could 'deal with it'. Her husband, Alexander Turner, was a man of calibre who had a distinguished legal career. By the time we knew them, Dorothea and Sir Alexander had their evening meal, then she would drive down to her room in the classics department, work there for a couple of hours, then return up the hill for an hour or two of Scrabble before they went to bed. I told her Neil and I couldn't play Scrabble, we always fought.

'But that's the whole point, Barbara, to impugn one's husband's education and knowledge.'

Impugn. Impugn. I went round murmuring the word all day.

I didn't think I had ever 'challenged or called something into question'. It seemed to have been a waste not to have done so.

Her clear-sighted intelligence and wit led to fun. As did her gift for friendship, and occasionally her sternness.

'No Barbara, I'm sorry but you're quite wrong.'

'But Dorothea . . . ?

A firm shake of the head. 'No.'

I had been reading J.D. Salinger's *Franny and Zooey* books (recommended by her) and liked the fragments of Sappho's poetry the author had used in one of them.

Raise high the roof beam, carpenter
The bridegroom cometh
Higher than a tall man.

'Dorothea, is there a good translation of Sappho's fragments somewhere,' I asked.

'Really, Barbara, you can't expect to get the true value of ancient Greek verse unless you learn the language.'

'Come off it, Dotty,' I thought, though did not say. Only very old friends called her that. More than that I should have liked to have impugned her comment, but of course didn't.

Far more often she gave us encouragement and enthusiasm. And wisdom. I learned from her virtues as diverse as fortitude, discretion and a concern for the words on the page. She had practical wisdom too. I asked her once whether she found that life was more of a muddle as one got older. She gave her dirty chuckle. 'It always was a muddle. It's just that we didn't notice then.'

One of our treats was to meet for lunch in Racquets, the café at the nearby squash courts, to talk long and hard about writers and other things of importance. It was always Dorothea who was first to read the new book by that interesting young New Zealand author.

Once when we were leaving a red-faced man came dancing up the steps. 'Had a good game girls?' he cried. Dorothea's look withered. He was never seen again.

Her judgements were often amusing. Words to her were things to play with, to savour. Once a young computer salesman was giving her the spiel on the virtues of his brand new model. This one, he assured her, was user-friendly. 'Ah,' said Dorothea, 'but I want one that's user-obsequious.'

After she and I had left university we continued to meet once a week in what she christened the Women's Collective, which now included Juliet Hobbs, another book eater. After one session at Juliet's house she was escorting us out to my car when Dorothea insisted on going her own way, and to Juliet's astonishment walked straight through a large bush and emerged on the other side seemingly unconcerned. She always walked with a stick and dealt with it with skill, which is easier said than done. They are tricky things, sometimes liable to wrap themselves around you. Dorothea had hers completely trained.

Nor did she ever make imperious gestures to motorists with her stick, but we could be walking along, inside or out, and without a word Dorothea would come to a halt, not suddenly, more like a well-oiled motor gently gliding to stillness. Then we would all stand staring ahead for a few moments. Nothing would be said, she was not puffed, or not that we could see. And then we would proceed, calmly, relaxed as ever, and conversation would be resumed. Our friend Dorothea was a joy and a wonder and I think her husband agreed. One evening she and I were talking at some legal gathering – which sounds a little odd, but anything is better than the term 'function'. We had arrived before Alec, who appeared at her shoulder, bowed at me and murmured to her ear, 'Consider yourself kissed.' A dear man.

At this time Anne McLean and I had discovered – or, more likely, our respective husbands had let drop – that the Air Vice Marshall Ewen Jamieson was about to make an official visit around the world to have talks with his opposite numbers in the USA, Great Britain, Germany and Canada. What the Black Admiral had called a 'swing around'. As he would be on official business he would be travelling in an RNZAF Hercules, and we might be able to hitch a ride.

To obtain something called an indulgence flight, we would need permission that we were welcome on board. Undoubtedly non-official people can be a nuisance. Like one of Damon Runyon's characters who said, 'I am known to one and all as a guy who is just around.' That would be us. Fortunately Ewen granted his permission. All that was required, from our respective husbands, was $587.

I had to explain my absence to someone in authority at the university and Bill Manhire was the one who swam into view. He looked at me with a firm eye. 'You're not going to do this sort of thing again, are you?'

'Oh no, certainly not.'

'Good.'

Our husbands remained calm at the temporary loss of their wives. After all it would only be four weeks. As Anne murmured to me as we boarded the C-130, 'They never thought we'd go.' All we had to do was go up those few steps.

Dorothea was delighted. If it had been possible she would have been waving us Godspeed with the biggest flag to be found. She was undoubtedly an early feminist.

Inside the plane was the Pod, an odd piece of work. It was literally a box inserted inside the aircraft to seat eight formica-lined on the inside; soundproofed, air-conditioned and with lambswool-lined seats. The officials, and us, were beautifully comfortable.

Anne was also studying at Victoria, so we settled down to write essays. Sitting in the Pod we must have looked so smug we were liable to burst.

In London I went to see Jeremy and Sue, his 'current girlfriend'. More surprises: the flat was both clean and pleasant. Sue was undoubtedly attractive though not as devastatingly as in photographs I had seen. Jeremy as ever was pleased to see us.

The next three weeks were a combination of 'What I did on my holiday' and a willy-willy. First there were friends: welcoming friends, 'Do come again' friends, friends I hadn't seen for years and with whom I immediately carried on half-finished conversations, real chew-the-fat friends. And favourite galleries, which like friends hadn't changed an inch.

Anne, as well as being alarmingly competent, had good ideas such as walking through the bright parks one Sunday at 8.30am to arrive at Westminster Abbey for morning service. I didn't know you could, why I can't think. Their only mistake was to have the wrong tune to 'Zion City of our God', but you must not make a fuss in abbeys.

After which I headed for Jeremy and Sue who were having a party. Jeremy was in the process of making blinies for me and his mates whom I knew and liked. Jane, for example, who sat with me on what I presumed was the master bed in the master bedroom while she told me about teaching the smallest girls in an Hasidic Jewish school.

The first mistake she had made was to put out her hand to shake the hand of the rabbi, the husband of the headmistress who had just engaged her. 'The poor man leapt up the curtains. I didn't know not to touch him.'

Jane was worried about her little girls; she felt they did not have much fun. Not only was their curriculum strict, but their behaviour must be also. And then when they left school, their hair was shaved off and they married and had infants in the hope of producing the Messiah, the promised hope of delivery for their race.

Jane had an idea. She asked permission of the headmistress to bring a goldfish to school, an idea to which the little girls reacted with something like hysteria and wild excitement, especially as they were going to choose a name for him – no one having mentioned a prospect of any other sex. Miss Elliot, who had been getting the goldfish stabilised at home, would bring him tomorrow.

'You'll never believe,' said Jane sadly.

'No!'

'Exactly. Gone belly up. Completely.'

'But what did you do?'

'What could I do? I thought of saying he was having a little rest but . . . Anyway Eddy' – her partner – 'dropped me off with the bowl with the fish still floating and the headmistress allowed us to bury him, but no, it was not nearly as much fun. They're hot on resurrection but . . . It wasn't *funny,* Barbara.'

Eddy arrived late. Jeremy introduced us. 'He's a brain surgeon, Mum. A profession which requires a certain amount of dedication. He's liable to be late.' It was a good party and showed no sign of ending. Eddy, though late, gave me a lift to the nearest tube station.

I arrived at the flat Anne had been lent feeling light of foot, but aware I had drink taken. Not too much by any means. Certainly not. After all I was my father's daughter, and all I had to do was to open the door with one of the keys Anne had given me.

Which was beyond me. Keys at home turn either this way or

that way, they don't sit in the middle and sulk. This one did. Eventually the only thing I could think of doing was to ring the bell long and hard as I knew Anne would be asleep. I continued for some time. Anne, obviously cold and sleepy, began shouting instructions as to how to make the damned thing open. None of which worked.

In the end I yelled at the door, 'I'll take mine out and you open with yours.' Anne, stunned that anyone could be so hopeless and getting colder by the minute, did so and we marched off to our double bed, me playing the drunken husband and Anne the unhappy wife.

Treats continued to jostle treats, however. The next day the sun shone and another of Anne's friends drove us down to Sissinghurst for the day. It was at the time when Vita Sackville-West's white garden was comparatively new and had launched a thousand replicas, even if some of us got little further than a grey pear tree sitting in the middle of a bed of white chrysanthemums. Rather to the disgust, surely, of the originator had she known.

Dorothea and Jill were pleased to welcome me back and we headed for Racquets for a mild celebration. Dorothea was in good form. She said that Godspeed is a good word for farewelling but one could scarcely offer a friend Godslow on return, or worse, Godwent.

I then went for a belated examination I had arranged with the English department before we left. Two memories remain: one of a question about Jonathan Swift's *A Modest Proposal,* that perfect use of enraged irony, and the other of the unfortunate invigilator's attempts to avoid going to sleep.

Jill and I met again that day. She had told me at lunch time she had discovered there was a course in Creative Writing. It had been in evidence for a few years. We exchanged comments. Fancy us not knowing – would you believe? Especially as Bill Manhire was in charge of the course and we knew him from ENGL LIT as being amiable, and, equally important, not boring.

I found a prospectus with speed. There it was: ENGL 252, Creative Writing = six credits, stage two, small classes of twelve. All we had to do was to send a portfolio of our work.

After some earnest discussion we decided not to tackle Creative

Writing yet. We had already planned to knock off Shakespeare and Middle English next year, and our new venture into Origins of Modern Art with Tony Bellette. We were already excited at the thought of it all. And perhaps all this good reading (and looking) might help us, in some mystic way.

Finally, happy as sandboys, Jill and I decided on two years of English and art before attempting ENGL 252.

Rear admirals and chiefs of navies have many tasks, one of them being to discuss matters of importance with admirals of friendly countries. Sometimes these discussions took place here, sometimes overseas, and sometimes Mrs Anderson might be able to accompany her husband.

The first admiral's wife I 'entertained' officially was Madame Nicketo Tan, wife of Admiral Sugito of Indonesia. The admiral's English was excellent, Madame's of the 'Yes' or 'No' variety, which could have made five days together heavy weather except for the presence of a young woman from the Indonesian embassy. From the moment Nicketo Tan Sugito opened the hotel room door I felt inadequate. Not only did the wardrobes bulge with teeming tiny model clothes, but the make-up jars on the chest of drawers positively bulged. There must have been twenty pottles and squeezers swathed about the neck in names gilded in French. How had Madame the time to get it all on, or more, get it off? My mother had just been playing about with Elizabeth Arden's products behind her Red Doors. How on earth could I keep Nicketo Tan happy when I was so keen to do so?

But all was well. Heather drove us to a New Zealand souvenir shop. With teeny whoops of joy our guests leapt out of the car and positively dashed into the shop. Nicketo Tan snapped up a paua shell kiwi clock set in wood, and paua everywhere: coasters, bracelets, necklaces, earrings.

Then I realised I was being ridiculous. Paua shell is beautiful, wonderful, and Nicketo Tan has not seen it before. Now she is doing what she is best at – buying things – and thereby keeping her husband happy by so doing. And think of the souvenir sales. We all relaxed, her smile widened, her English improved. 'My eyes are too big,' she laughed as she flung hundreds of dollars at the till.

Happy times continued through the day but not at quite such a quivering level. I felt things were good as Heather drove Nicketo Tan and her handler plus me and another wife to make things even, and we went to Waikanae to gaze at the beautiful New Zealand scenery and have lunch at Country Life. Nicketo Tan's smiles continued but less widely. Her triumph this time was in pointing at bored-looking white animals and saying, 'Sheeps.'

I whispered to Heather and we stopped at another souvenir shop on the way home, and so the entertainment continued to the north and back.

Admiral Neil Anderson was making small talk to Admiral Sugito at the farewell function. 'The first thing Barbara did when she arrived home was to water the garden.' Admiral Sugito looked puzzled. 'But surely your servants water the garden?' Gifts were exchanged later. Admiral Sugito presented Neil with an exquisite filigree silver Indonesian boat and me with a similarly handsome silver dish. Neil retaliated with two sheepskin rugs. I felt there was something symbolic about the exchange, though I hoped Nicketo Tan might be glad to nestle up against the skin of a sheeps occasionally.

An invitation to Neil to the United States included Mrs Anderson, who leapt at it like a bounding doe. America when we were young was where every good thing came from. Films at the Cosy on Saturday Mornings with Colin and me and Barbara Landels glued to our seats as the injuns cantered by on their ponies with no saddles, and sometimes slipped themselves over to one side to avoid the whiteskins' bullets, though Colin worried for their steeds. Then followed *Crime Does Not Pay* and a licker in the foyer afterwards.

I was not deterred by the news that I would travel economy class and Neil first – not from virtue, anyone could see that, but because Neil would be working and I was going to see America. To keep up appearances I would be ushered into first class before landings, the first of which was Hawaii, where we were greeted by friendly people and shown into the guest house for visiting senior officers.

Neil's escort officer appeared next morning, a young woman, Susan Murdinger, a lieutenant in the US Navy. My height, slim as a bluebell, smart as paint and funny with it. Later on I couldn't resist saying, 'Susan, you have the most wonderful green eyes I have ever seen.'

'Mrs Anderson, I have the most beautiful green contact lenses ever seen.'

Our flight from Hawaii to California was courtesy of the US Navy, a beautiful experience. The P-3 (Orion), as Neil told me, had bunks, plush seats and antimacassars with four stars embroidered around USN in each corner in case anyone was muddled as to whom this beauty belonged. The young Philippino steward loved Neil and attempted to brush his uniform every time he moved.

An unexpected delight in Pasadena was the Huntington Library, which, it fortunately being Sunday, Neil could see too. The docent who had volunteered her services led us round this wonder, where we moved along from a 1460 Book of Hours to *Piers Plowman,* after whom we had named our son Piers –

In a somer season, whan softe was the sonne

and then around a corner or two to David Hockney's etchings inspired by Wallace Stevens's poem inspired by Picasso, which I had just read!

The man replied 'Things as they are
Are changed upon the blue guitar.'

Round more corners and more surprises. Some early silver, by which they meant a 'fifteen-century woodrose spoon with a wild man of the woods on the top'. (If you happened to know what a woodrose is, or which wild man.) Then finally into the gardens, herb gardens (shades of my meagre Herbert Garden in Newlands), and old rose gardens, down to the Japanese garden, with the house open on each side.

Everything which wasn't outstanding seemed to be fun. Outside stood a bright pink bus with large eyes and huge eyelashes painted around its head lamps. It was called the Nudie Cutie Courtesy Bus. I should have guessed. That morning we had read in the *New York Times* that the Tutankhamun Exhibition had finally closed. The headline read *Tut Tut Tutsie Goodbye*. Could the *Dominion* match that? Though of course the Tutankhamun Exhibition had never been there to de-tut.

On our last night in Washington the New Zealand Ambassador to the United States of America, Mervyn Norrish, and his wife Francoise gave a dinner party for us in the embassy. A happy evening and an excellent rack of lamb, I remember.

Neil's official visits to the Pentagon and other naval VIPs were now finished and we flew in a dolly little plane to New York, where our dear American handlers gave us a last farewell and flew home, and we checked in to the Gorham Hotel in the centre of the city. Ye Gods. This hotel was a perfect set for the lonely hotel where the heroine takes the overdose in the last reel. The reason for this being we were paying for it ourselves. The room was filthy; Mum could not have possibly have put a foot on the floor. The cold water was off, but fortunately came on by the time we had had a walk down Fifth Avenue.

On the day we were to leave New York, 2 October, the Pope was to arrive and there were dire predictions as to the traffic tangles which we were assured would be extreme. Pope or no Pope, Neil was due at Rhode Island for a Sea Power Symposium for the Chiefs of Naval Staff from over the Free World. And no, I didn't know what it meant either.

Arrangements were made for us, vis-à-vis the Pope, to be driven by Captain Tempero, our New Zealand Naval Attaché in Washington, to Newport where Neil would meet his next escort officer, male this time, equally charming and efficient, who talked to me about Wallace Stevens. More than that, he gave me his own book of one of his poems. 'I can get another, any time. Please, Mrs Anderson, I would like you to have it.'

Mrs Anderson thanked with shy enthusiasm.

Where do they *get* these men?

Flying from one side of America to the other is relatively painless as long as you are used to being cramped, crowded and eating plastic meals. We arrived in San Francisco and the hotel was both reasonable and clean. Added to which we found a café that included window views of a sensational sunset beneath the Golden Gate Bridge and us with two Bloody Marys to hand. Next day we flew from San Francisco to Los Angeles International

Airport, which was very nasty indeed. With conflicting signs, confusion, and walking for miles, we found we had arrived in the right place where we sank a gin. Eventually, at boarding time Neil walked firmly into first class while I peeled off into second. After some time the American chief steward appeared to apologise but there was no way he would be able to move me up.

Me: 'Not at all.'

Him: 'And I notice that your husband is determined not to come sit with you?'

Me: 'Mumble, mumble.'

Him: 'He must be a brave man or has an amazing wife.'

Me: 'But you're not a New Zealander.'

Him: 'Is that how it is? I'll emigrate immediately.'

CHAPTER 22

Anyone who had fought there in the war could never have forgotten the Battle of Crete. The official fortieth anniversary was in May 1981 and the main commemorations were to take place at Galatos, the scene of one of the most bloody and heroic battles of all.

The minister of defence, the Hon David Thomson, was to represent the government and he would also make official visits to Singapore and Kuala Lumpur *en route*. He would be accompanied by his wife June, Neil (and me), and Denis McLean, but regrettably not Anne as she was now teaching and thus tied to her post. The ministerial party were joined *en route* by representatives of the Crete veterans from New Zealand and a colour party from Singapore, to travel by Hercules to Crete.

The flying was better than I had dared to hope. No Pod this time but perfectly comfortable. A lot of noise certainly but earphones dealt with that and I was working on *Sir Gawain and the Green Knight* for Middle English.

The first day in Crete held several joys. One was to meet our friend Ann Thomas, who was now living in Crete and had come to stay in Hania to be at the ceremonies of the fortieth anniversary and to see me, and Neil when he was not being official.

Other treats followed. Having landed at Hania, we discovered that our hotel was right on the Porto Veneziano, the beautiful Venetian harbour with the lighthouse at the end of the mole.

We found also that after lunch all who wanted to could rush back to 'our' aircraft and scream off to Knossos for literally three quarters of an hour and worth every minute of it. Knossos is a magical place, even I knew that. We then had five minutes in the Heraklion Museum, a glimpse, but at least we saw the bull water clock.

Then back to Hania to the appropriately named Hotel Hercules, and at the appointed hour Ann Thomas appeared, the same mind-blowing good mate as ever. She was with us at the first of the ceremonies next morning in a small mausoleum in a minute, almost nonexistent village where we saw our first traditionally dressed Cretan men, bandaleros with bobbles across their foreheads, around their waists dagger type swords, and black high boots into which were tucked knee breeches. For some reason one leg was always placed forward. One old hero had a New Zealand plaque slung around his neck.

Then on to the next ceremony at Galatas, the scene of the epic battle where the New Zealand troops, many of them Maori, retook the town in fierce hand-to-hand fighting and where Lieutenant Charles Upham won his first VC. The atmosphere was tremendous. When we sang 'God Defend New Zealand', that sadly uninspired national anthem, I bellowed it with pride and declined for some reason to sing 'God Save the Queen'. The bugle player in his lemon squeezer hat stood up on a flat-roofed house and sounded the Last Post while the Greek flag fluttered above him. So many dead, so many young. It was heartbreaking.

There were wonderful moments. When one old Cretan in full fig discovered two of the New Zealand veterans, he kissed both their hands, four in all. I saw it.

We left feeling proud to have met such people. Neil then went to another ceremony and Ann and I back to the Hercules to catch up with our talking. We sat cheek by jowl on the little balcony gazing at the Venetian lighthouse. 'Tell me more, why were you so determined to live here.' 'No it's your turn, how's Wellington.' 'Superb.' 'Liar.' 'Not at all.'

Eventually Neil came back and we all took a taxi to a taverna on the beach. Simple tavernas are a Greek triumph, especially when by the sea. A sheet of plastic was thrown over the wooden table by a friendly host, a few peanuts and broad beans both still in their shells followed the plastic, wine came in something like a more elegant milk bottle and orders were taken. Ann ordered tiny fish and real Greek salads.

Glorious.

The last ceremony of the day was at Souda Bay. As we drove down with the windows open I sniffed. 'What's that wonderful smell?'

The driver stopped, jumped out and handed me a bunch of wild thyme. 'Oregano,' he said. I told you Cretans are wonderful.

The day was becoming cooler as the last ceremony came to an end. It was quieter with many of the Greek sailors from the Souda Bay training school participating.

Then came the Folklore Festival where the spirit and gaiety of the dancers of all countries lifted the heart. It was also interesting to have to go to Crete to discover that Scotsmen do not wear anything under their kilts. I suppose I had not sat directly below a stage before, or the rules at the highland dancing competitions at the Hawke's Bay Agricultural and Pastoral Shows were different.

On Sunday we went to the Greek Orthodox cathedral with Ann. Like many things in Crete it was faintly similar, yet very different: highly ornate carvings and statues of unknown saints adorned the walls, there was much chanting on all sides, and elaborately dressed white-bearded priests.

On we went to Kolimi to a ceremony on a hillside in the memory of cadets in training during the war who were too young to fight, fought anyway, and were killed.

Lunch was at the Officers Club and I was lucky. I sat beside a New Zealander who was knowledgeable about the Greek political situation, the endless jostling for positions, the dire problems, and how to ease them.

Ann appeared again at the hotel later in the afternoon. Neil went somewhere official and once again we talked, drank coffee and stared at the lighthouse. She then led me into the town to the navy museum to see an exhibition of historic photographs which had been taken in the war, including one of a German firing squad killing 108 hostages. The most appalling thing was the half-smile on the face of the German officer in charge.

We walked on up and around an old wall, past cottages and little gardens. Obviously in Crete one must walk. And certainly we must come again and explore further with Ann.

Another of the pleasures was getting to know the 'Vets', as they were always called. The plane that had flown from home carried one general, two brigadiers, a colonel, two lieutenant colonels, a major from the Maori Battalion, and a colour party of ten from the 2RNZIR in Singapore led by the sergeant major and the bugler. Captain Upham and Dan Davin, war historian flew from England.

We talked of different things; between themselves they must have been in different worlds. The ones who talked with me quite often were General Gentry, Brigadier Burrows and Colonel Fountaine, who came from the Coast where my Grandfather Jackson and my mother came from. He endeared himself to me by agreeing with Mum's story; he too as a child had heard of the carthorse with a straw hat with holes for the ears to come through. He also said it was high time I revisited the Coast. Which I did later.

Brigadier Burrows and I talked about teaching, which he had done all his life and as a territorial when he was not at war, in the same way that General Kippenberger had been a territorial and lawyer before war broke out. Both of them also came from the South Island.

Teaching, the brigadier and I agreed sitting side by side in the Hercules, has its pleasures and its displeasures. He thought if I had taught longer in one good school I would have liked it more. I agreed. We moved on to books, and especially poetry. Did I like A.E. Housman? Very much, especially since I had been often to Shropshire. We chanted snatches we could remember to each other.

My other friend, if I may call him that, was General Gentry. He talked to me about how difficult it must have been for the wives all those years when their men were away, then went on to tell me how he had been surprised to find that Mrs G. had kept all his letters.

'But of course she would.'

'Do you think so?'

Then he recalled a particular letter in which he told his wife how much he would be like to be in their garden planting broad beans (his favourite) and he would hear her call, 'Tea's up', and he would go round, pick up his cup, flop in his chair and say, 'Nearly finished.' Then he'd remembered what hell the following few days had been and that it was days before he could get that letter away.

'I never told her of course,' he said, almost shyly, 'but it was odd wasn't it.'

'Yes.'

The sergeant major, who was the only chap who could iron the lemon squeezers to parade ground perfection, was also friendly. 'I'll show you next time. They're quite tricky,' he said. They were too.

Another person I met was Patrick Leigh Fermor, who with William Stanley Moss masterminded the kidnapping of the German General Kreipe in Crete with Cretan andarte assistance.

There were others, including a few women. One of them – who stays in my mind as having an unusual name which eludes me – was a film reviewer for the *Observer*. They all had stories to tell, as did each of the vets.

Farewells to Crete came with determinations to come again, especially to see Ann as she stood in front of her hotel in front of a row of baby octopuses hung on a line to dry.

Flying home in the Hercules I had plenty of time for thinking as well as keeping in touch with *Sir Gawain*. I didn't do heavy thinking often. Nor do many unless thinking is their trade.

But as the sun sank before the blazing horizon in Australia I was wondering why I had drifted from both the political ethics and the religion of my childhood. Like my father I had never been keenly interested in politics. It seemed to me as I grew older that my vote would go to the party which did the best for the most.

The subject had never surfaced until brother David mentioned supporters of Bill Rowling, the Labour Leader who had taken over as Prime Minister when Norman Kirk died, who had begun an organisation they named *Citizens for Rowling*. Some left-wing doctors in Wellington carried on with a similar group which they called *Physicians for Rowling*.

David was enraged. 'Who the hell do they think they are!'

'They have every right.'

'You don't mean you vote Labour?'

'Yes.'

'Good God. What did the old man say?'

'Not much.'

Similarly the lapse from the faith of childhood, the 'Gentle Jesus, meek and mild / Look upon a little child' prayers each night, followed by Sunday School at St Matthew's, then weekly worship at St Luke's, then daily matins at St Francis of Assisi. All had slowed down to me in faith as the years rolled by. Neil and I marched our children to church at Newlands occasionally and always at Christmas like so many others. 'Presents come afterwards, you know that boys.'

Our sons were confirmed as their parents had both been. And that was as far as it went for them – while their mother drifted along thinking about God.

I still wonder why so many men and women have died for their faith. I have never liked the sound of Abraham, who was preparing to sacrifice his own child to prove his love for God until God stepped in and said that was enough.

And look at alternatives like Voltaire: 'If God did not exist, it would be necessary to invent him.'

Stevie Smith, the poet I met in ENGL 109, gave me many pleasures, and her 'Not Waving But Drowning' is now a classic. She also had other talents such as writing letters. One of them finishes with the perfect adieu to a fellow writer: 'I hope you are well and writing like stink.'

Glorious.

And then there were her views on God. She too grew away from contented faith. She too loved the music in the church, the psalms, the wonderful words.

She too must have chanted, 'I will lift up mine eyes unto the hills, from whence cometh my help', or better, 'Be still, and know that I am God.' I miss such words, and miss, and miss. There was no agony, no grieving disillusion; it was just that I didn't believe any more. And nor did Stevie Smith. But she got in first.

This heavy thinking faded away as I thought of seeing Jem and Piers when we landed in Auckland. That would certainly be good.

Three weeks later an ANZUS meeting was held in Wellington. It fell to Neil (and me) to slip lightly up to Ohakea in a plane and greet Admiral and Mrs Long – he, Bob, was the Commander in Chief, Pacific Command, and Sara his wife. It seemed to me an odd way to kill Saturday but Neil assured me it would be appreciated. Then the four of us flew back to Wellington. I liked Sara immediately, cool and visibly so. I had not met a cool American woman before and Bob was sweet, though I don't suppose the Admiral, Pacific Command, would be pleased to be thought so.

Sunday was spent with more hovering to meet the Australian

Chief of Defence Staff and his wife. We had met Tony and Anne in Australia and they were pleasant as ever. All merry so far.

Tuesday was Anne McLean's and my day to officially welcome the wives. We whooped it up at a luncheon at a restaurant called Windows on Wellington, a place of which we had heard good reports. It must have been sabotaged – the food was appalling.

Mrs Haig, wife of the dreaded General Haig, Secretary of State, looked completely stunned as well she might. She probably was wondering what country she was in. A faded, reserved, sad-seeming woman.

Neil told me later that General Haig played tennis at 5pm and again at 7am. Raewyn, his driver who had taken over from Heather, gave a mangled chuckle as she heard a mutter from the back seat, 'Musclebound creep.'

Then it was my turn to host a dinner party. This time the food was cooked by the ever-blessed men from Shelly Bay and it was a good party – the Longs, the Synnots, the McLeans and ourselves. All you need is good food and interesting guests. Bob Long, that dear man, gave us a print of an early US warship and three pineapples.

Two hospitable people in Wellington were Earle and Rosemary Riddiford, who then lived in an old house set in a large garden by the sea. Earle was one of the strongest mountain climbers around. He had been the driving force behind the New Zealand expedition to the Garhwal Himalayas in Northern India and also with Eric Shipton, the leader of the Everest reconaissance in 1951, both times beside Ed Hillary.

The Riddifords must have been nudged by 'higher authority' and thus Anne and I and the ANZUS ladies, Sara Long and Anne Synnot, went to lunch at Orongorongo. The four of us were driven to Wainuiomata, and down to the coast road to the sea and on to be welcomed by our hosts. After coffee Earle directed us to a Land Rover. Not his wife of course, Rosemary was now to attend to the lunch. The Land Rover also had a final touch in the form of a corporal driver complete with his coloured stable belt, the history of which had always interested me. Something to do with different colours on the belts of each regiment. He drove the five of us at a fast clip across the paddocks and on to vast boulders towards the sea. And then the seals. A dramatic and wonderful sight. Twenty? Thirty or more. So many seals lumbering and staring at us, so close to the capital city.

As the belted corporal drove back at a more stately pace Earle told us a fine story. His great great grandmother had seven daughters and she realised they had little hope of marriage (only one man had appeared at Orongorongo during the previous year). Like Jane Austen, Mrs Riddiford knew that 'a single man in possession of a good fortune, must be in want of a wife'. Mr Riddiford was not interested in this problem so his wife made arrangements for two Maori war canoes and their crews to paddle the family (except her husband) to Petone, where bachelors were many. The only loss to the story was Earle not knowing the tally of success.

Seals, corporal in stable belt at high speed, tales of seven maidens paddled by friendly Maori in war canoes and a beautiful garden, made a good morning. Then duck soup with orange, followed with other delicious food. A glimpse as to how it can be done.

After the Synnots left for Australia Neil and I (and the air force) took the Longs for a perfect flight on a perfect day. We saw both Mt Egmont and Mt Ruapehu clearly as we flew over the Southern Alps and around Mt Cook. Flying up Milford Sound was not only dramatic but exciting, scenic wonders everywhere. When we landed at Queenstown it was cold, but the air, we all agreed, was like wine.

The next day we went to the airport for other scenic delights, this time by helicopter. A bossy young woman briefed us about them – Bob referred to her later as 'that marine sergeant' – but as he was in command of all US forces, army, navy and air force from the west coast of the US, across the Pacific to the Middle East, he did not require much briefing. He also gave a nice touch to things, one typical of Bob. Just before we climbed into the helicopter he shook hands solemnly with his flag lieutenant, as one departing on a deeply dangerous mission.

Undeterred we all took off for more wonders and the pilot made the most of them: the jet boat rides on the river, the glistening mountains, the purple hills melting down to the golden tussock.

We were sorry to leave the Longs at Christchurch airport.

*

The ANZUS meeting finished in June 1981, and shortly after occurred what came to be known as the Molesworth Street incident.

The Springboks were touring New Zealand, and thousands of people, led by HART (Halt All Racist Tours), were protesting, not wishing the country to be associated with apartheid. The match before had taken place in Hamilton, and the anti-Tour protesters had won a victory. Four hundred had managed to get into the ground, then linked arms for two or more hours while the police could do nothing but trot around them, and the game was called off. Prime Minister Rob Muldoon, who was in the UK, sent a message back: 'Such events must not be repeated.' And they were not.

Men and women who gathered at Molesworth Street about five o'clock that day linked arms and began to march up the street past parliament, to be greeted by nervous young policemen with batons.

I had not planned to march there. I had been busy rearranging the chairs in our tiny parlour so a few friends would all get a good view of the Royal Wedding – that most romantic wedding seen on television since the Queen's. It was not until next morning when we heard the wireless and opened the *Dominion* that we learned of the bloody batons and broken arms and faces. We were stunned with disbelief. New Zealand cops did not beat up innocent citizens.

Responses to the Molesworth Street incident were varied. The protestors became better organised. From then on all were wearing helmets and protective clothing. The police next brought out their most frightening weapon, well-trained police dogs. Then we heard allegations that Muldoon had called in the SIS to assist law and order.

Other unexpected results occurred. Some men who loved their footy – men who felt, as John Mulgan wrote in *Report on Experience*, 'Rugby football was the best of our pleasures: it was religion and desire and fulfillment' – decided this was too much. A few such men were now marching with the protestors, as were women who had never thought of saying boo to a policeman.

The next march to stop the Tour was before the Test at Wellington's Athletic Park. The nearest rallying point to us was near the National Museum. Anne McLean and I agreed to meet there.

'Apartheid,' I said when we met, 'is legalised racism condoned by law.'

Anne nodded. She had read it too.

By the time we arrived there was a large crowd milling around, many stamping their feet. Why, I wondered? Judith and Helen who had been watching the Wedding with us were there, and other friends. Some in the crowd were exhilarated, some eager, most earnest.

Finally a tough-looking marshal who wore an armband, a motorbike helmet and a homemade shield and carried a loud hailer jumped onto a nearby truck. He told us what to do: link arms, hold tight, keep in step and stay near a marshal at all times, if we could. Squads were marching from all over Wellington, he yelled. Eventually they would converge on Rintoul Street, join forces at Athletic Park, break through the barricade, stop the bloody Test, break and head off for a beer. Right?

We roared again.

He continued: 'Finally, if things get rough, keep your heads down and stay calm.' We all roared again.

All clutched arms as we set off, led by the chanting marshals in their gear. Up Taranaki Street we went and the chants grew louder and more aggressive. Now we were in Wallace Street. Citizens, some of whom had never thought of appropriating a disabled carpark, were now shouting –

One, two, fuck the cops
Three, four, fuck the cops
And more, fuck the cops
One, two, fuck the . . .

Tension mounted. We were strong, marching against racial discrimination seven thousand miles away and proud to do so. I knew that, absolutely. But . . .

'I don't want to fuck the cops,' I yelled at Anne as we marched past the old Winter Show Buildings.

'What?' she yelled back.

'The cops, I don't want to fuck them.'

'You don't have to. Get real.'

The pace was now much slower, and I drew to a halt as we headed down the slope towards Adelaide Road.

'That chant. I have every respect for the cops, or had until recently. It's Muldoon and the thick-headed oafs of the Rugby Union who should be impregnated.'

'It's a chant for heaven's sake.'

'My father always said you should not be carried away by the idiocy of others.'

Anne looked at me in sorrow and ran on.

In the sneakiest part of my mind I had another reason for leaving. I had an essay for Middle English due to be handed in tomorrow. Yes, on *Sir Gawain and the Green Knight*. I would never get home to finish it at the rate we were going.

I felt worse when I heard of the scene at Rintoul and Luxford Street. More violence, more bloody long batons, more beatings. This time the police had used slashers to cut down the protesters' grappling hooks, with which they had planned to gain access to the match through the barbed wire.

The South Africans won the Second Test in Wellington 24–2.

And the essay? It was marked B+. One of those 'could do better'.

CHAPTER 23

Dorothea foregave me for not protesting till the end. Her anger was that she and her walking stick would have been unable to march for long. She must have felt like Boadicea without her chariot.

The Springboks went home in due time and the Tour was over.

Two games were cancelled by HART and their followers.

Mr Muldoon's government was re-elected but with a reduced majority.

Then summer came, the long hot summer when citizens of the country look forward to holidays and Jeremy and Piers came home with their sagas of marches and wounds. Jeremy had been manning a medical tent organised by HART but the marchers and cops passed at such speed that the obvious thing to do was for him to pick up his bags and chase after them.

Not having a daughter I have not known much about young women of the time but sons delighted me. They were fun, told me many things but not all, and made me laugh to excess. Which didn't stop them giving me extreme surprises occasionally.

Neil and I had been in Auckland for some reason and planned to pick Piers up early in the morning from the flat which he was sharing with others. I was slightly surprised by the strong language chalked on a blackboard in the kitchen, but more so when through an open door I saw two young men asleep in a single bed.

At this moment Jeremy drifted in from his nearby shared flat. He patted me kindly on the shoulder. 'Culture shock, Mum. Just culture shock. Good guys.'

Which they were and still are, and am I not a fan of Auden?

Lay your sleeping head, my love,
Human on my faithless arm.

Perhaps it was the smallness of the bed or the influence of the Hays Office in my youth?

We finally dragged Piers from his bed and headed for Wellington where Jeremy joined us later. Their visits were varied. Once they helped Neil who was painting the house and another time joined with their father in hiring morning suits for their cousin Diana Wright's wedding.

And as always they brought their favourite records (no CDs then) for me to hear. Their taste was perfect. The enigmatic Grateful Dead, singing 'Mama Tried': 'I turned twenty-one in prison doing life without parole . . .' followed by 'Mama tried to save me but her feelins I denied, but Mama tried, Mama tried, Mama TRIED'.

I embroidered the colourful album cover of the Grateful Dead on the back of Jeremy's blue denim shirt which was gratefully received and much envied. Like a good Mama, I had tried.

There were many others. 'Six Days on the Road' by the Flying Burrito Brothers, and Johnny Cash was not to be missed, especially 'Man in Black' – surely the most moving piece of ham ever sung. Gram Parsons was another favourite – 'We'll Sweep Out the Ashes in the Morning' being one, and a sad song, 'The Streets of Baltimore', which tells the tale of a young man who sold his farm in Tennessee because his darlin' wanted to live in Baltimore and it makes a man feel good to keep his darlin' happy but when he came home from work at the factory with every muscle sore he realises his darlin' loved the streets of Baltimore more than she loved him.

We drove through those streets with Denis and Anne McLean while we were staying with them much later in Washington on our way to see Alan Bennett's *The Madness of George III*. But I didn't sing it. I didn't think they would have appreciated the young man's grief.

Another of those expeditions which Bill Manhire had once described as 'this sort of thing' took place in April when Neil was invited by the Japanese defence forces to visit their establishments and have discussions with Admiral Yata, Neil's opposite number. I was also invited. How many women are invited officially to visit Japan? Good luck, Anderson.

And it was the most interesting ten days I had ever spent. Completely different in so many ways – beauty in unexpected places, cities hideous in smog and crowded beyond words, traditional differences from sitting to sleeping, from eating to bathing, and wit and friendliness from both men and women I met everywhere. I had expected formality, and there was that, but I had not expected such laughter.

We were met at the airport by Ross Craig from the New Zealand embassy and Rear Admiral Oki of the Joint Staff Council (who spoke perfect English) and Major Sugimoto (almost as good) who wheeled us around the enormous airport to the driver waiting to take us to the residence. Then began the hellish traffic to meet the New Zealand ambassador, Rod Miller, and his wife Pam. I had met enough members of Foreign Affairs to realise that part of their job is to help New Zealanders abroad, and sometimes to have them to stay in the residences, which they have all done with friendliness.

I woke up to a fresh spring day and a beautiful garden, then after breakfast Pam and I walked their dog amongst narrow streets and private houses with glimpses of places I would never have seen, including miniature gardens in pots right on the street, which were endearing.

Then back to the embassy driver who drove us to a department store where we shot up each floor, with young women bowing saying, 'Good Morning Madam. Welcome to the Something Something Store', which I found a bit odd but possibly it was the speed of the escalators. It was worth every minute, though, as Pam showed me *yukata,* a simpler version of a kimono, made of cotton not silk, and not nearly as elaborately decorated. The ones I chose were two male ones, one being for me. The young saleswoman looked alarmed . . . Madam should have more flowery patterns, girls for girls, there should be no messing up the sexes. However, I was firm; I had never been a floral matron and I liked the idea of the hard-working Japanese man slipping into his when he came home, and also of wise New Zealanders slipping into the lightest dressing gown ever known.

Next morning Neil went to sign the book at the Emperor's Palace while I was conducted around the garden by a diminutive woman – my height was a shock to many in Japan but their politeness restrained them from showing too much alarm.

One of the highlights of the garden was the bonsai garden where my guide told me there were one hundred varieties of tree.

I have never been a bonsai fan, but the results in the Emperor's garden were delightful, including miniature quinces, apples, and cherries in full flower. My guide told me volunteer gardeners come to work in the Emperor's garden for three days, there was a six-month waiting list, and on the last day they met the Emperor. We watched the lucky ones at work in wide aprons and big white hats.

This was interesting but watching a thousand-year-old looking gardener giving a bonsai its daily pruning was better. The process took some time, during which he glanced not an eye to either of us. He knew his priorities and had plenty of time.

Next day we left Tokyo in the bullet train on our way south to Nagoya. Ceremony here was not forgotten. Neil was greeted by the station master and the rest of us followed into the imperial family's waiting room where we drank tea. Then, after an exchange of cards, and in my case feeling like something out of a Monty Python sketch, we slid onto a mile-long red carpet and were ushered onto the train, with officials sweeping small people out of the way.

Admiral Oki showed me notices inside the train. 'The train is travelling at 150 kilometres per hour,' he translated.

'Goodness.'

I liked more an advertisement beneath the speed notice where a young Japanese man with a crew cut and a lasso glared at me while he smoked his Marlboro cigarette. More goodness.

However, the polluted air made the perfect cone of Mount Fujiyama rather dim as we flashed by. I had expected it to look like the calendar that had hung in Nana Jackson's dining room fifty years earlier.

We disembarked from the bullet at the city of Nagoya and again with immaculate timing Major Sugimoto swept us all to visit Heian-Jingu Shrine (The Shine of the Sword) where we were met by a swashbuckling priest in pale turquoise trousers, the effect being strangely macho. After him we met the high priest, another charmer in occidental rig. Eventually he excused himself to go to a conference, having offered us rather bitter thick tea like pea soup. I liked it, rather like campari. Perhaps also the small sticky cakes were to see him through his conference.

I still felt, though, that everything must be perfect or heads would roll. Not the high priest's nor Admiral Oki's, but Major Sugimoto seemed ill at ease if a fly sneezed. For example, when the bullet train had swept into the station, at a word from Admiral Oki the major had leapt from it and run at speed to meet the entourage who then were sweeping forward to escort us to the correct waiting room.

By now Neil was getting into the swing. He seemed to know where to stand, to move, to be greeted. But from then on we travelled more slowly, which meant there was more to see than speed flashing by. I enjoyed the Japanese women with huge baskets on their backs, and the school children in their uniforms. On this day hundreds of paper kites were flying for the boys, Admiral Oki told me. It was their festival and I was assured there were girls' festivals, but, no, they did not have kites.

Our next stop was Kyoto where we visited the Palace Garden. Any place in Japan with palace in its name is liable to be good. 'Boss stuff,' as Major Sugimoto told us and he was right. It was a beautiful garden but rather a speedy visit. The Major discovered we had been too quick as we had walked around it. We now had five minutes to spare so the thing to do he thought was to do it again. After some more thought it was decided it would be better to have a mini lecture from a Japanese guide (in Japanese) for a few minutes, which eased the anxious major.

That night we stayed in a *ryokan,* a Japanese inn where all was total peace and calm. They are, of course, made for small ladies and gentlemen and sleeping on the floor takes a little getting used to and the bathing arrangements were unusual. First we took turns sitting naked in a deep wooden tub full of hot water, then into showers, then again in red hot water. Why red this time, we wondered. There were things I would have wished to own, from the little stool in the bathroom to a low table near the sleeping arrangements. Perfect simplicity everywhere you looked.

Suitably cleansed we put ourselves into our two handsome yukata – they must have been sent from Hokkaido, the northern island where people are taller. Then we sailed along to Admiral Oki's room for a Japanese-style meal which meant we would be eating on our knees which I thought would not be my forté. Not so, and the food was excellent and a happy time was had after a wonderful day.

Five new things:

1. The exquisite little Japanese garden outside our window.
2. *Shibui*, the Japanese word for good design.
3. *Wabi,* which means 'melancholy' restraint.
4. The sign on the minibar: 'Please choice cheerfully.'
5. A giant Pink Panther gesticulating with writhing pink limbs above a garage nearby.

Neil had expressed a wish to see a place called Miyajima, a little island on the Inland Sea where he and two other midshipmen had had photographs taken thirty-five years earlier.

Things swung into action with speed and a second photograph with Neil and Admiral Oki was taken. When Neil had last seen Miyajima it was a small fishing village with a shrine and the famous Torii in the sea where the first photographs had been taken. Now it was the Polperro of Japan – thick with Aunt Lillias's 'trippers' – but today with a couple of odd-looking large people with funny voices. A polite teacher asked me if her high school students could practise their English on me. Certainly. Certainly.

Later I refused Major Sugimoto's suggestion I should visit with him the Peace Museum in Hiroshima while the other men were working. He was very disappointed. It was excellent he told me.

Another admiral appeared at this stage: V.A.D.M. Nagata, an amiable man with beautiful western table manners which I found odd. He was in command of the Kure naval district and hosted the dinner that evening. We were all sitting on chairs, which was easy for everyone, but his knife and spoon drill was as good as Little Lord Fauntleroy's, as if his mother had knocked him into shape.

Next morning was another triumph of organisation for Major Sugimoto who arrived for us at 8am. Then we drove through more pollution through wisteria and azaleas growing wild, cascading down the hills to the sea. Neil peeled off at the naval headquarters and I met Mrs Yata and we departed for Etajima, a small island of the Inland Sea, by the admiral's barge. There is a pleasing ring to the phrase admiral's barge, whenever it is heard. This one belonged to Admiral Sugata who was in charge of this beautiful island, the site of the naval college and naval museum. He made Mrs Yata and me welcome which was kind of him as his wife had recently died. Another female covered with Japanese brass on her uniform would escort us to the museum, the most memorable part of which was the Kamikaze Pilot Memorial for about 2,000 young men. Our guide told us that any expert pilots who volunteered, as many did, were rejected. They were needed as able pilots, or instructors, or escort pilots. That was why the kamikaze were as young as seventeen, and very few more than twenty. We saw photographs of them singing around a piano, others swimming naked, fooling around, laughing. One tying his comrade's white headband for him as the latter sat in his cockpit. His *hachimaki* – similar to those worn by samurai warriors – was a symbol of coolness and courage. They all wore them on their last mission.

A large photograph of the final ceremony covered an end wall. A young man in an old-fashioned flying helmet, with his face calm, drank his last toast to the Emperor. Both of his hands were raised to lift a small white saucer to his lips. The next kamikaze behind him waited his turn.

The last toast to the Emperor is always drunk in water.

I felt sick. Enraged for all victims of all wars. 'For what they did to our boys.' For what we did to them. I should have gone with Major Sugimoto to the Peace Museum.

'They were so young,' said Mrs Yata as I blundered out with my shoes clattering on the tiled floor.

Next day, in smog like Los Angeles on a bad day, our object was to visit the Shinto shrine, very fine and crowded with the usual chattering children. The thousand-year-old gingko tree with a huge rope around it took me back to Neil's parents' gingko tree at 110 Frederick Street, Hastings. It also flourished and had done so for some years, though not thousands.

This young priest was again attractive, wearing the same swash-buckling turquoise trousers and wooden sandals. I complimented him on his rig. 'Uniform,' he said.

Nice. Perhaps all men look better in uniform.

We then took tea in a Japanese teahouse. I had met them before with plenty of wabi, that kind of melancholy restraint of which the Japanese are so good.

Nearby was the aptly named Giant Buddha, hundreds of feet

high and into which we were shown. The private house of the head priest of the temple was beside. There we met a, charming, English-speaking old lady. She told me which is *tokonoma,* the alcove, and which is *kakemono,* the hanging screen. Beyond this open room was another enchanting garden and again I didn't have a camera. Major Sugimoto was good at getting everyone to leap to attention and compose themselves but was not around at small gardens.

Admiral Oki was always a help in explaining things to me. Yes, the Buddhist temple we had seen was calm and beautiful and built in 793. I told him I wondered whether I was getting a glimpse of both religions available in Japan, to be fair to both.

He smiled. 'Shinto is the most attractive,' he said. 'It has no sin and is useful for things such as the blessing of young babies, marriages and, of course, deaths.'

'And Buddhism?'

'Buddhism,' said Admiral Oki, 'is more complex.'

Another thing he told me was that Japanese men find the nape of the female neck seductive. That was why the courtesans in Utamaro's work all have low necks at the back rather than the front. The admiral's hand then gave a sweeping curve. 'Very seductive, that is why young geisha have not such a low back necklines. She could be called a midshipman geisha. She is learning, you see.'

I told you Admiral Oki was an interesting man.

CHAPTER 24

Jill and I, those two colour-coordinated old dolls sitting side by side near the front, had launched ourselves into our third year in our bachelor of arts by taking Augustan Literature (of which I remember little) and Romantic and Victorian Lit (which I wallowed in) and Tony Bellette's Origins of Modern Art, which was splendid. Tony also allowed in people who wished to hear his lectures and see the slides but not take the exams. As long as there was plenty of sitting room for all. The wife of a retired lawyer was one of these. Jill and I met him once waiting for her. He told us it made him feel young again, which seemed both unlikely and patient. 'Not at all,' he said, 'when I was studying I spent hours waiting for Betty when she was doing her BA. It takes me back to those days.'

The time came for applying for the creative writing course. Bill Manhire met us in a corridor one day – Jill and I always travelled two by two – and suggested one of us should apply again the following year, the reason being, he told us tactfully, or as tactfully as anyone could, that two students of our age might upset the demographic balance in a class of twelve, though he didn't use that word. Because I had several cross credits from Otago University and the next year was my last at Victoria, I would be the first to take ENGL 252.

Handing in my portfolio gave me pause. I hadn't thought of anything other than poetry, but which sort? It was no use discussing this with any other than my friend Jan who was now living in retirement in Taupo with her husband Bill Drake. All she did now, she said, was look after grandchildren, garden or go fishing in their boat – happily named *Sir Francis*. And, of course, read. She couldn't think of anything worse than attempting to *write* poetry. 'The whole point of poetry is to read it,' Jan wrote back firmly. 'Preferably aloud.'

I had written poems for years but knew they would not be good enough to read aloud with satisfaction. Poetry, I now think, is the hardest form of literary endeavour. But many attempt it. Perhaps it's because poems can be shorter? Easier to 'give it a bash'.

Undeterred, I had a go at W.H. Auden, the one who said his face looked like a wedding cake left out in the rain and, more alarmingly, announced that of course everyone peed in the bath. He also wrote poetry like a dream.

Or the more austere T.S. Eliot perhaps. One of Jan and my favourites was the demise of 'Aunt Helen':

> *. . . and the undertaker wiped his feet –*
> *He was aware that this sort of thing had occurred before.*

All I can remember about my deathless verse was a poem about wind tossing rubbish bins about with skill and clouds billowing high in the sky. Which now seems rather odd.

Presentation was important too, Jeremy told me, according to his now permanent girlfriend, Heather Buchan. People are put off if they are faced with a mess and it doesn't take long to make the thing look good. This was interesting advice and also simple to achieve.

I was delighted to hear I was accepted, but not surprised. For some reason I had thought I would get in, not from the excellence of my product but from a sense that I *had to*. It was now or never.

Neil retired from his job as Chief of Defence Staff (Vice Admiral) in 1983 at the age of fifty-six. From the day he left the navy with a guard of honour as farewell he made it his business to take over my typing, and in time he joined Senior Net to learn 'basic wordprocessing'. I was all set.

Some of the writing exercises Bill set were unexpected, sometimes odd and occasionally alarming. The other students were twenty or thirty years younger than I, and all seemed possessed of considerable talent. Some of them are now well known: Anthony McCarten, Dinah Hawken, David Geary. Dinah is a poet and the men both playwrights. Others had been 'getting something down on paper' since they were in the primers. One had a parent who wrote down her infant's first stories to encourage her.

One of the first things I learned is that writing of any kind takes a great deal of time – preferably in a room of one's own, somewhere where you can write and rewrite and rewrite again.

Perhaps the discipline of endless marking helped me, I thought, but no, I loved writing from the first.

I don't know how Bill made the class work so effectively any more than I know how he writes his poetry, but I do know that ENGL 252 gave me my start as it has done for others. For me Bill was the impetus, which my dictionary tells me means 'the driving force, the energy which makes a body move'.

I have mentioned that good teachers are interesting people. How lucky those of us were who had at least one at school, how we will remember old X, Y, or Z until the clods fall over us. Their mannerisms, the way they talked, walked, occasionally wiped one side of a nose with a finger folded in thought. Another trait such teachers have is an ongoing interest in those who enjoy their subject. They may tell them about a book of interest, ask them how things are going. Bill Manhire is one of those.

I had assiduously been doing the unusual exercises we were given for homework, and 'writing like stink' (Stevie Smith) at the poems I would be handing in when the time ended. I was sure I must be getting better – I had been working hard and enjoying myself.

Various visitors came during the classes to tell us about their various trades: a writer of fiction, a poet, another writer, and Brent Southgate from the *New Zealand School Journal* who spoke to us of the importance of never patronising our readers. Fatal, children catch onto it at once. We all nodded our non-patronising heads.

At another class Jeffery Thomas, a Radio New Zealand drama producer, appeared. We discussed the craft of dialogue and as he packed his books together at the end he invited us to send mini-plays to RNZ. Short ones, he said, were always welcome.

My incipient play for radio was about a child's fantasy friend who was becoming a minor bore to his parents. One of the 'Don't sit there, Dad, Eric's sitting in that chair' kind. The parents had come to the cunning idea of telling their son that Eric couldn't come with them on their camping holiday; there would be no room for him with all their gear. The child wistfully agreed until they were putting up their tent when the he cried out, 'Look, look, Eric's got a lift in that yellow caravan just arriving. See, he's waving.'

Two lines I liked:

Mother: 'Who ever had a phantom friend called Eric.'

Father: 'Yeah, but have you ever had a child who called a cat Betty?'

'Eric' brought glee to the home. The news fell through the letterbox – not only that, but the letter told me I had an ear for dialogue. It also contained the usual small payment.

As it was obvious that Bill and the other assessors were less enamoured of my poetry, the next thing must be for me to write plays. I had always loved seeing them since the good news appeared in the Bay when I was working at the Napier Hospital in 1948: the Old Vic Company were coming to Wellington with Laurence Olivier and Vivien Leigh, brought here by the impresario D.D. O'Connor. The plays were *Richard III,* Thornton Wilder's *The Skin of our Teeth*, and Sheridan's *The School for Scandal.*

I climbed onto Mr Newman's Service Car (remember them?) with a return ticket. When we stopped at Palmerston North an elderly man beside me turned and said kindly, 'Do you want to go?'

I declined with thanks.

'I think I'll give it a go,' he said. 'You never know, do you.'

The weekend was wonderful. A complete wallowing on my part, especially when Olivier turned left front, revealed his hunchback, and began:

> *Now is the winter of our discontent*
> *Made glorious summer by this son of York*

It was the *words* which made me sit bolt upright in my seat, although Olivier knew his audience loved him even if his character was a plotter of deepest direness.

Think of many other playwrights. Harold Pinter's first page in *The Birthday Party* for example. A man and woman are together. The woman speaks.

Meg: *I've got your cornflakes ready. Here's your cornflakes . . . Are they nice?*
Peter: *Very nice.*
Meg: *I thought they'd be nice.*

The first three pages of *The Birthday Party* verge on hilarity until they become more and more macabre. A critic described

Pinter as writing plays which have 'a weasel behind the cocktail cabinet'.

I had no illusions as to my ability to write great plays but it gave me excitement beyond days as well as sweating in my boots.

I began writing full-length plays which I hoped would be played by real actors in real theatres. I had dreams right back to the days of the Muni – the Municipal Theatre in Hastings – and the chorus singing 'At the Balalaika' and my cheek rubbing against the blue velvet on the front row of the circle.

At that time Playmarket (good name) was workshopping a few plays every second year, and my full-length play *Bonnie and Bru* was one of those chosen for 1984. So off I went in September to the Auckland Teachers College with Byron's 'heart for every fate', which was just as well. The workshops must have cost a lot of money, with playwrights, directors, actors, dramaturgs. One and all flew around the country and had a merry time. We were well fed, well bedded and delighted with ourselves. Later in Christchurch one producer said that in his opinion the whole thing was a pack of wankers having a holiday but we thought that was most unkind.

Bonnie and Bru was about two women who loved each other. They taught dancing, the only profession I could think of where two women would work together. Until one of them left the other to marry a man. Bru was to be tall and dark and lithe and Bonnie to be small, blonde and gentle. A cliché waiting for an author. And I was proud of it.

One of the moments which had displeased some of the audience was when an elderly farmer was explaining the situation to his wife. 'They are like albino turkeys, you know, it happens from time to time. Being different.'

Renée – who preferred to be known by one name and whose *Wednesday to Come* was undoubtedly the best of the other plays presented – and her supporters attacked me verbally at the end. There was an uproar and *Bonnie and Bru* collapsed.

To my shame (and rage) I burst into tears. I had been proud of my slow farmer and his metaphor but not of his views. But I was artless and naïve and thus I copped it.

Pamela Tomlinson, who was Editor of Victoria University Press, a publisher of New Zealand plays, was my dramaturg, and was admirable in soothing the situation, as was theatre director Sunny Amey.

Nevertheless, I wrote in my commonplace book the poem I had found by Judith Wright:

> *Whatever the bird is, is perfect in the bird . . .*
> *Whatever the bird does is right for the bird to do . . .*
> *But I am torn and beleaguered by my own people.*

Pompous by me but a good poem.

The creative writing course was in the past and also my BA, but I went back to take another of Tony Bellette's courses, so our kitchen table was covered with plays and Baroque and Neo Classic. This would be my last gasp at Victoria University but I knew that Dorothea and Jill would continue our social life at Racquets.

One day I met Bill Manhire upping or downing in a lift somewhere and he asked how the play was going. 'Finished,' I said, as surprised as he was. 'Why don't you put it in for the J.C. Reid Memorial Prize, at Auckland University. It's plays this year.'

'Oh, thank you. I will.'

And so I shared the 1985 prize with Brian Turner. His play was about cricket and was called *Fingers Up?* Which shows you he can write plays as well as good poems.

My play was called *Truthkick*, which some man said was the maddest title he had ever met for a play. After reflection I agreed. It was selected for the 1986 workshop, and director, dramaturg and actors did their best, but *Truthkick* sank with its name.

But as I sat in a bus waiting to go from Christchurch to Lincoln College, Renée, who appeared this time as a dramaturg, was smiling cheerfully with her 'Hello, Barbara'. 'Hello, Renée.' So all was well there.

I then began writing plays for Radio New Zealand, and later on short stories. Sometimes I still get a polite notice telling me one will be replayed at 3am on Tuesday next, but no more money.

I also wrote a frolic called *Gorillas* which has been played a few times before puzzled audiences, and some not puzzled at all. The players and Neil and the non-puzzled liked it. The beginning is superb.

*

So I was now back to the kitchen table, this time writing short stories.

My father in his earlier days had enjoyed short stories, many from *Blackwoods* which he had subscribed to for years, though not 'for the surgery'. He had also worshipped Sherlock Holmes, in both long and short lengths, which he later gave to Piers. My introduction to him at the proverbial early age included wading my way through *The White Company*. Dorothea was pleased to hear my father was also a fan. She told me that when she was sixteen and her family were in London the first thing she and her father had to do was to track down Baker Street where Holmes and Dr Watson lived.

More than those I found new short story writers from university modern literature courses. Writers like Raymond Carver, Donald Barthelme and Grace Paley, and my friend Stevie Smith once again. People who weren't concerned to tie up the ends of their stories, whose characters could be as free as the air – even if their readers can occasionally be puzzled.

My short stories progressed, and occasionally I won a prize and other times I didn't. I played bridesmaid three times: to Kate Flannery (later de Goldi), Fiona Farrell Poole (later just Farrell), and another whose name I shall remember soon. People enjoyed my stories and I loved writing them more than anything. Bliss at the kitchen table. And that's not a nod to Katherine Mansfield's 'Bliss' either.

I met Bill Manhire one day in yet another lift. 'Why don't you get a collection of your stories together and see if you can find a local publisher. They might accept them as a book?'

'Oh, might they?' Moving from writing individual stories to thinking of them as a collection. Imagine.

'Well, you might as well try. I get off here. Goodbye.'

'Thank you.'

Moving from writing individual stories to a collection was exciting but rather alarming, like producing quadruplets instead of one chaste infant.

The obvious choice of publisher was Victoria University Press. Fergus Barrowman had taken over after Pamela Tomlinson had died suddenly, and I had met him at various book launches. Dorothea enjoyed book launches but had strong dictums about them as she had about many things. Never go to a book launch unless you are going to buy a book.

'Never, Dorothea?'

'Always. I'll come to yours.'

'Thank you.'

So when I had enough stories I sent them to Fergus and Damien Wilkins who worked there in their shed-like office as the university students thundered by.

Not long later the news came back. Acceptance, Acceptance, beautiful Acceptance flew through the spring air of '88 to our letterbox in Beauchamp Street, Karori.

Now I had the bit between my teeth. Or rather bits. I was already beginning a novel called *Girls High* and was as happy as a sandboy doing so.

One day months later I had stopped for coffee and was reading a magazine called *Bird and Bush* or some such name. Jan had sent it to me and it was and is unexpected. For Jan, birds and bushes should be strictly New Zealand. This one was about unusual ways of behaviour all around the world. The Lilypad Hopper for example minds the chicks and when he goes to feed they tuck themselves up in his front feathers with only their legs sticking down below to indicate their presence.

So there.

I had moved on to the Mouth Brooder (female) who carries half-fertilised ova in her mouth, when the telephone rang.

It was Fergus. The book was getting near to blast off and it had no name. Little things like that were needed. Could I come down?

Certainly. Almost as soon as I arrived Damien had thought of *I think we should go into the jungle*. We all decided it was a brilliant name, taken from 'Shanties', one of the best stories.

The cover had been chosen and again was appropriate – a painting by Janet Paul which showed a domestic scene of her daughters sitting around a table outside. But what was her friend Ormond Wilson doing creeping around on his knees in the background? Weeding for Janet, of course, tidying up the jungle.

*

And then came the time for the launch. Dorothea spoke as she had promised, with her usual combination of sense, wit and enthusiasm. The event was held at Unity Books which in those days was on the corner of Willis and Manners Streets and was owned by Alan Preston, a good man who had always been interested in New Zealand writers and was admired in return.

And Neil the typist was there of course and friends and relatives and brother David who said, 'Wouldn't the old man have liked it, Bub?' and I said, 'Yes!'

Then came the reviews and they were good. Very good. The one which made me skite most and blush from ear to ear came from Ian Reid in the *Listener*:

Its unerring economy of effects suggests at times the quality of a Flaubert, a Patrick White, a Grace Paley. To have achieved such brilliance in a first book is remarkable.

'Mackerel Charlie!' as Uncle Freddy would have said.

Another ace came later from Michael Hulse in the *Guardian Weekly* when the book was published in 1993 by Secker and Warburg. The best bit was 'this must be the sharpest collection in English since Carver's *Cathedral* in 1984. Anderson has an important gift: she notices everything . . . When a woman suddenly obsessed with death turns the talk to Mantegna's *Dead Christ,* her partner replies that in the morgue they tie your name on your big toe – the right one – for identification.'

And so it seemed the jungle was meeting the waterfront. The next printing was in train, and the next, and soon it was on the shortlists for both the New Zealand Book Awards and the Wattie Book of the Year.

There were other pleasantries. Once when I was asked to give a lunchtime talk at the university, Douglas Lilburn was sitting next to a friend and at the end he turned to him, saying, 'This woman can *write*.'

And one more. A friend of ours aged ten or so was discovered by his father reading the book late at night. When he heard 'Lights out', the boy replied, 'But I can't put it *down*, and Barbara says something really *rude* about the hollandaise.'

But don't we all occasionally.

*

And there were treats. Dorothea took Jill and me and another friend to celebrate again at the Taishan, another eating house of which she approved. I had parked the car on the other side of the road and she and I and her retinue stopped as Dorothea was wont to do for a few seconds in the middle. To my relief the nearest car was some distance away, so we walked across calmly and the evening was as good as ever.

It was about this time Dorothea introduced me to a useful form of nomenclature. If she liked or admired a person they were 'a good egg'. If she did not, and she could be a good hater, they were 'a bad egg' and she had no wish to meet them, or, if having done so, made quite sure she never made the same mistake again.

Victoria University Press continued in their small shed-like place where Fergus sat on one side of a desk and Damien on the other. I had read somewhere that Robert Browning and his wife Elizabeth Barrett Browning sat on either side, and had thought it an unusual way to write poetry. Fergus and Damien, however, had no space anywhere else.

One day when I had visited them I met Bill Manhire on the road outside. I told him I had just seen the two baby-faced killers to tell them I'd be away. We were going to see Jeremy and his wife, Heather, in London.

'Why don't you try to show your book to a literary agent while you're there?'

'A what?'

'Literary agent. I'll give you a couple of addresses.'

'Oh, thank you.'

Jeremy and Heather had a flat in William Goodenough House, that haven of overseas students at reasonable rates and in pleasant surroundings. The flat was full and Neil and I slept on a futon with comfort. I loved the nearby garden and liked being on a second floor looking onto green plane trees, but was puzzled as to why women must carry keys into their bathrooms.

'To stop men walking into them, Mum,' said Jeremy kindly, 'when the women are in the bath.'

'Oh.'

A nearby pleasure, which their friend Daniel recommended, was to take tea at the Russell Square Hotel on a Sunday afternoon.

The foyer was very grand but the hall carpets less so. In we went to meet a roly-poly waiter scurrying about attending to ancient people who looked as though they had been sitting taking tea and cakes forever. I wished I had been able to make a play about it all, but unfortunately Jeremy and I became slightly hysterical and I forgot to watch harder. To me the place was the Hawke's Bay Farmers' Tea Rooms gone haughty.

The next day three letters arrived for me in the post (not mail). One was from one of the literary agents Bill had suggested, who said they did not take short stories except from their established writers. The second was from Alan Ross of *London Magazine* to say he liked my story 'The Trinket Box', and would accept it, with a considerable cheque. And the third, ah, the third, came from Caroline Dawnay of Peters, Fraser and Dunlop, who would like me to go and see her while I was here.

Glorious.

So on Monday 13 November 1989 I went to see Caroline at her office, which was then at Chelsea Harbour. After instructions from Neil I caught the wrong bus. Having realised this after some time, I stepped off and caught a taxi. I like London taxis, they know where they are going and there are lots of them around, but they do charge real money.

Dropped off at the correct building I sailed up to the fifth floor, marched through the door marked *Women* and tripped over the cleaning lady with her mop. She was understandingly displeased. 'Didn't you see the notice outside?'

'No, I just thought . . .'

'Some people!'

Apologising profusely I backed out and tried to get through the door marked *Peters, Fraser and Dunlop.* I began by knocking then realised I should be dealing with a series of talking-into buttons. Mad, they seemed to me, completely mad and utterly incomprehensible. After a few minutes an amiable young woman with wide vowels and blonde hair let me in and said she would fetch Caroline. Which she did.

Caroline Dawnay arrived smiling and pleasant and friendly and started the conversation by saying how much she liked the book.

'Did you *really* like it?'

'Yes, I really liked it.'

I liked her more immediately and forgot the morning's dilemma.

She then told me the bad news. No British publisher would publish a book of short stories by an unknown New Zealander. She also told me, gently, that she was not my agent until, or unless, she had sold any of my work. And had I anything else I could show her?

'A few chapters of a new novel, but . . .'

'I should like to see them if you would let me.'

'Of course. Yes. Of course.'

Half smiling, half tottering, I left the building filled with euphoria and caught a taxi to St James Park to see the pelicans which I had planned to do. It was probably the best walk I have ever had, that brisk amble through the misty autumnal air of the park. And the pelicans were as surprising as I hoped.

The next few days were hectic. I finished one chapter and wrote another by the simple expedient of not going to bed until the early mornings. Neil thought I had gone mad, which I ignored. However, he was good enough to take the new chapters to PFD at the right place and make sure they were handed over to Caroline.

A few days later we were still so elated we took our young to a restaurant near Russell Square and the four New Zealanders became more elated, especially as Jem was becoming a wine buff and recommended a new season Beaujolais, a thing his parents knew little about.

The only time my parents had a glass of wine was at Christmas when my father 'broached' a bottle from the mission at Greenmeadows.

Mum's usual routine was to take a large sip (if there is such a thing), make a pained grimace and hold it out saying, 'More.'

Six days later we were in Hampshire seeing good friends. Cedric, who had been in HMS *Saintes* with Neil, and Iona who had been kind to me and our small boys, made us welcome again. Cedric greeted me with the news that my agent wanted me to ring her.

'I haven't an agent,' I said. 'Caroline said they're not unless they sell your stuff.'

'That's what she said. And to ring her at home. Here's the number.'

I rang Caroline. It was true. I had an agent. 'A well-known

publisher in London' had offered me an advance for *my first novel* on the evidence of the first five chapters my agent had shown him. He liked them. The first person I rang was Bill in Wellington at 11.30pm Greenwich Mean Time. It was the obvious thing to do.

He then told Fergus at Victoria University Press to ring me. Which he did immediately. He was glad too. He told me to go for it.

I couldn't understand why I wasn't completely off my head with delight. Think of it. If wallowing time ever was, then it must be now. From the days with Colin and the People to the age of sixty-three I had wanted to write books and hell's fangs now I'd done it, written one and pledged another. I had asked Caroline what would happen if I couldn't finish *Girls High*. She gave her gentle smile and said, 'Then you would be in breach of contract.'

Oh.

I rang David and Jenny. David's reaction was, 'Wouldn't the old man be pleased. And that *Jungle* thing seems to be selling well.'

Good.

I had an appointment at 10.30am with Dan Franklin of Secker and Warburg – he being the 'well-known London publisher'. They were ensconced in the art nouveau Michelin Building in Fulham Road. I pressed the right buttons this time, but Dan Franklin came down the stairs to shake hands, saying, 'I just adored your stories.' Which again was a good start. 'People,' he continued, 'are queuing up to read them.'

'Oh.'

'Shall we go up? Oh, is this your jacket?'

'Oh yes, thank you.'

Then we moved into his office and he began.

The novel would be hardback and paperback in UK and Australia and there was always the States. Also they would like me to fly over for publication, about February '91. They would get on to 'our man in Australia'. The whole thing was beginning to sound like *Our Man in Havana*.

Then in came the queuing-uppers. Robin Robertson, whom Dan had mentioned as the toughest, hardest to please editor in London with two books in the Booker Prize shortlist this year. 'I loved your book,' he said. 'So fresh, lively, refreshing after so much that is dull.'

'Thank you.'

Followed by Serena (publicity) and Elspeth (paperback) who came to shake the hand and pass the card.

All were enthusiastic as I sat wondering why all young women in London publishing houses had gentle names, blonde hair and clarity of speech.

After this astonishing session I walked to the ICA where I had a piece of chocolate cake to celebrate before I listened to Bobbie Ann Mason being interviewed by someone called Gordon Burns who, I thought, was bordering on the rude in his queries.

GB: 'Don't you think there is now a backlash to your type of writing?'

BAM: 'I don't regard MTV and TV as junk.'

GB (undeterred): 'Don't you think there's a danger of your work being incomprehensible in ten years with your present use of brands.'

BAM (still undeterred): 'No.'

Afterwards I asked bravely for her American agent's name, which she gave me with a smile.

GB: 'So you're a writer?'

Me (casually): 'Yes. I've just been at Secker and Warburg.'

GB: 'Oh. Dan Franklin.'

Me (still casually): 'Yes. He's taking my book.'

Still filled with glee I walked to St James Park to see the Canadian geese, bizarre ducks I had never seen before, milling around in the chill crisp air of London, making an unusual honking.

Jeremy came early to say goodbye in a handsome charcoal-grey coat with a long reddish scarf, looking like a cross between the Toulouse-Lautrec poster and his maternal grandfather in his well-clothed days. He also told us the Berlin Wall had collapsed. That Mr Gorbachev and President Bush had said, 'The Cold War is over.' All astonishment and excitement, said Jeremy, and why hadn't we heard?

Because we had been head down bottom up packing to leave the next day and our thanks to him and Heather for giving us such a wonderful time.

'Not at all matey, and get on with *Girls High*, Mum,' said Jeremy.

CHAPTER 25

Jeremy's wise advice about *Girls High* was deferred to see friends in America.

First of all a brief return visit to Bob Long and his wife Sara. Bob, who was now also retired, was the one who had played the mocking hero, to the confusion of the bossy woman at the helicopter pad in Queenstown.

Sara and Bob looked exactly the same, if not several years younger, which seemed a bit unfair, but they were glad to see us again as we drove to Annapolis, the naval college. There we ate crab cake, which was disappointing after the one Anne and I had met in Seattle. Crab cake or no, the overall impression for me at Annapolis was of excessively *keen* youth. One could certainly visualise them throwing their caps in the air when they passed out – in the correct sense.

The commander who showed Sara and me around told us he was glad to have the privilege of teaching children the Bible every Sunday while their parents were at church. I wondered how many naval officers would do so at home. Apart from anything else it had been women's work at St Matthew's, Hastings, where David asked the lady why Jesus looked like a sissy and I why his hair was always parted in the middle.

The young Commander also showed us John Paul Jones's tomb, which had been discovered in Paris and 'broughten back'.

After which Sara and I peeled off to meet those whom I had come to think of as 'the *Girls*'. This time, however, there was only one, a friendly woman who was neither alarmingly smart nor thin.

Next morning Sara appeared in her 'breakfast robe', which was a useful garment made of red velvet with frills to demonstrate it was not a beat-up old dressing gown. Bob, she told me, had given it recently. I said that was nice of him.

'Yes,' she answered, 'he's fun to live with.'

How many wives would say that, red velvet or no.

The pleasant time with our lone Girl was repeated next morning.

She said she was a grandmother to twin granddaughters. As I was about to get into cooing mode she told me her daughter had called one Brandy and the other Sherry. She herself did not approve, but of course she didn't say so to her daughter. Having agreed with the nice elderly Girl I wondered if I could use Brandy and Sherry in *Girls High* – but no, there are limits and no one wants to write silly stuff.

Fond farewells on all sides and a drive through heavy snow took us to the Washington airport.

Jeremy had warned us that ASH were pretty aggressive in the USA and Britain was catching up, but as usual Neil headed to smoke his pipe in the non-smoking area. A young woman appeared and asked him to desist.

Neil: 'Why?'

Airport person: 'Because this is a non-smoking area.'

Neil: 'Then why are there ashtrays?'

Airport Person: 'Because they were there before the ban was enforced. Would you move over there please.'

Neil (with bad grace and *sotto voce*): 'Bugger.'

When we were in the air again he was planning his attack for when we landed at Denver, the mile high city. He would head for the bar, they must let you smoke there. But no, even a mile high city did the dirty on him.

San Francisco is one of our favourite cities and remained so, despite a recent earthquake. Jill Barton had a cousin, Sally Billinghurst, who lived there. Jill assured us that Sally and her mother and daughter would be delighted for us to stay with them for a few days. Sally continued to love New Zealand, its occupants and all true good things about it.

She had lived in San Francisco for years, had begun as a volunteer helper in the San Francisco Opera and risen to a high position, and a few years later would be programme manager at the New York Metropolitan Opera. She had grown up on a farm near Waverley, a region for good land and racing horses. As a small child she remembered running around the gorse on her way to her primary school. Later she boarded at Marsden where I had taught Science with a capital S. Sally married in New Zealand, followed her husband and had two children in San Francisco, where the marriage ended. The astonishing thing about Sally is that she makes everything seem simple, and not only that, but fun.

She also gave us tickets to the opera. I had never been to one before, not even in the Hastings Muni in the olden days. And to come to a superb *Madam Butterfly* – magic to hear.

The local earthquake damage was to be seen, so much of it that Neil would compare it with Hawke's Bay when he was three and his tricycle kept knocking him off. However, he was glad to see the authorities in San Francisco were getting the damage under control.

Sally's friends were not only friendly but interesting. All the men seemed to be writing as well as being psychiatrists. Someone called Peter was writing a biography of Nijinsky, having already written one of Schumann. A Dr Wolf was writing about Thomas Mann, a Pierre had written several books, his most successful one called *Passive Men, Wild Women.* I was not surprised to hear that good titles sell books. Alexandra, Dr Wolf's wife, also a psychiatrist, told me more interesting things. She had never heard of a male patient having an affair with his female psychiatrist but knew many cases of the reverse. There was also a James whose profession I didn't know but whom I liked a lot. He was chatty, gossipy and camp.

All of them, he told me, were Jewish intellectuals, opera lovers, and were glad to tell me the members' contributions, which ranged from the Medici Circle at $25,000 to the Gold Circle at $49,999. And this was per annum and in American dollars

On our last evening we were invited to a party with Sally. By the time we arrived the party was jumping, with wine, food and to us unknown people. Then 'everyone suddenly burst out singing' – just like Siegfried Sassoon wrote in his poem, only these were carols, sung by the members of the chorus of the opera company. Thank goodness I had the sense to keep my mouth shut, and just love Sally and her friends.

As we stood in the endless queue at the airport next morning a blonde woman behind me said, 'Pardon me, but do you come from Noo Zealand?'

'Yes. Yes, I do,' I said wondering which bit of my luggage on the trolley had identified me.

Blonde: 'See Hank, I said.'

Hank: 'Yeah.'

Blonde to me: 'I guessed. It's your voice, so funny. And I believe it's so pretty, Noo Zealand.'

Me (thinks, Bully for you lady): 'Yes, it is.'

Blonde: 'And there's some track, like a hike.'

Me (thinks, even better lady): 'Yes, the Milford Track. Four days' walking, three nights in huts. And the rivers, of course.'

Blonde: '*Rivers*. Hear that, Hank.'

Hank: 'Yeah.'

She sounded as though we had knocked off Kipling's 'great grey-green, greasy Limpopo River'. I remembered the beauty, the sounds, the wonder of the track.

'You'd love it,' I said.

'It's a pity now though,' she said, nodding towards Neil who was lighting up his pipe. 'He'd never get over there now would he? Not if he smokes.'

'Lucky sod,' said Hank.

'Hank!'

More and more people were 'giving it up' at home and everywhere else we had been. Now Neil would go through the routine of asking a hostesses if she 'would mind'. Most people were under the illusion that pipes were all right, not like those smelly old cigarettes. The time had not yet come when some people with strong convictions had cards printed: *No smoking please.*

Then smokers would have to retreat to balconies, if there were any. One kind wife used to follow her unremitting husband, presumably so he would not be lonely.

Problems, problems. And there were others for hostesses.

One who enjoyed entertaining despaired at the damage to her parquet floor by stiletto heels, which had just come into fashion and which were death to any uncarpeted floor. Being an astute woman our hostess had a larger card printed which guests would see when they arrived at the door. She thought it would be ridiculous if only women were made welcome in this way, so the card read *Please Remove Shoes.* All went well until an unfortunate man removed shiny black shoes and revealed a large hole in the sock of his left big toe. After which a discreet pair of black socks were kept at hand, which was even more ridiculous.

But parquet floors are rare in Wellington. It was the smokers who were the real problem when we returned to Wellington.

Most happy travellers feel good when they fall into their own bed once more, but I had more reason. I was now a fully paid-up writer who wrote books, well a book. Euphoria bit me. All I wanted was the scrubbed kitchen table before me, a chair and a blue Bic in my right hand.

Dan Franklin and Fergus Barrowman agreed with me that the name *Girls High* should have no apostrophe. These things are important.

As Anita Brooker wrote somewhere, 'Writing a novel is like sitting an exam. You have a certain amount of time and do it as well as you can.'

Me. That's me. I'm not scared at exams. Never have been – with the exception of those at Woodford. Now I found a novel was like a short story but different. A keen eye is useful for both but especially for short stories. Thinking, meditating, working things out are required more for novels. But who can say, who can say, who can pontificate.

Neil was now ensconced in Pop's old room, his fingers banging at the updated computer he'd brought from England. The only occasional snarl came from one or the other as to whose turn it was to make the sandwiches for lunch (not luncheon).

The only loud noise was the roar from Ted, the mowing man and his machine who, like me, only sang when no one else could hear him. Neil loved him. 'It was time I gave the thing up.' He paused. 'I think I'll go to see Peter sometime.'

Peter was our general practitioner. 'Why?' I said.

'People do occasionally,' he replied.

He came back with instructions to make an appointment with a heart specialist at Wellington Hospital as soon as possible. Which he did, with the result that the heart specialist after examining him made another appointment for Neil to see a heart surgeon, Mr Sharma, who had helped set up the Wellington Hospital with the 'beating heart' surgery unit. He said Neil must come as soon as possible for a triple bypass. As long as he gave up smoking, of course.

But Neil had smoked a pipe for years, well before he had a heart attack twenty years before. 'Pipes,' he said firmly, 'are all right.'

'Nonsense,' said Mr Sharma. 'No smoking, or no bypass.'

Neil quit that day.

At his last visit before the operation I was to come too. Mr Sharma welcomed us, showed us diagrams, told us what he and his team would do. He gave me an image of a heart about the size of a small cup, with aorta, right ventricle, left ventricle, etc, marked.

I knew about hearts – what went here and what went there. I had visited Ngauranga freezing works when I was teaching Science at Queen Margaret College and we were doing *Man and the Vertebrates*. I felt dissection was essential. I drove to the works, where someone had once painted on a large sign *Haere mai te Queenie* in welcome to the Queen Mother when she visited our country and my hat was squashed forever in the bus going home. A man at the works met me cheerfully – 'You can have them free, Dear', and I drove back in triumph to tomorrow's expected combination of squeals and interest in my hearts.

All I wanted to do now was to drop Mr Sharma's pretend heart, grab Neil and get him out of the place. Thank kind and brilliant Mr Sharma and all go home. But we didn't.

Then came the day when the operation was over and I was allowed into a large room with few patients, with a nurse at each bed. Mr Sharma showed me Neil sound asleep, then he gave him brisk slaps on each cheek. 'Wake up, wake up.' Rather like the old days when a sailor called 'Show a leg, show a leg' to make sure women had left the hammocks and only sailors were on board. Though I didn't think about that at the time.

Neil continued making a good recovery. He had to be in hospital for ten days to allow the stitches to be removed.

Convalescence was a pleasure for all when he came home. Friends and relations came to visit and Jeremy and Piers gave good advice.

Jeremy, Heather and Zoë were now in Dunedin and Piers and his wife Sally and Sam and Harry were in Auckland.

And then there was more good news. By another helpful suggestion from Bill Manhire I had applied for the Victoria

University writing fellowship for 1991, and got it, which meant that in a few months' time Neil would have the house to himself and I would have a room of my own for a whole year.

Soon I would be writing like stink once again which we know is the best way.

About five weeks after Neil came home we went to see an exhibition at the Tinakori Gallery, which was then still in Tinakori Road before it moved into town. There was a hint of spring in the air as we walked across the road to a local restaurant. The paintings had been good. I remember that, but now neither of us has the slightest idea of who painted them.

My salmon arrived (I always remember food). 'I haven't seen you look so well for years,' I said.

Neil agreed. He had never felt so good either. We clinked glasses to each other, then to Dr Sharma, and then went home.

There are many ways men and women get up in the morning. He is up first every morning so He makes Her a cup of tea. Or She is up first so vice versa. Or maybe *neither* wants tea, but there must always be one who gets up first. Neil is both up first and tea first. It would be very odd to sleep with one who was neither, though I suppose one would get used to things in time.

One morning Neil was late. The first thing I heard was an odd noise in the hall, then he came into the room, crawling. I leapt up, tried to drag him into the bed, muttering, 'It's all right, all right. I'll ring Peter.' Madness all around, but Peter Moodie came immediately.

I don't know when he mentioned the word 'stroke' but I must have known what it was although I had never seen a case. Peter rang a specialist who lived nearby. He too was quick and efficient but what could they do? What could anyone do?

I don't know why Neil didn't go into hospital. I suppose it would not have helped this strong man reduced to puzzlement and trying to smile.

Friends arrived with food. When in doubt New Zealand does. And not only women. I remember with affection a young man who arrived with a warm casserole and a small daughter dancing at his heels who asked me if I had any children she could play with, and if not, why not.

Another helper, one who I had never met before, was Fionn McClennan who came from the Stroke Foundation. She lent me a book written by Roald Dahl. Not another of his well-loved and sometimes alarming children's books. Roald Dahl was also the husband of Patricia Neal, a film star who had an early stroke. Being an intelligent man, Dahl designed various techniques to increase her speaking, to help her learn how to read the time again, and many other everyday things which had to be relearned. He was determined not to sacrifice his work, but her friends were willing to help. As were ours. Stan, Helen, Beverly, Jenni Burns, each came one day a week, I took the weekends and Neil had one day off which seemed only fair for him.

Beverly who had worked with stroke patients said she knew he would get well from the moment they started. Many, she told me, find it so hard at the beginning.

Neil was also given help by a young woman called Sally Claridge, a speech therapist for outpatients at the hospital. She helped Neil in practical as well as theoretical ways. He went to her every Wednesday for two months.

Sally also gave me a recipe for an exotic-sounding Zucchini Chocolate Cake. I have not made the cake and probably never will. For one thing it is too late for three of the true-blue mates. Bless you again Stan, Jenni and Bevo.

Another essential was what Jeremy and Piers called the *Get Dad Well Plan*. They gave good advice: 'Do what they say. Do lots of walking. No, not at the beginning. All will be well. Good on you, Dad.'

Everyone we met said Neil was doing well. And so he did. And so he did . . . but there were bumps along the way. When they would not let him drive, for instance. He could not stand the thought of *me* driving him for six whole months. Also there was not much point in going to the flicks. They didn't seem to make sense for him. One evening we did go to a film at the Penthouse which had been so simple that Colin and I would have enjoyed it at the Cosy Theatre. 'Another flop,' said Neil as I drove home. I parked the car in the garage and we walked down the back steps to find the door open. We had just missed the burglar, or burglars, who had thrown a brick through the kitchen window.

Their loot was a little turquoise ring and a box which had once been Mum's. The rest of its contents scattered on the floor. The only other thing was a bottle of whisky which Neil was not drinking. 'They always go for those things,' said the insurance man who arrived next morning. 'And the TV, though this one's is a bit small and old I suppose.'

So we were lucky weren't we? Luckyish.

CHAPTER 26

Neil rose again to his usual good health and amiability after what he called The Last One, so off we went to London for the launch by Secker and Warburg of *Girls High*. We arrived an 23 January 1991, in chilly and inclement weather, but to me that was nothing. Launching a book is a good thing and going abroad to fling one is pleasing.

The Gulf War was in full flood and I was worried but not as much as I might have been. We were booked into the Royal Commonwealth, in a room Serena the publicity director from Secker and Warburg had filled with flowers. And people everywhere were *kind*, especially at the BBC, where I thought of Pop and the Gulbrandsen and wondered how on earth I had managed to get here with interviews on every side.

The best thing was seeing Caroline, who was as ever good, and Dan Franklin, the publisher with good advice. I remember him saying to me, 'You are not always too obvious in your writing Barbara.' I was beginning to apologise when he added, 'And don't ever change that.'

Dan had a small drinks party to launch *Girls High* at their house. His wife, Lucy Hughes-Hallett, is also a writer, and their two small twin girls were happy too. It was a wonderful evening, and as we left Dan said there might be a review tomorrow in the *Sunday Times*. 'But these things are never sure.'

We fell into bed and slept, Neil like a snoring baby, me like something more edgy. Eventually I heard a gentle thud outside the door. I had ordered the *Sunday Times* the night before, and here it was as large as life, and beautiful. The reviewer said of *Girls High:* 'Even its contents page is irresistible . . . This critic will stick his neck out and say that *Girls High* is the most enjoyable book he has read so far this year and that Barbara Anderson is a born writer.'

Good for you, Nick Hornby, whoever you are.

Neil woke up. 'What's it like?'

'Have a look.'

'Hmn.' Long pause. 'Not bad.'

*

I was soon ensconced in my own room, this free gift, this bonanza where no one else could come within a 'bull's roar', as David used to say when we were young and foolish. And look, there is a view, a glimpse past the Hunter Building and down below to the town, but who needed that when writing books.

Both my *Jungle* book (apologies to Kipling) and *Girls High* had been a pleasure to write, but *Portrait of the Artist's Wife* was more so. Some reviewer wrote that the book 'had a dash of feminism in both title and story'. Which pleased me. I had wanted to write about a man and woman who had a rocky and non-rocky marriage. Another wrote it was a comedy of manners, which surprised me. Satirical and farcical, was that me?

What would novelists do without the two sexes. We have a lot to be thankful for.

The part of which I was most proud in *Portrait,* and for which I had little kudos, is a poem. A fragment at the end.

> *How is it love arises from the heart*
> *And then torments the heart that bore it?*
> *Just think of rust and iron; rust's born from iron*
> *What does it do but gnaw it . . . gnaw it.*

It was written by a Persian poet, Bu'lfaraj, in the eleventh century, and translated by Dick Davis. I had read it in the *Times Literary Supplement* and wrote to Davis to ask if I could use it. He wrote me a kind letter back to the effect that he would like Bu'lfaraj's poem to have an airing. And I was glad to find something which characterised Sarah and Jack's lives together.

I finished the book at the end of my time at Victoria University and it was published early the next year. Later the same year, 1992, it won the Goodman Fielder Wattie Book Award. That was the Wattie award's twentieth anniversary, and four years later with a change of sponsor it would become the Montana New Zealand Book Awards.

I suppose to win a prize is always pleasant – the only other one I had ever achieved was *The Maori As He Was,* about forty years before, which was a considerable gap. I thanked Mr Wattie's representative as I took the splendid cheque I was given. My 'searching for blows' with Pam Cashmore would have come in useful in my thanks but I thought it would have been unfair to mention something as unwanted as 'blows' in Wattie's cannery. Nor did I mention Mr Wattie's dictum: 'Work eight hours a day and have no worries / And in time you will become the Boss and have all the worries.' I was grateful for Mr Wattie's prize, and furthermore I didn't lose his money like the first time.

The ceremony was shown on TV in those days and one who saw it was Danny, the woodwork teacher at the evening classes Neil was attending. Apparently Danny was a great teacher, an amiable cove, and Neil was progressing splendidly. However, when Neil appeared next week Danny greeted him with 'What does Barbara have to do to get a decent kiss out of you?'

Decent or indecent Neil has always been a generous host and the party in our Auckland hotel room was booming before long. Bill Manhire and his wife Marion were there of course, plus Fergus Barrowman and his wife Elizabeth Knox who was pregnant. It was not long after that Jack Knox Barrowman arrived, another win.

The judges that year were three enlightened book people. Well, I would say that. One was the publisher David Elworthy, another an able woman from a bookshop. The third was Nigel Cox, who had worked at Unity Books for many years. Many years younger than me, Nigel published his first novel about the time I started writing. By 1992 he was in Auckland at their Unity Books, and whenever he came down to Wellington we were liable to meet for a pie or a pud. Nigel was writing, and writers like talking with others as long as they don't keep telling you how magnificent their present work in progress is, when yours is lingering.

'Mouldy Pig,' as Piers said when young.

None of that with Nigel. He told me agreeable things such as that the three judges had been as one. Had been prepared to fight for the same choice. That sort of thing.

One day Nigel was even more cheerful than usual. He told me he had met the most wonderful young woman. I congratulated him. Wonderful young women, I told him, are not always easy to find.

He nodded. Gave a seraphic smile and murmured, 'And she *reads*.'

I insisted on paying for the pies that day. What else could I do with my friend Nigel?

I had sent Caroline some of *Portrait* before it was finished. She had liked it and sent it on to Dan who was still at Secker and Warburg. He wrote to me. Quote: 'The most important news is that I've read the pages from Caroline from *Portrait of the Artist's Wife* and I think they are wonderful. I spent most of y'day enthusing to Caroline. It's clever, funny, beautifully observed and somehow much more moving than *Girls High*. You are wonderful.' End quote.

Sometimes I think English men have different minds from New Zealand men. If they think a woman has done a good job they say so, with enthusiasm. They are not afraid the said woman might become a 'skite', that dreaded disease of my youth. The word is not even present in my *Shorter Oxford Dictionary* but it is there in the *Dictionary of New Zealand English* edited by H.W. Orsman. First noted in 1857, 'To boast, to show off.'

I don't know how English men deal out compliments to women they love. Perhaps the French are the most dedicated. I read somewhere, in translation, 'You are a little too fat, my love. I enjoy "pour faire l'amour" but you are a little plump when dressed.'

Or perhaps Frenchmen are just the bravest.

Let me tell you now how my first letter from the United States of America arrived. It came in 1991 from someone called Lizzie Grossman who worked at the impressive-sounding firm Sterling Lord Literistic Inc, who did business with Peters, Fraser and Dunlop and therefore with Caroline Dawnay. Lizzie told me how much she had loved *Portrait of the Artist's Wife*.

It was, she said, simply one of the best novels she had read in ages. Not only that, but she had read it straight through on the plane home from London and, although it might sound silly to say so, it had made her both laugh and cry.

Good on you, Lizzie.

She continued: Sarah Tandy was now firmly lodged in her gallery of favourite characters. She particularly liked the wonderful irony with which I had recounted the character's evolution.

Goodness me.

Also I must be pleased to know she had seen Dan Franklin in

Frankfurt at the Book Fair and he couldn't stop telling her how much *he* liked the book. She then finished by looking forward to a successful sale of the book there. She also hoped Neil was well on the road to recovery – 'and again congratulations on a superb novel.'

The next letter came in February 1992 from Gerald Howard, an editor at W.W. Norton and Company, New York. He began by saying his assistant Emma Lewis and he were very pleased to introduce themselves as my American publisher for *Portrait of the Artist's Wife*.

Me too, Gerald. Me too.

He continued by saying that both he and Emma were passionate about the book, which was both smart and powerful. There was a touch in it of Virginia Wolf's thesis in *A Room of One's Own* – though there was nothing in the least didactic about my book. These, he wrote, 'were real people, caught up in the messes of life'. It was quite an accomplishment he told me and they would be proud to be able to publish it.

Too kind. Too kind.

Gerald then talked about matters of business including the fact that he would like to see *All the Nice Girls* at some point. Then he finished by saying welcome to W.W. Norton, and congratulations on my 'smashing novel'.

The next letter from abroad was from Caroline from Chelsea Harbour, where I had nearly fallen over the unfortunate cleaning lady some time before. She told me Lizzie Grossman had confirmed her acceptance of Norton's offer for *Portrait of the Artist's Wife*.

She also told me Gerald Howard had said, 'We'll show them.' With her usual perspicacity, Caroline thought his comment might mean his editorial board might be less enamoured with the book – a thought which had never occurred to me, and what was an editorial board anyway? I knew nothing of such a beast I did not like the sound or smell of it.

However, as Gerald Howard had told me in one of his affable letters, publishers were the slowest creatures on earth so they would not be publishing until spring of 1993. Which would be good for us as Neil would be completely well again and able to travel.

In the meantime letters came from Emma Lewis. She told me

Norton were so excited about being able to print the American edition of *Portrait.* Also she said Lizzie Grossman should have a cheque from them very shortly – the request had already been drawn.

Yippee!

Emma also enclosed an author's questionnaire. (*Who she/he?*) Would I mind filling this out for them? (*Not in the slightest.*) They were, continued Emma, rather tiresome as I knew (*I didn't*), but they were quite useful.

Emma then thanked me very much for my time and looked forward to being part of this project.

What is that bit in *The Tempest*?

> *O, brave new world*
> *That has such people in't.*

The ones I met in New York were knee-deep in courtesy.

The next letter came from Lizzie Grossman. She thanked me for my letter with that wonderful stamp on it. She was looking forward to seeing me and having seen Gerry Howard at Frankfurt she had suggested we should all have lunch on one of the days I was here.

Good thinking, Lizzie.

The American version of *Portrait of the Artist's Wife* came out in April 1993. Its jacket showed a black-and-white photograph of an enigmatic woman with water up to her neck, her hair long and dark and her eyes shut. On the back I found she was named *Eleanor, Chicago, 1949,* by Harry Callahan, courtesy of Hallmark Photograph Collection, Hallmark Card, Inc.

Gerald had asked Janet Frame to give him a few words and she kindly did. 'Acutely observed, furiously gleeful, compulsively readable – and the work of a natural writer.'

Even her comment, the hard efforts of Gerald and presumably all at W.W. Norton – nothing prevented *Portrait* from sinking.

We went to the lunch of which Lizzie had spoken. It was not a merry one but Gerald, one of the nicest men I had met for a long time, was apologetic down to his bootstraps. Apparently there was not one, *one,* review of this book all over America. He had never heard of such a thing.

The thing which passed my mind was that Caroline had been right. The editorial board had been correct.

Other things I remember. One was thinking to myself, 'Worse things have happened at sea.' Another asking if I could have a glass of wine. It was a foolish thing to do, because liquor at lunch/luncheon always has bad effects on me. Anyway Gerald looked slightly startled – neither he nor Lizzie had any.

Here is the last letter I ever saw from him – via Lizzie – via Caroline:

Dear Lizzie,

I began All the Nice Girls with real anticipation because I knew I was in for a fine read, but also with trepidation because I knew that there would have to be some special quality to the book that might help us overcome the dismal performance of Portrait of the Artist's Wife. I have finished the book now and I am afraid that my trepidation was justified. This is just as acute and compelling a look at marriage as Portrait, but it lacks the scope of the earlier novel. If we found it as hard to get across a novel about New Zealand literary life as we did, I completely despair of making any more of a dent with a novel about life in the New Zealand Navy. I would get precisely nowhere with the board on this novel and I think that would be an entirely justifiable decision.

This is a pretty sad ending to something that begin with all kinds of high hopes on all sides and some energetic spade work on this side. I can only point a blaming finger at the market place, the ignorant book reviewers, and the fates. Please tell Barbara that I deeply wish things were otherwise, and good luck in finding a new customer.

All best,
Gerald Howard.

I told you he was a fine man.

However, B. Anderson's *Portrait* was lost forever in New York – I began to say 'in the Big Apple', but I thought that would have been silly. Also, later on I did see two copies in a bookshop, in San Francisco!

CHAPTER 27

When Neil had been promoted to Vice Admiral and Chief of Defence Staff in 1980 it seemed we would be living in Wellington for the rest of our natural lives.

This had not appealed to either of us in earlier days, when we had bought a section near the beach in Milford, Takapuna, with a full view of Rangitoto Island. The house we bought was a wreck and we hired, if that is the correct word, a female architect who was also enthusiastic about the sea and a five-minute walk to reach it.

The tenant who lived there had always wanted to buy our handsome result. 'No,' replied the Andersons, who also wished eventually to be living there. But that was long ago, and by the time the tenant had decided his drive over the bridge and back from Anzac Avenue each day was killing him I wanted to live in Wellington, and Neil remained calm. Writing was what I now did and I wished to do it there. We sold Milford and committed ourselves to Wellington.

In 1986 we bought one of the cheapest baches in the road of Fieldway, Waikanae. It was no more than an hour to drive from Wellington to come to good swimming in the sea across the road. The one bedroom could just fit one bed. Next door was the ablutions block: shower, tub/handbasin, and a serviceable lavatory. The other room had a small sink and a minute stove called a Baby Belling. It was inept as an oven but it did have a hotplate, and the best feature was that cooking was easier done on a barbecue and this was Neil's department. It was one of the early kind and he became an expert outdoor cook. Some men are brilliant with barbecues, some are not. David, for instance, was hopeless. Piers has inherited his father's skill, but now his latest model is so elaborate it looks as though it is about to take off to the moon, and back with all beautifully cooked.

Neil's barbecue had another good point. He had set it up in the carport so he could operate in all weathers.

I divided the kitchen/dining room/sitting room by stitching together bright patches of colour to make a vast curtain. Mrs

Munro in Swanmore, who taught me how to do long-legged cross stitches, also told me never, never, never to throw away good pieces of colour, and I haven't.

The old man who sold the bach to us asked us if we would mind if he took the stuffed trout above the curtain. Not at all, we said. Not at all. Please do.

We both loved our Fieldway bach and the first thing to hunt for was an old caravan, which became my writing room until six o'clock. Then the News came on, from the equally ancient television which lived there until people came to stay, when it hid in the toolshed till they left.

Televisions were not in every beach house in our early days. Another ten-year-old friend, Toby Manhire, enjoyed watching the rugby, or sometimes cricket, with Neil. Bill would bring him round and Neil drove him home. Marion always noticed how Toby reeked of old tobacco smoke but that was in the early days when puffing was allowed.

It was also where we began what Jenni Burns used to call our Annual Dinner and Dance, a summer picnic which has continued ever since, where babies rolled about on the grass and the adults took care not to tread on them and a good time was had by all. The venue later changed from Fieldway to Rangihiroa Street but the menu was the same. Though now it is more 'Ladies a plate, Gents a bottle' in true Kiwi fashion. It was also where we had more room for our grandchildren.

Piers and Sally had the first and the news of Sam's arrival was brought to us over twenty years ago by a friend, as we had no telephone in Fieldway. Sam was the first to know the tub/bath. Later Harry arrived a few months earlier than Zoë, Jeremy and Heather's first child who was born in England. A few years later Lucy arrived to Sally and Piers. A daughter should be in every home, though there is something beguiling about males as I have always known. Joseph was born in Australia four years later than his sister. It was Joe who particularly liked Fieldway. He took especial pleasure in bathing in the tub with a wine biscuit so he could watch it melt on his pink stomach. As his great grandfather would have said, 'We all take our pleasures differently.'

*

The next, and probably our last, permanent establishment, the one from which we hope to be carried out feet first, was in Oriental Bay in 1995. When we bought it it was called a flat. Now flats are known as apartments. Why I don't know – but once again we were lucky to find it by the ocean. Neil is a kind of a sea creature, not some sinister monster but an amiable sea beast, a serpent perhaps of a gentler type snuffling the sea air. I sometimes come across Neil early in the morning at an open window catching the sea smell or listening for a coming storm or watching one of the lipstick-coloured tugs as it set off on its duties. Birds are not bad either. Stormy petrels, say. Why do they fly so much lower than the black-backed gulls. I also like to watch. Why do the gulls continue to pad about on the sand, but when they come onto the pavement for more scavenging are much quicker so you can't see their feet at all? They have the speedy grace of Russian female dancers whose feet are never seen, as if some mechanism is making them whiz around. And children are an unending pleasure to watch. The sea and the sand are both there but the sea is Neil's best.

We found a larger and more comfortable place in the older part of Waikanae which should be called a cottage rather than a bach. It had a pleasant garden with many trees but I still needed my room for writing. I said I would not move from Fieldway unless the caravan came too. Neil said it would fall to pieces. I said nonsense, like Mr Sharma. Neil consulted Bob from the garage. Bob said it would fall to pieces.

Bother.

Then Tilly Lloyd from Unity Books told me of a place that sold caravans, many of which were second-hand. Thanks Tilly. Too kind, or words to that effect.

So we bought one. But there were still problems. Our cottage took up all the level area at the top, then there was a steep fall to the orchard down which the caravan could not be moved by anything or anyone. It must live on the flat level below. So the next thing was to ask our neighbours below if we could have the caravan towed through their property. I found the owner's telephone number in Auckland and with some trepidation rang him.

'Go ahead,' said the voice. 'It's only a bach.'

The vendor then towed it across the next-door property and

through a convenient gap in the hedge near the pear tree to its new home. And very handsome it looked too.

We found later our neighbour was a judge. The best sort, we agreed.

Neither Jill Barton nor Dorothea saw our new establishment. Jill, who was younger than I, died in 1996 and Dorothea a year later. That is one of the sorrows of one's own ageing. I didn't meet either of these good friends until I was in my late fifties and their deaths were a sad shock to me, to say nothing of their families.

One unworthy thought came to me at Dorothea's funeral. Everyone present knew how musical she had been, how she had been both player and critic. She had chosen some of her favourite composers for this well-organised occasion: Haydn, Mozart and Bach, all were present. My wish when I shoot through from this interesting world would be to follow Dorothea's choice, though now being deaf as a coot I am now not musical. But I realise there will be a pleasing noise coming from Dorothea's wisdom.

And Dorothea would approve. Or perhaps.

'Really, Barbara.'

'But Dorothea . . .'

'Well, perhaps? In this case.'

What a friend she was to me.

After the trauma of Neil's illness had ended and my time in the writing fellowship room had finished, I wanted to write somewhere other than home.

I visited several real estate agents who showed me one or two small offices but at high monies.

But once again came Luck. Great Luck, lodes of it, Luck wearing funny hats and waving them.

In the nineties disused large offices were occasionally available for small rent with short tenancies. This was because several individuals could share them. And if a light bulb popped or worse, the heating system fell apart, that was our collective problem. Though I can't remember being asked to do anything of this nature. Being in your sixties occasionally has its better moments.

We were a mixed gang – I could tell that from our first summit meeting. Some insisted on closed doors, others enjoyed a chat however busy. They were all quick-witted people, bright, fun to be with and good at their trades.

One of the major heroes in this plan was Stuart McKenzie with his wife Miranda Harcourt. It was he who approached me to join these heroes. For some reason my father disliked the word 'approached'. Perhaps because a young man we knew was always telling us how he had been 'approached' again, the result of which was always a better job. 'Has Michael been approached lately?' Pop would ask in a dry tone.

Another early hero was Danny Mulheron, a playwright, and later William Brandt, an actor beginning to write. The first time I met William was in the lift, holding his mountain bike in one arm and a baby under the other. Also there, at times, were Jim Barr and Mary Barr.

The first place we rented was one level of a building in Kent Terrace where we each had our office. Eventually the whole building was sold and converted into apartments, one of the first inner city ones known to man, woman or beast.

For me there were many advantages. I could walk there and back from Oriental Bay. And on one occasion I needed to describe a night out with a heavy metal band. No feeble imitation would do, no pale simulacrum. The obvious thing was to go with Neil, but he declined. Flat. There were lines which he would draw and one of them would be to pay money to listen (or avoid listening) to something called heavy metal.

'But I *need* it for the book,' I cried. 'It's an essential moment when Emmie and Robin get together, almost halfway through. It's essential.'

'Then find someone else.'

Stuart heard this story, both of my feebleness for not going by myself and the distaste of Neil. He volunteered to go with me.

The place where Shihad was going to play was round the corner of Kent Terrace and they were to begin about 10.30pm. I thought the best thing to do was for me to stay working at the office and for Stuart to pick me up. Which he did but was surprised to find me asleep on the floor.

I enjoyed the evening immensely, possibly because I heard the music – completely.

Here are two of the extras I needed for *The House Guest*:

It was too long since he had been surrounded by such a blast of sound, such beat. The hedonistic anarchy of the sound was therapeutic.

A thin guy, a mosher, scrambled onto the stage in front of the bass guitar, dashed across the stage, was chased by a man so tough, so beautiful, so trained to kill, that Robin's heart moved.

Music as she is won.

And then Stuart having picked me up dropped me off on his way home. Thanks Stuart.

Our next move was another great effort for Stuart. This was to the sixth level of the National Mutual Building in an arcade on the other side of the city.

Here again were Jim Barr and Mary Barr who stored some of their works of art in an enormous safe that was known as 'The Safe Sex Storage'.

Once again the occupants staged various exhibitions as they had done in Kent Terrace. And again there was a lot of what used to be called merriment, and hard work and occasional balls-ups.

People came and went. Neil Pardington was there and Fenn Gordon and Rachael Mansfield and Vivienne Plumb. At one stage the set design for Stuart's short film *Snap* was marked out in masking tape on the open space on the floor where the table tennis once was. One had to be careful.

But mine, my room, had a lock.

Another drama occurred when Michael Parekowhai's huge sculpture I AM HE was found to be too big for the lift and jammed in the door. Whereupon all the heroes had to carry I AM HE six flights down the stairs and words where heard and sweat was sweated and men were far from happy.

But then developers developed after two years and we, the National Mutual Appreciation Society, had to leave, all in different ways this time. I found another well-shut-up room, this time in the Hope Gibbons Building, which now has a bungy jump outside. Occasionally it swings high and low but did not when I was there. I would not have been tempted, either by bungy or jumper.

And then again it was 'Scribble, scribble, scribble! Eh, Mr

Gibbon?' as King George III's brother the Duke of Gloucester said to the author of *The Decline and Fall of the Roman Empire.*

No relation to Hope Gibbons I think.

And I was happy as another sandboy as long as words went well and was miserable when they didn't.

The only other person in Hope Gibbons Building on level four whom I knew was the playwright Ken Duncum, who had been in Bill Manhire's class the year after mine and was now in the room next to mine. He told me my room had once been occupied by Aunt Daisy, the icon, if I dare the term, of Radio New Zealand, who five mornings each week burst upon housewives crying, 'Good, good, good morning, good morning everybody and what a beautiful morning it is today', or alternatively, 'A nasty day today but never mind.' Or words to that effect. Then off she went with recipes, excitements, lack of excitements, interesting news or lack of same, on she went, year after year after year. A national treasure, long dead. Ken showed me evidence of her presence, a bit of iron bracket sticking out from the wall.

I told this news to the only other man I ever met on our floor. He too gave me news but not so interesting. He brought a large bottle of water each day by train from Petone because Wellington's was disgusting. I hadn't noticed but told him Hastings had the best water in the country. He didn't seem impressed. But that was before bottled water hit the market.

That was about all I learned at Hope Gibbons but I wrote a lot.

CHAPTER 28

In 2004 Jeremy Anderson, Professor of Epidemiology and Biostatistics at the University of Melbourne, with his colleague Don Campbell, director of Health Services Research, were driving through Sri Lanka where they had been giving workshops at the medical school, Jeremy's being an 'evidence based' medicine course. The van was comfortable, the countryside interesting, when the driver began whistling a song Jeremy thought he knew. He asked the man, who said it was one by Mr Presley. Jeremy, like his mother and several million others, enjoyed Mr Presley. He then located the song on his iPod, transcribed the words and serenaded his companions with the classic 'Wooden Heart'.

There is not much point in this story other than it is typical of Jeremy.

At his funeral nine months later there were eulogies. Professor Sally Green, director of the Australian Cochrane Centre, told of the great affection in which Jeremy was held, how he led with generosity, humility, enthusiasm, not to mention questionable musical taste. He was renowned internationally for his innovation, scholarship, creativity, and good sense of humour.

Professor Terry Nolan, head of the School of Population and Health (professors were everywhere), described Jeremy as a 'sweet, generous man . . . someone who had a real creative edge that was evident in all aspects of his life'.

The main 'aspect' to Jeremy's life was Heather and his two children, Zoë, aged fourteen, and Joseph, ten. He loved them all so much, was proud of each and every one. During Jeremy's illness, Joe won a short story award. His parents were present when the prize was given and Jeremy told me later that he wept. 'Mad, I know, but I felt I was letting them down.'

Mark Thomas, one of his best friends, also spoke. 'Heather had never given any sign of being other than madly in love with Jeremy – and his occasional eccentricities.'

Neil and I and Piers all said goodbye that day. It was easy for me to remember him from the beginning: 'Jeremy was an amiable child, and like all children was interested in anything. "Where my book-a-read," was an early phrase, I remember. He also liked the fun of working things out. About fifty years ago he came to me saying, "Mum, I can do a joke."

'"Great," I said. "Tell me."

'"Ha, ha, ha."

'After seven schools, the freedom of university, and the strong and lasting friendships he made there, opened new worlds. It was also at Auckland University he met Heather Buchan, the best thing that ever happened to him.'

Piers also had memories: 'Jeremy's quickness was evidenced from the outset; aged eight, he learned chess by watching the old men on the boat coming home from Britain. Then he taught me, aged six. I remained cannon fodder for his bishops' and knights' moves thereafter.

'He was always the herald of the new in everything. The latest amp, the most subterranean sub-woofer, the iPod no one else had heard of, the next food style, the best chopping knife, the new second best restaurant in Melbourne, the lot.

'My bro.

'Jem.'

And Neil read from the book of the Apocrypha, the Wisdom of Solomon.

Jeremy had come back from Sri Lanka feeling very unwell. His doctor examined him and said his colon should be looked at as well. When Jeremy returned his friend told him the bad news. He was diagnosed as having colon cancer and, worse, the cancer had metastasised. Nevertheless he continued academic and clinical work until November.

He also continued to email his wide circle of friends.

In December he was 'looking forward to shrugging off patienthood for a summer's worth of personhood at the beach'.

In early February he wrote of his rapid deterioration: 'Previously I was a man who, faced with a life-threatening illness, smiled politely, looked it firmly in the eye and walked on by. Without wanting to be melodramatic, my current response now has more of the Robert Johnson about it – "went to the crossroads, fell down on my knees".'

Dr Buchan (Heather), chief executive of the National Institute of Clinical Studies, spoke last at the funeral: 'And most of all I want to thank Jeremy for twenty-one amazing years we shared. Right at the beginning I felt enormously lucky to have Jem as a partner and that feeling never left me. A friend who rang from London said Jeremy was very good at treats and encouraging people to enjoy themselves. And our life together was really one long treat. Finally I want to thank Jeremy for creating and nurturing two terrific children of whom we are both very proud.'

As Jeremy became more and more ill it became obvious he would have to go into hospital. Heather also said, 'In Jeremy's final days Myra, John and Daniel provided comfort around the clock, and he was never alone.'

And Heather. And Heather.

When we were there I occasionally took over at about 9pm, to be followed later by Heather.

It was tragic to see him, but always he grinned if he could and said, 'Hullo Mum', followed always by, 'Where's Heather?'

'She's coming soon. Why not sleep?'

He would shut his eyes. 'Ah, that's better. You're sure?'

'Yes.'

'Good.'

One evening Heather arrived having tucked up the children and leaving Neil in charge. I swear Jem opened his eyes as the door opened. 'Heather.'

I had a cab on the way home and always sat in the front seat as Jeremy had advised. 'They think you're going to stab them if you're in the back. Front seat every time, Mum.'

There was a cricket match going on at the time and the driver was lauding the brilliance of Shane Warne. After some time I asked if all Australians were so enamoured of the man. He looked at me with something like shock. 'Lady,' he said, waving his right hand in the air, 'if Shane shook me by this hand it would never be washed again.' 'Oh,' I said. 'Third on the right. Thank you.'

Jeremy died next morning, five days after his fifty-second birthday.

EPILOGUE

Recently it has occurred to me that I am old, about the same age as Dorothea was when I knew her. Yes, I now have a stick like the stick without which she never moved. It is not for striding about the countryside like Major and Mrs Duncan, whose sticks are evidence of their owners' ease.

Dorothea's stick was not a thing of beauty, and neither is mine, but sticks are needed, on flat or hill. They can, however, be disturbing on buses. You press the button for leaving and find the stick has disappeared and the driver is displeased. He thinks you are old, ergo nuts. Whereas the real problem is that the stick has gone under the seat and thus, to use David's phrase again, has 'done a flit'.

Which brings more sorrow. David died suddenly ten years ago. He had a bad cold and moved into another bedroom to avoid Jenny catching it, and she came in the next morning to find him dead. A death perhaps easier for the one who died but dreadful for the one who is left.

Everyone loved David, but Jenny and their daughters Diana and Lizzie had to battle on.

One of his colleagues said to me, 'It's so damn unlike Dave.'

And yes. I remember the odd things he said. Once when I was with him driving up to Hastings a man shot ahead then cut back in front of us. David looked at his rear end and said, 'My dear old tosh', and on we went. Though sometimes his reaction could be very different.

I also remember Pop's reactions to motor cars. We were in Devonport when safety belts had just come in. Like Dorothea when she died, he was around the age I am now. He disliked 'this business' and his reaction was to flap the thing at me, saying, 'You put it on, Bub.' Usually I did, but one time I was having a slight problem finding the other half to join together. Pop lay back saying, 'Never mind, Bub, it will probably be easier not to have an accident.'

Other things sneak up on me. Now back seat safety belts are required by law as I discovered when I was in the back seat with Joe. The silly thing was flapping about and instinctively (or was it hopefully?) I handed it to Joe, and he put it together with the kind words, 'It's quite easy when you get used to it, Granny.'

I thanked him, and was glad Joe was around. Though sloth may be one of the Seven Deadly Sins, it is on my side. We may ignore things in the hope of getting away with it. Why spend time and effort working out things which are of little use to the old in the hope of being thought to be *trying*.

Mum and Lillias had another sister, Jeannie (or Jinny), who was very different from them, although Jinny also married an Englishman, Ronnie Whitworth, and they had four sons. Many years ago she was incensed by the change to decimal currency. One day she shook her purse at me saying, 'Look at all these little brown buggers, Bub. Useless. Quite useless.' History is repeating itself. The only difference is that the little brown buggers I now have are smaller and don't go any further.

But many of the elderly will have none of this nonsense, one of them being Lillias. She insisted that things should be as she required and nearly always they were. When she came to live in Havelock North she continued to travel abroad, even though 'abroad' was now Queensland. She also always flew with what she called 'my Qantas', presumably because she had shares in them. Once, before she was going abroad for a holiday, she spent a day or two with each of her nieces, Uncle Freddy's daughters, Joy and Rosemary, and their husbands in Remuera, and Neil and me on the North Shore. All had had their turn and then Neil had taken Lillias to the airport and made sure all was well with her Qantas. Then he came home and after a glass of home brew he rang Joy's husband, Jim. He then lied like a flat fish and told him that the Qantas in question had collapsed and all passengers must leave and return tomorrow. And as Remuera is a great deal nearer to the airport than Devonport and we had a previous engagement, perhaps Jim would go out and collect Lillias and take her home.

Jim, who is known to one and all as a man of exceptional kindness, gulped. Joy was not home at the moment, three small children were lining up for evening baths, and he was in the process of frying oysters for a Friday night treat. Though of course he would get out there when Joy arrived home.

Whereupon Neil finished his beer, rang Jim again and told him all was well and he hoped Jim and Joy would enjoy the oysters.

For which Jim thanked him and said it would have been a case of oyster-interruptus.

Aunt Lillias enjoyed Queensland again, but it was too hot. She was quite glad to get back into her Qantas. Then she told us all about the holiday and why we should go there, though it is quite difficult to see a koala unless you looked carefully. In the wild of course.

Lillias was one of those who kindly tells you things. Like the young man with an American accent who revealed to us everything about Black Madonnas in a church in Italy. Real Ancient Mariner stuff. Black Madonnas are indeed interesting but this one was his. He continued to tell us that a shepherd had discovered it lying around somewhere, had taken it to a cathedral, and it had disappeared again, and after that . . .

Perhaps the young man was doing his PhD or something, though some men like telling things. Once when I was in the Courtauld Institute, in one of those almost-empty rooms, a man came up to me and said, 'I thought you might like to know. Princess Margaret has issued a statement. She will not be becoming engaged to Group Captain Peter Townsend.'

'Oh.'

'Not at all,' he replied and went off to spread his news to another lucky woman.

But the nicest men who have offered information have been of small age. Neil and I were in the Brera Art Gallery in Milan in 1995, hoping to get background information for *Proud Garments*. The woman behind the desk asked us where we came from and we replied, 'New Zealand.' Some small boys were bored stiff and I had been feeling sorry for their guardian nuns. At the words 'New Zealand' they leapt to their feet with knowledge and cried, '*Lomu, Lomu!*' We nodded with pride and sailed on.

But back to age. What about eyes, ears and things of that nature?

'I'm glad you asked, Bub,' as a friend of mine used to say in tones of deep sarcasm.

Both David and Pop had bad eyesight. David once picked up the ball in traditional rugby manner and ran, ran fast, but unfortunately his eyes led him to the wrong goal-line.

And Pop, ah, Pop's eyes. Another memory: at breakfast Pop sat taking off his spectacles (as he called them), blowing on each inside lens and giving it a good huff with a clean white handkerchief, while Mum sat looking pained – why, we never knew.

I, Barbara, was the one with 20/20 vision. When I first went to an ophthalmologist he told me I had 20/20 and with his enthusiasm it sounded as if it was a Good Thing.

But now the good thing has been and gone. My 20/20 vision has done a flit. Why didn't I regard it with pride while I had it?

It is the same with my hearing. I was diagnosed with hearing loss when I was about thirty, and these things are liable to get worse. But all I knew about deafness when I was a child was when I met Deafy Jones the plumber. Deafy answered to the name and the world bellowed it back at him. He had no evidence of help, no hearing aid, no trumpet. If anything Deafy Jones the plumber was a bit of a laugh in Hastings.

Mum was a kind woman who liked all (with one or two exceptions), but I heard her telling Bub Landels the saga at the back door: 'It was all I could do not to laugh, Bub, when I heard poor old Deafy bellowing inside the safe. "It's the *ball*cock, Mrs Wright, it's the *ball*cock, see."'

Things are a great deal better now than that for anyone who has to bellow about ballcocks, but all I remember of seventy years ago are ear trumpets which old men (never women) occasionally put to their ear and hoped for the best.

I have had various and varying jobs and I have not been aware that my deafness has been much of a handicap. Nor, of course, has it been a help. Speech can be like some esoteric form of Esperanto that no one can handle. But to me one of the sillier things we deaf can do is to say, 'People mumble, everyone mumbles, they don't speak properly.'

It's a lot more ridiculous not to be able to hear the mumbles that can be heard by others. As usual Shakespeare has the answer:

The fault, dear Brutus, is not in our stars
But in ourselves.

Still, deafness is not a barrel of laughs. Film festivals are welcome because they bring subtitles, but speakers, regrettably, do not.

I have given a few How to Write courses under the auspices of the Centre for Continuing Education, which also organises inspiring study tours around the world.

The last time I tried anything like teaching was years ago in a large cold room. One student brought a large, coloured duvet because, she explained, she wrote better lying down. Another woman never stopped explaining about how she had a wonderful plot but it was just a question of getting it onto paper and what was I going to do about it? There was only one man: a large one in a sinister raincoat who looked as though he was about to cry. However, the day went well I thought, or did for most, and we were about to leave once again on terms of mutual respect. I began packing up and so did the students. There were farewells. As they left they handed in something about how the day had gone for them for the centre to look at. I did not look at them but I have to admit the last student's – not the one with the coloured duvet – caught my eye. She said she thought the day had been helpful but she thought it would have been better if Barbara had a hearing aid.

I could have kicked her.

Hard.

Since then I have been wary about being a writer talking to readers. There was one time at the Sydney Writers' Festival when the woman who was introducing me and my books had obviously not read any of them. However, she sailed amiably on and I had a fine time meeting other writers – Briar Grace Smith, the New Zealand playwright, for example, whose play I had seen at home.

Another person I wanted to meet was J.M. Coetzee, who some years before had burst upon an astonished world. He was pleasant, usually silent, but asked firmly for orange juice when the rest of us visitors wallowed in excellent wine from the nearby Hunter Valley.

It was good to be with such people. Another I would never have met and whom I liked was Dionne Brand from Trinidad. The woman who introduced her said cosily, 'How wonderful it must be to write for your people.'

To which Dionne said, 'Yeah, but sometimes I think the hell with it.'

Nice.

Writers and Readers Week began in Wellington in 1986, and inspired others around New Zealand. It started with the work of three people, Bill Manhire, Ann Mallinson and Elizabeth Alley, who worked like Trojans, though that was a long time ago.

Our festival became regarded as excellent by visiting writers. Of course as a nation we have always been friendly and kind.

A particularly warm memory is of August Kleinzahler, a fine poet and a delight to meet. He came from New Jersey and someone had spotted him, like a star, from far away. Augie is not large and is good at telling stories against himself. He told me that just before he came he had been at some *function* (the first time I heard the word used like that) which was about the importance of good sexual relationships between men and women – or something inexplicable like that. He told this to his mother. 'When I told her the subject her mouth kinda dropped. Then she said, "*You,* Augie."'

He asked for laughs and got them and was wonderful. He was also about the same height as Gary Glazebrook, my cheerful first dancing partner in Hastings. However, Augie fell immediately in love with Jenny Bornholdt, but that was understandable because they liked each other's poetry.

I met Augie wandering around one day with his small black unopened umbrella held in front of him as though it was a surfaced periscope. We greeted each other outside a café and he asked me something. Ever helpful and often wrong I thought he was talking about the quality of the fare. I told him it was expensive, there was often no place to sit, and frankly I wouldn't go there at all.

He looked at me with puzzlement, both hands still clutching the umbrella, and said, 'The *Boys'* Room, Barbara?'

'Oh. No. That way.'

But our friendship remained till he left. I came across a poem of his again in my commonplace book the other day, from the *London Review of Books* in 2001. It is called 'The Old Poet, Dying'. The last lines are:

> *– Well, of course, he says,*
> *taking my hand,*
> *his eyes narrowing with malice and delight:*
> *– That's not going to be just any old snowflake,*
> *now, is it?*

The old man reminded me of Pop. The taking of the hand, not the malice. Though of course Pop was no poet.

I have a good friend who often confides in me, usually when I want to confide in her. Confiding requires not only the right person but also it can be of vital importance or of much lesser substance, but in either case honesty is all.

Such as: 'Is my hair a mess?'

Careful inspection from friend. 'Yes. Since you ask.'

'What should I do?'

'I can't imagine, but you could have a perm.'

'A perm! I haven't had one for years.'

'Yes, but they can be a help for the mess. Conceivably.'

'Ah. Conceivably.'

Some people can manage without friends but not the majority, I think. The importance of friends begins at primary school and I was not good at it. I had taken *Flower Fairies of the Summer* to show Miss Linsey. Bad mistake, sucking up to teacher, and seen by Josie Black who threw the fairies in the mud. I punched her, which was unusual, and Josie said I couldn't take a joke and I was outraged. I *could* take a joke, even David said I could occasionally. I walked home with the still-muddy fairies, hoping for sympathy.

Fat chance. Mum was making pastry – always a tricky moment to appear. She gave me a brief glance and repeated that awful lie: 'Sticks and stones can break your bones, but names can never hurt you.'

'But they *can*,' I shouted.

'And don't shout! And don't touch the book, I'll clean it, you'll make it worse.'

Things improved in time and I was no longer like the small boy who came back from school and told his parents the boys there went round in twos and threes but he went round in ones.

The heartbreak of loneliness is hard to forget, and worse, much worse, when grown up.

So friendship is the thing, though I can't think of becoming part of a friendship with a woman who was athletic. Think of her pain as she watched me, useless at serving, but so keen and eager. Or her sorrow as I attempted to get the ball in the hole.

But books, books are the thing. You can have friendships sitting forever. Then you may talk things through.

'Tell me the title again, Damien.'

'*Stoner.*'

'Never heard of it.'

'Well you should!'

You can of course have disagreements over books.

'I've always thought *Lady Chatterley's Lover*'s overdone.'

'What on earth do you mean by overdone?'

'Just that. All those loins for a start.'

'Loins? There's hardly a loin in sight, except when she sees him washing at the beginning.'

Friends interest me who have a sense of direction. Neil had one long before he became a navigator, from the days when he and his friend Terry Goldfinch crawled along on their stomachs to find and pinch Mr Dykes's watermelons – ones he had hidden among the pumpkins in the middle paddock. Neil's sense of direction was useful at an early age.

Another friend with this gift of which I have not an ounce was Ann Thomas, with whom we travelled in Crete at the reunion of the vets in '81, and again in '87. Our ace travelling friend now lives in Auckland and we see her but not enough. Apart from anything else it was she who introduced me to Sappho before Dorothea.

The moon has set, and the
Pleiades, it is thereof
the night and time passes
time passes and I lie alone.

Are friendships different from how they used to be? Also manners? Nothing now is more dated than an elderly man opening a car door for an elderly woman. Though I suppose the Queen of

England would be surprised if it did not happen for her. Would she have to clamber out somehow, or would she sit there forever?

True manners involve true caring. Listen to Sir Philip Sidney as he was being carried wounded from the field of battle. When he saw a dying soldier looking at his water bottle he gave it to him with the words, 'Thy necessity is yet greater than mine.'

Four centuries later Padre Spence of the 20th Battalion 2NZEF caught the eye of Colonel Kippenberger, who noticed the padre had several bottles around his belt. Kippenberger thought he had them for himself and tried to avoid sarcasm, but the padre replied that he carried one or two in case any of the boys were short. It was then Kippenberger noticed that the padre's lips 'were cracked and parched and his face grey with fatigue. He had not touched water for a long time.' Kippenberger later wrote: 'I think it was the most Christ-like thing I ever saw.'

Manners come from the tough, and the less tough. Men or women who hold heavy doors open for me and my stick in Courtenay Place delight me.

Another thing. When I was young if anyone made me a compliment (usually an older woman) I would go all coy and blush with shame. If it was clothes they mentioned I would mumble, 'This old rag', or something equally idiotic. Not so now. I tell a young girl in all honesty how delightful she looks and she will say, '*Thank* you.' Then I feel like saying, 'It's not as good as that.'

And incidentally, have you noticed how much taller the young are now? And so beautiful the tall young men are, although many look similar.

After I was asked to leave the second floor of the Hope Gibbons Building and Aunt Daisy's shadow I found another second floor of a building which faces Courtenay Place. Here the front rooms get all-day sun. I am at the back all by myself and face the trees on the high hills beyond. I have been here for years and years and new books appear occasionally and I am glad. I am happy in my own patch, Courtenay Place, which is mine from 11am till 4.30pm daily, five days a week.

Still the De Luxe blossoms. The T-shirts now have *Deluxe* in one word, but otherwise all is just the same as when Stuart and Miranda and the rest of the gang worked in Kent Terrace, and it is still mine each morning when I buy my lunch, drink a coffee and read the paper if I can snatch one provided by the establishment with my good manners before the last one has gone.

One of the reasons I know I have been here for such a long time is because when I began I was able to see the peak of the Byrd Memorial which stands at the top of Mount Victoria – a triangular shape pointing to the South Pole in memory of the American explorer who was the first to fly over it.

Now I can't see it. The trees have hidden it.

ACKNOWLEDGEMENTS

Thanks to Fergus Barrowman, Bill Manhire and Damien Wilkins for all things. Thanks to Mary Varnham for information I had forgotten about Woodford House, and to David Poole for discovering Yeddie and unknown breeds of Jackson. Any mistakes are mine alone.

Grateful thanks for permission to reprint from the following:

James K. Baxter, 'High Country Weather', courtesy of J.C. Baxter.

R.A. Copland, 'First Reading: Only Meeting', *Islands*, vol. 6 no. 3 (March 1978), edited by Robin Dudding, courtesy of the author.

August Kleinzahler, 'The Old Poet, Dying', *The Strange Hours Travelers Keep* (Farrar, Straus and Giroux, 2003), courtesy of the author.